MW01196333

St. Seraphim of Sarov
A Spiritual Biography

by

Archimandrite Lazarus Moore

New Sarov Press
1994

Printed with the blessing

of

His Grace Bishop HILARION

Russian Orthodox Church

Outside of Russia

Cover Photo: The Diveyevo Portrait of St. Seraphim,
painted during his lifetime.

NEW SAROV PRESS
Blanco, Texas 78606-1049
U.S.A
ISBN 1-880364-13-1

Acknowledgment

With deepest gratitude to Bishop Hilarion, Dianne Cranor, Catherine Penn, Malcolm McElvaney, and Edward A. Cortez, Jr., without whose help this book could not have been published.

PORTRAIT OF FR. LAZARUS MOORE
by **ALEXEI ANTONOV**
Courtesy of St. John's Orthodox Cathedral, Eagle River,
Alaska

Contents

Introduction

by Catherine Lucinda Penn

Saint Seraphim of Sarov (1759-1833) is among the best known and most beloved Saints of the Orthodox Church. He is beloved of the Russian people, and of all who know him. With the publication of this *Spiritual Biography* by Archimandrite Lazarus Moore, many people will come to know him even more intimately.

St. Seraphim lived at the beginning of a spring time in the life of the Church in Russia. In his century monasticism would flower and with it, the faith of the people would flourish. During his lifetime thousands of pilgrims thronged to the Sarov Monastery to see him. They came from all over that vast land. Seventy years after his repose, love for him had so taken root in the Russian people that hundreds of thousands attended his Canonization.

This great Saint radiated the love of God to all who came to him, peasants and nobles, lay men and women, Monks and Nuns. Just to be with him strengthened, cheered and healed them. Several of his spiritual children were blessed to see a further radiance. They relate how his face was so luminous, that it was even impossible to look upon it.

One of his greatest gifts to mankind, his teaching on the goal of the Christian life--the acquisition of the Holy Spirit--was given in such a moment of radiance. This account alone, included unabridged in this biography, is unforgettable. The profundity of this

11

St. Seraphim of Sarov

teaching, however, can only be fully grasped in the context of his whole life.

So, while joy and brightness are our most powerful impressions of the Saint, Fr. Lazarus sets forth in vivid detail the source of his effulgence. He shows the grace of God in the Saint's life and the mystery of that grace. He also chronicles the refinement of this gift of God in monastic obedience and in a furnace of awe-inspiring asceticism.

The story of his thousand days and nights in prayer on a rock hidden in the Sarov forest is familiar to those who know of him. Fr. Lazarus helps us to take in this feat, and his battles with demons, and he also makes tangible the less dramatic myriad other acts of self-sacrifice for the love of Christ. We follow the whole flow of his life--of a devout youth in the world, to life in the Monastery, to ever greater reclusion, and finally, "when the fruit was fully ripe," to his cell door opening to all mankind.

The Mother of God was markedly present in St. Seraphim's life from early childhood to his death. She showed him inestimable love, healing him from grave illness more than once and appearing to him twelve times. In one of these appearances she gave him the miraculous spring whose waters healed thousands of pilgrims from all manner of illness during and after his earthly life. He constantly instructed people to turn to her for help and consolation. He was renowned himself for the maternal tenderness he showed all who came to him in sincerity. Instructing

Introduction

a future Abbot, he once said, "Be a mother and not a father to the brethren."

With unwavering devotion to the Saint, the author lets us see his difficulties and temptations. With full devotion to the Church and to monastic life, Fr. Lazarus relays how troubles and temptations arose within this setting. He describes the frailty of most people when set in proximity to great sanctity, and how this led to misunderstanding and even hostility toward the Saint. The author in no way judges those who were offended by St. Seraphim and caused him difficulty. In this humility he follows the Saint's own example.

Clearly, this is not a biography in the ordinary sense. Fr. Lazarus Moore does so much more than recount the life and teaching of the Saint. His interaction with the Saint is felt on every page. It is as though he were at St. Seraphim's side, learning from his Elder's acts and words. When the Saint withdraws from human view to immerse himself in the mystery of God, his disciple waits and reflects with us on that which exceeds our comprehension. The ineffability of seclusion was familiar to Fr. Lazarus, for he himself had spent many years in solitude in India.

The history of this book is itself remarkable. The text was originally sent to Fr. Benedict, publisher of New Sarov Press at Christ of the Hills Monastery by Bishop Hilarion when the Monastery was about to be received into the Russian Orthodox Church Outside of Russia. Vladyka Hilarion said to Fr. Benedict, "I'd

St. Seraphim of Sarov

like to send you a biography of St. Seraphim to publish. It's the most amazing biography of St. Seraphim I've ever seen. I think it's perhaps the best biography that's ever been written. It's never been published. How this manuscript came to me is in itself an unusual story. The text was mysteriously found at Novo-Diveyevo. I have the original here. It's obviously thirty or forty years old. It's yellow and crumbly and it's typewritten, with handwritten corrections indicating several edits."

Fr. Benedict was going to publish it as an anonymous work, but susequently Vladyka Hilarion said, "It could be that this was written by Fr. Lazarus Moore. I have no way to really know." Fr. Benedict wrote to Fr. Lazarus, and Fr. Lazarus answered that he did not believe it was his. He was very old, he said, and could not remember.

In late August--early September of 1992, Fr. Benedict was going to Alaska to see Fr. Lazarus on church matters. He did not take the manuscript with him, but he did mention it to the aged monk. Fr. Lazarus responded that, yes, he had written a biography of St. Seraphim, but it was long ago and he hadn't seen the text for maybe twenty years. There had been two copies of it. One, he thought, perhaps Archbishop Andrew of Novo-Diveyevo had. The other, a more recent edit, had been given to a spiritual daughter in Australia. He had lost contact with her, and so that one was completely lost. He asked Fr. Benedict to send a few pages to him--he would try to see. His memory was poor, for he was already dying.

Introduction

Fr. Benedict sent a half dozen pages when he got home. Fr. Lazarus was intrigued when he received them. He said it must be his work. It was his footnote system from years previous, when he had worked on the Holy Scriptures, a system he had since modernized. Others commented that the translation of St. Seraphim's conversation with Motovilov in this manuscript was virtually identical to that published by Holy Trinity Monastery and known to be Fr. Lazarus' work.

Encouraged by this, Fr. Lazarus and Dianne Cranor, who is his spiritual daughter and the trustee of his literary estate, were most eager to see the whole work. In a few days a choir director from St. John's Cathedral in Eagle River, Alaska, would be flying to the Lower Forty-eight on business. He then extended his flight to San Antonio to spend a weekend at the Monastery and hand carry a copy of the manuscript back. Dianne Cranor gave it to Fr. Lazarus. He was fascinated with it and said, "Yes, this must be my work." After looking at it a few days he was really convinced that this was an earlier edit of his lost biography. He was asked if the work was complete. He answered that, no, the writing was finished but the book still needed some work. By now it was mid-October, just weeks before his death. He was already too ill to do that, or even to guide someone else in it.

The editor of this biography has chosen to publish it essentially as Fr. Lazarus left it. In some places there is a lack of polish to the language. There are a few repetitions in the accounts. These have all been left in. In this reader's opinion, the roughness is in character with the personal nature of the work, and even perhaps enhances its action of involving the reader's heart and soul.

The vast amount of Holy Scripture used by Fr. Lazarus presented another editorial problem. The author was a Scripture scholar and translated the Bible himself. For this reason it seemed useless to check various translations to find what were exact quotes and what were paraphrased uses of scriptural texts. Again the editorial choice was to follow the author, and italicize only what he underlined.

A few anomalies in the text were changed where the intent seemed clear. Where it was not, they were retained. The only other significant changes were for the sake of specifically Orthodox formulation, as, for example, from the word "Assumption" to "Dormition."

It is with deep gratitude to Fr. Lazarus that we bring this *Spiritual Biography* to the public. St. Seraphim of Sarov can bring us all untold help and grace. We need his guidance and his prayers. Fr. Lazarus brings him not just before our eyes but into our very hearts.

Fr. Lazarus Moore was born in Swindon, England, on St. Luke's Day (October 18), 1902. When he was 18, he was sent to Canada where he worked at many jobs and eventually became a Canadian citizen. Then he received a call from God, and returned to England.

Introduction

Over the next several years he lived in a Monastery, spent time on Mt. Athos, then went to Yugoslavia and was tonsured a Monk in the Russian-Serbian Monastery at Milkovo. He was ordained Deacon and later Priest in the Russian Church Outside of Russia, and sent to serve in the Russian Mission in Palestine. He was Priest in charge of a Convent of about one hundred Nuns. In 1948 the British Mandate ended and their army returned to England. On the same day, the Israeli-Arab war broke out and the Israeli army made the Russian Mission their headquarters for the duration of the war, and then handed it over not to the owner but to the U.S.S.R. The Church lost everything. He was sent to the United States, and then to India in 1962. Later he went to Greece and then finally, Australia. In 1983, Fr. Lazarus moved to the United States at the request of Fr. Peter Gillquist to help the Evangelical Orthodox Church become Orthodox. He lived for six years in California. In December, 1989, at the request of the St. John's Cathedral parish, Eagle River, Alaska, Father Lazarus moved in with Deacon Harley Mark and Dianne Cranor with over two thousand books, numerous manuscripts and very few clothes or personal items. He finished his earthly life in Eagle River, and reposed on November 14/27 of 1992. Fr. Lazarus is buried there in the cemetery at St. John's Cathedral.

**The Wonderworking Kursk "Root" Icon
of Our Lady of the Sign**
Before which St. Seraphim was miraculously cured. Today, this
Icon is in America where it continues to work miracles to this
day.

Chapter I

Under His Mother's Roof

The native place on earth of this truly heavenly man, of whom the Mother of God herself said: "He is one of us," was the city of Kursk, mercifully protected by her wonder-working Icon of the Sign, called 'Korenaya'[1]. Under her special care Saint Seraphim grew up to great and high sanctity and was granted to hear from her the most sweet and glorious appellation: "My Beloved!"

His father was a pious merchant and industrious builder, Isidore Ivanovitch Moshnin. He had his own brick-works, and he was engaged in building stone Churches and houses. For this business a strong and prudent soul is required; but Isidore Ivanovitch was further distinguished for firm faith and solid piety. Still more adorned with virtues was the mother of the future Saint, Agathia Photievna, who was a true servant of God. She was noted for her charity. All orphans and poor children of both sexes enjoyed her special care; to them she was in the fullest sense a mother, and she attended to their maintenance, upbringing and Christian education. When the girls grew up, if they evinced a desire to marry and she could find a suitable bridegroom, she arranged their weddings and gave them dowries without demanding any repayment. And her only reaction towards all ingratitude was love. But besides this she was gifted with deep understanding and a courageous soul, as we shall soon see.

---

[1] "The Sign" refers to Isaiah 7:10-14. It is called the "Korenaya" or "Root Icon" because it was found at the roots of a tree.

St. Seraphim of Sarov

Three branches sprang from these parents: the first child Praskovia, the eldest son Alexis, and his younger brother, the future light of the world, Prochorus.

Nothing happens by chance in God's world. Even apparently small events have their significance. The future God-bearer, the flaming Seraphim[2] who was glorified while still on earth with the light of the glory of the Transfiguration of Tabor, was born on the night of July 19 to 20, that is on the day of the glorious Prophet Elias, the great Old Testament ascetic and contemplator of God on Horeb, who conversed with Christ the Lord on Tabor. At his Baptism the child was given the name of Prochorus, one of the seventy Apostles and first Deacons of the Church (Acts 6:3) whose memory is celebrated on July 28, that is on the ninth day after the birth of the chosen child. According to the law of the Church the holy name must be given on the eighth day (Lk. 2:21); here it was given a day later. When we meditate about this heavenly protector of the Saint, this Deacon or "minister" of the Church and guardian of the poor and widows (Acts 6:1), naturally comes the thought of the holy Father who called himself the servant of the Mother of God, and by her special order created the Convent for the Diveyev "orphans"--virgins and widows. As a true "guide of Monks" and Nuns and teacher of grace to the whole world, St. Seraphim fittingly received his name, which means "Choir Leader."

---

[2] The name "Seraphim" literally means "flaming".

Under His Mother's Roof

Under the patronage of the Mother of God, the Prophet Elias and St. Prochorus, the good qualities which the child inherited from his strong-spirited father and his kind-hearted mother began to grow and blossom. But most of all he was guarded and brought up by Holy Church, to which he was devoted from his earliest childhood. His father, while still in the prime of life, died at the age of forty-three, and the child was left to the sole care of his devout mother.

Incomprehensible to us are the ways of God, but it is undoubtedly true that the Lord Who "with wisdom profound orders all things with love, and gives to all that which is useful," as is sung in the troparion for the dead, called His servant to Himself at the right time. Was it pleasing to Him that the future Saint should be brought up by his more pious and meek mother? Or would the Saint have been tempted to follow the practical way of the world pursued by his father, the builder? Or was it that his father would not have consented to his son's leading the monastic life, although he had been chosen by God for that purpose? This is known only to God.

Without inquiring into the judgements of God, the young widow Agathia humbly accepted the hard cross. Without yielding to faint-heartedness, she took into her courageous hands the three young orphans, all the complicated housekeeping, and the particularly responsible business of building a Church in honour of St. Sergius and Our Lady of Kazan, which was started by her husband in 1752 and was finished under her direct supervision. All that time Prochorus was

21

St. Seraphim of Sarov

never away from his loving and beloved mother, whom he respectfully honored till his death. The whole of his childhood and youth was spent under her influence and under the auspices of the prayerful Church-building which unconsciously drew his pure soul from earth to heaven. "The House of God" became for him his native Monastery. And later we shall hear from the Saint himself that he was always loath to leave the Church and the Divine Services.

It was about this time that the first miracle happened to the seven-year-old boy. While looking over the bell-tower, Agathia went up to the very top. Prochorus went with her. Suddenly, having heedlessly gone to the edge, from the tremendous height, he fell to the ground. In horror the mother rushed headlong down, expecting to see her son lifeless. But to everyone's astonishment, he was standing on his feet perfectly well and not hurt in the least, exactly as though he had been borne down on Angels' wings! Thus the grace of God protected His chosen servant, according to the Psalmist: *He shall give His Angels charge over thee to guard thee in all thy ways. They shall bear thee in their hands, that thou dash not thy foot against a stone.* (Psalm 90:11-12). Later the same divine power will lift him above the earth.

It is worth noticing that the completion of the building of the Church coincided with a change in Prochorus' life. In 1777, Agathia found a tenant for the Church; in the following year she gave up her son to the service of God, and he went to the Sarov Monastery for the All-night Vigil on the Feast of the

Under His Mother's Roof

Presentation of the Mother of God. One hundred and twenty-five years later in the same Church near which the Saint spent his first years, a chapel was built in his name. Wonderful are the ways and works of God.

Soon "the Mother of God's chosen" servant experienced his second miracle. When he was nine years old, Prochorus fell ill. His mother lost all hope of her son's recovery. But her son told her that he had had a dream, and that the Mother of God had appeared to him and had promised to visit and heal him of his illness. Many years later the Saint was openly granted the most extraordinary apparition of the Mother of God and the Saints, after which he said to a Nun:

"See, Mother, what grace the Lord has granted us poor creatures! In this way I have already had twelve apparitions. What joy we have attained! We have reason to have faith and hope in the Lord! Conquer the enemy--the devil. Invoke the help of the Lord, the Mother of God and the Saints. And remember poor me."

Did his mother pray, or did the boy himself call upon the Queen of Heaven? Anyway, this is what happened. The wonderworking Icon of Our Lady of Kursk was carried through the town. The procession went down Sergiev Street where they lived. All of a sudden it began to rain heavily. To make the way shorter, the Icon was carried through the Moshnins' yard. The mother quickly picked up her sick child and carried him out to the Mother of God. And the Heavenly Queen kept her promise, for the boy soon

St. Seraphim of Sarov

made a complete recovery and zealously gave himself up to his studies.

By nature he was gifted with exceptional capabilities--bright mind, strong memory, impressionable heart--which he retained to the end of his life. That is why whatever he undertook he mastered quickly and permanently. So it was with his school studies. According to the wise and pious custom of old times, the instruction always began with the Service Books and the Psalms of David. Then it passed to the Bible, the Lives of the Saints and other spiritual books, feeding the mind with knowledge and the heart with devotion. Prochorus soon learned to read and write, and all his spare time that was free from prayer and work he devoted to reading. From his very childhood he had been serious. Like many other Saints, the boy avoided the ordinary children's games and amusements, and he looked for friends of similar spirit. Five of his friends were to devote themselves to the monastic life. Two of them would accompany him to Sarov, and two others would choose other Monasteries. Only one was to stay in the world, and that was because on the death of his parents he had to look after his five brothers and three sisters. It was in such a family and circle of friends that the future light not only of the Orthodox Church but of the whole world *advanced in favour with God and men* (Luke 2:52).

At the same time, there was a servant of God then living in Kursk, a fool for Christ's sake, who had a beneficial and holy influence on young Prochorus.

Under His Mother's Roof

His name is unknown to the pages of history. Previously many of these fools were scattered over the face of Holy Russia. And unnoticeably they did a great work by drawing people from earthly attractions, and teaching them better than any book detachment from the world, Christlike humility, and the martyrs' patience under all privations, besides foretelling the future, comforting sufferers and sometimes convicting the stony souls of sinful people.

One of these "Men of God" met Agathia when she was walking in the town with her two sons. Fixing his attention on Prochorus, the "fool" said to the mother:

"Blessed art thou, widow, that thou hast such a child, who in time will become a strong intercessor before the Holy Trinity and an ardent interceder for the whole world."

From that day he became strongly attached to the boy, and in later years influenced him for good. Prochorus absorbed all that was holy and good from the servant of God, just as dry land soaks up the rain. His pious and Orthodox-minded mother could only rejoice at all this and welcome it.

True, her work needed the help of her younger son. Besides the brick-works and the Church-building, they owned a shop in the town. The Saint afterwards related: "I am from the Kursk merchants; and when I was not in the Monastery, we used to deal in the kinds of goods that were most needed by the peasants: shaftbows, harness, iron, ropes, straps, and so on."

St. Seraphim of Sarov

Young Prochorus never refused to work, but his heart was already given to God. In the beginning he tried to combine the two. Early, in winter before it was light, he would hurry to Church for the Morning Service, and then he would spend the day at his trade. But as time went on, the young Saint became more and more convinced of the impossibility of combining wholehearted love for God with the service of the world. "It is impossible," he afterwards taught, "to immerse oneself wholly and calmly in contemplation of God, to meditate on His Law, and to ascend to Him with all one's soul in fervent prayer while remaining amidst the incessant noise of conflicting passions in the world." And therefore his soul had for a long time yearned for a quiet and solitary Convent where he could give himself up wholly to the spiritual life and flaming, seraphic love for God. His friends of his own age with whom he shared his thoughts supported him in these aspirations. Books showed the way. Examples around attracted, for at that time many people of Kursk were saving their souls in near and distant Monasteries. More than one had already reached even the dense forests of Sarov, and had attracted thither the hearts of those who sought silence and a strict monastic life. Among them Father Pachomius was particularly outstanding. He was one of the Kursk merchants Leonov.

The pious Agathia had long ago noticed these holy aspirations, and she did not oppose them. No matter how much the mother loved her son, she could not forget the miracles God had worked for him. She

Under His Mother's Roof

could not help seeing his extraordinary zeal for prayer, his love of solitude and his indifference to earthly affairs. So her heart had long since prepared itself for the sacrifice. Therefore when Prochorus reached the age of seventeen and revealed his cherished dreams to his beloved mother, she was not surprised but meekly accepted this cross, seeing in it the divine will. The saintly mother willingly agreed to give up her son to God. Then the holy youth procured a certificate of discharge from the society of Kursk so as to enter monasticism and, like a free bird, decided at first to go to the Kiev-Petchersk Monastery together with his five like-minded comrades.

A tender and touching farewell took place between the Saint and his family. At first, according to pious custom, they sat in silence. Then the holy youth rose and bowed at the feet of his beloved mother, asking for her blessing for the monastic life. Weeping profusely, the mother first of all gave her son the Icons of the Saviour and the Mother of God to kiss and then blessed him on the way of the Cross with a large copper cross. And this blessing cross the Saint always wore openly on his chest till the end of his life. With it he died.

Having left the quiet home of his parents and his native Kursk, the six pilgrims thoughtfully made their way to the cradle of Russia, the divinely preserved city of Kiev.

Nearly eight centuries previously, to the same Kiev and from the same Kursk, another great ascetic had

27

St. Seraphim of Sarov

run away secretly, the "iron" Theodosius of Petchersk, "the founder of community life." But that was against the mother's will, while this time it was with her blessing.

What awaits pure souls burning with holy love? God knows. But now they have *chosen the good part.* (Luke 10:42).

Note. By the established and generally-accepted calculation of the sequence of events in the life of Saint Seraphim, his birth is usually referred to the year 1759. But, according to information obtained from the Spiritual Consistory of Kursk at the time of the opening of the relics of the Saint for the Canonization, it appears that this date, as also many others, must be re-examined. First of all, from the birth and Baptismal registers it was discovered that the Saint's father, Isadore Ivanovitch Moshnin, died on the 10th May, 1760, at the age of 43--not in 1762, the third year after Prochorus' birth, as has been written hitherto in all the biographies of the Saint. Then his mother, Agathia Photievna, died, not during his novitiate, but much later, on the 29th February, 1800.

Next, when Prochorus was in Kursk to make collections for the Church between 1784 and 1786, if he was at his brother Alexis', then he certainly saw his mother, too. But usually it has been written hitherto that she was dead by that time and that he just visited her grave.

Under His Mother's Roof

But a more important question concerns the year of the Saint's birth. In the Confession registers found in the Ilinsky Church (of St. Elias) where the Moshnin family made their Confessions, the following was noted: That in 1762, Alexis was eleven years old and Praskovia fourteen, while nothing is said about Prochorus. We may suppose that he was only three years old at that time and that he could not yet confess. But surprisingly, by 1768 in the same Confession registers there is the entry: "Widow Agathia, fifty years old; her children: Alexis, seventeen, Prochorus, fourteen, Praskovia, nineteen years old." If this is correct, then Prochorus must have been born not in 1759, but in 1754, that is, five years earlier; and in 1760, on the death of his father, he entered his sixth year. Consequently, in 1762, he was seven years old. Although by custom children of seven can already make their Confessions, yet he was just entering his eighth year and Confession still lay ahead.

Perhaps the figures of the Confession registers are incorrect. It is natural that they were written without special care according to what the Confessors said. There are foundations for doubting these figures. Agathia died in 1800, at the age of seventy-two, as has been already noted. Therefore in 1768 she was forty years old, and not fifty as it is written. Or else she died at the age of eighty-two, which is less probable. But then the other dates 1768 and 1762 regarding Alexis and Praskovia agree (a difference of one year in the case of Praskovia is unimportant as it depends on the month of her birth). In that case, there is a very

St. Seraphim of Sarov

great foundation to suppose that Prochorus was born five years earlier than the usually accepted time; and then all the other dates of his life, from the pilgrimage to Kiev until his death, must be moved back five years.

Later history must solve this question.

St. Seraphim Being Healed Before the Wonder-working Kursk "Root" Icon of the Mother of God.

Chapter II

On the Way to Sarov

The pilgrims reached Kiev safely, prayed to the Mother of God, venerated the relics of the Saints and visited all the holy places. Standing on the threshold of a new, unknown life, no doubt they sought experienced Elders who might give them wise advice regarding their proposed monasticism and as to which Monastery to enter. And they were told that in the Kitaev Monastery, ten versts from Kiev, a clairvoyant ascetic called Dositheus was saving his soul. To him Prochorus hurriedly directed his steps. Looking at him, the Elder saw in him the grace of God, and peremptorily blessed him to go to the Sarov desert. At the same time he gave him this testament:

"Go, child of God, and stay there. That place will be to thee for salvation, with the Lord's help. There thou shalt finish thy earthly pilgrimage. Only try to acquire the unceasing remembrance of God through the constant invocation of the Name of God thus: Lord Jesus Christ, Son of God, have mercy on me a sinner! Let all thy attention and training be in this: walking and sitting, working and standing in Church, everywhere in every place, coming in and going out let this constant cry be on thy lips and in thy heart; with it thou shalt find rest, thou shalt obtain spiritual and bodily purity and the Holy Spirit Who is the source of all blessings will dwell in thee and will direct thy life in holiness, in all piety and purity. In Sarov the Superior Pachomius is of God-pleasing life; he is a follower of our Antony and Theodosius."

St. Seraphim of Sarov

In these few words not only was the place of his asceticism prophetically shown to Prochorus, but also the chief monastic "training" was defined--the interior activity of the Prayer of Jesus. But it is particularly remarkable that St. Dositheus clearly pointed out to him the basic aim of the whole spiritual life: "The Holy Spirit will dwell in thee." Such was always the Christian doctrine, beginning from the Lord Himself Who promised to send *the Comforter, the Spirit of Truth* (John 14:16-17; 16:13-15), that *living water* (John 7:38-39), through the Apostles (Acts 10:44-45; Rom. 8; Gal. 3:14; 4:6; Ephes. 2:22; 5:9; Heb. 10:29), then through all the Holy Fathers to St. Gregory Palamas with his teaching about the grace-given "light of Tabor." On this only true view all the true Orthodox Christian ascetics were brought up, experimentally guided by God's Holy Spirit, and instructed by the constant tradition of the Orthodox Church. Such a man was the clairvoyant Dositheus.

The attentive and fervent Prochorus accepted and took to heart this inspired testament with the firm intention of carrying it out. Many years later, in a striking conversation with N. A. Motovilov, we shall hear from himself the same testament: "The aim of our Christian life consists in the acquisition of the Holy Spirit of God." Wonderful spiritual aim!

not union c̄ God?

In this way the question of monasticism and Monastery was decided for ever for Prochorus. God expressed His will by the lips of the clairvoyant. It may be said that here in the Monastery of Kitaev the spiritual anointing of the Saint took place; the good

On the Way to Sarov

seed of his whole future life was sown, and his ascent to the glory of God. Here, invisible to the world, the hand of God rested upon him. The cell belonging to Dositheus became a monastic font for Prochorus. In it was mystically accomplished the monastic betrothal of the Spirit of God with his own spirit. Thence the Saint came out already essentially a Monk. The later ceremony of Profession only sealed openly the choice by the Spirit. And just as Christ, after His Baptism by John, was led by the Spirit into the desert, so that by temptation He might be prepared for His ministry, so too Prochorus did not immediately go from Kiev to Sarov, but returned for a time to his mother's home, his native Kursk.

The reason for this delay is unknown to us. Perhaps the youth wanted to test and examine himself more, to see whether he could take upon himself the monastic "sweet yoke" of Christ (Mat. 11:29). Or did he wish to prepare gradually for the parting with his loving mother; or had the clairvoyant Elder given him such advice; or did something else providentially retain him? Anyway, Prochorus continued to live under his mother's roof for about another two years.

But he lives there now only with his body, while his soul has begun to die to everything earthly. He still goes to the shop, but he does not take any share in the business. He spends his time in prayer, silent meditation, reading books, and in soul-saving conversations with visitors. And undoubtedly it was while he was still there that he began to carry out the testament of Dositheus regarding the "unceasing remembrance

St. Seraphim of Sarov

of God," and the constant "Prayer of Jesus." His home became the portico of the Monastery.

The test is finished. Prochorus gets ready to go. It was hard for his mother to part with him; and, having lost all hope, she says to her son:

"You should have buried me first, and then gone to the Monastery!"[3]

But he had already buried everything two years ago in the cell below Kiev. His mother had nothing to do but to give her blessing once again to Prochorus and, as she thought, never again to see him on earth, for Sarov was too far for her. Prochorus was accompanied by two of his fellow pilgrims from Kiev, while two others had gone earlier into other Monasteries.

It was autumn. The trees were shedding their leaves. The rains had started. In Kursk it was still warm; but to the North, nearer to Tambov, the cold was making itself felt more and more. Winter had drawn near. The way was not easy. And ahead of the Monks there lay the difficult life of struggling to mortify the passions, in the name of pure snow-white dispassion, so as afterwards to live in the Spirit.

The future ascetics walked in silence, secretly saying the Prayer of Jesus. They reached the forests of Temnikov. The aged pine forest received some new

---

[3] If he had obeyed his mother, he would have had to wait till 29th February, 1800, when Agathia died, and when he had already finished his monastic effort.

On the Way to Sarov

spiritual fighters, and by its high, dense wall of huge pines, sometimes four or five arm's-breadths in girth, it cut them off from the past.

They were nearing the mysterious Sarov. On the 20th of November, 1778, towards evening twilight, the three young pilgrims approached the gates of the Sarov bell-tower.

It was the eve of the Presentation of the Mother of God which is pre-eminently a monastic feast. This is the day of the consecration of the holy Virgin Mary to the greatest service of God for the salvation of the human race; her departure from the world for the salvation of the world; the feast of virginity in preparation for the Incarnation of God. This is the feast of the dedication of the Bride of God for her education by the Spirit to be the Mother of the Son of God.

This was not a chance coincidence. The holy youth had come from his earthly mother to his Heavenly Mother. From the hands of the honest widow, he was taken by the Immaculate Virgin. From the roof of the Church-builder Agathia, he came under the protection of God, into "the most pure Temple of the Saviour, the very precious bridal-chamber," into the embrace of the Mother of God. And one is again reminded of the Saint's wonderful conversation on "the acquisition of the grace of the Holy Spirit" as the aim of life. This is clearly sung in the same kontakion of the feast: "The Virgin is today introduced into the house of the Lord, bringing with her the grace which is in the Divine Spirit."

St. Seraphim of Sarov

"And the Holy Spirit will dwell in thee"--the prophecy of Dositheus is again remembered. Through the gates of the bell-tower the pilgrims entered the Monastery. They were at once surrounded from all sides by the buildings of the cloister, like living arms warmly welcoming and embracing the new inhabitants. It was as though the door to the other side of the world had been closed behind them for ever. Now their home, family, Father and Mother were here.

Before them in the middle of the Monastery enclosure, stood the enormous five-domed main Church of the Convent in honour of the Dormition of the Mother of God, rebuilt only a year previously in the time of the Abbot Ephrem. In appearance it reminded one of the distant Church of the Dormition in the Kiev Lavra. The gates of the Temple were open. The pilgrims directed their steps straight to the place of God's dwelling, to the house of the Queen of Heaven, who invisibly ruled the Monastery from there.

Their cherished desire had been fulfilled. The seekers of the City of God were in their quiet harbour. The recently appointed Abbot, Father Pachomius, celebrated the solemn Service of the Presentation. Everything was done in order and according to regulation, for the Superior was strict in keeping the Church and monastic rules. Prochorus' soul rejoiced. He had found his place. And now he could say in the words of the Psalmist: *The sparrow has found herself a house, and the swallow a nest...Blessed are they that dwell in Thy house, O Lord* (Psalm 83:4). *This is my*

On the Way to Sarov

repose for ever! Here will I dwell, for I have chosen it (Psalm 131:14).

Icon of the Presentation of the Lord
Russian, ca. 1500, Moscow School

The Monastery of Sarov
Above the Monastery is depicted St. Seraphim kneeling in prayer
before the Icon of the Mother of God, "Compunction". At the top
are depicted the various Churches of Sarov. *Left to right:* Church
of St. John the Baptist, Chapel over St. Seraphim's Relics, Chapel
of the Spring, Church of All Saints, and Chapel over the Relics of
Sts. Zosima and Sabatius.

Chapter III

The Novice Prochorus

On the following day all three pilgrims paid a visit to the Father Abbot. He gave them a warm welcome, and joyfully admitted them into the Monastery. He particularly turned his attention to Prochorus, whose parents he had known well in Kursk. Seeing in him the great spirit of the future Saint he handed him over for spiritual direction to the experienced hands of his closest colleague and friend, the wise and love-filled treasurer, Father Joseph. From him Prochorus received his first obedience--that of a cell attendant.

Thus was begun the monastic life of the Saint, which lasted for 54 years. It was fraught with hard struggles, but was crowned with a glorious and holy end. The light service of the Father-treasurer was only the introduction. Soon the Novice Prochorus, like other inhabitants of the Convent, was given different, more physically difficult obediences. He worked in the bakery, at prosphora making, and in the joiner's shop. Then he did duty as the bell-ringer, both to call the Monks and for the Church. He also sang in the choir, and went on general obediences such as wood-cutting, sewing, etc. Most of all Prochorus used to do joinery work, in which he gained great skill, so that among the brethren he was mostly known as "Prochorus the joiner."

His interior life in this novitiate period, when the foundations of monastic education are laid, is little known to us. We mostly have to conclude as to what it was like from the Saint's later counsels to others (which we must think were given from his own experience), and only in part from the occasional and insignificant testimony given by himself about his past life.

First of all, Brother Prochorus was distinguished for his absolutely unmurmuring fulfillment of his obedience. Moreover, by the nature of his exact character, he did everything with zeal, accuracy and all possible perfection. This is just what is required of new Novices in order that they may learn from the start to break their worldly pride, that root of all the other passions and the basic malady of the fallen soul.

That is why the Saint afterwards instructed the Diveyev Nuns chiefly in obedience: "Remember always," recalled his words Xenia Vasilievna Putkova, who later became the Nun Kapitolina, "obedience surpasses everything. It surpasses fasting and prayer! And we should not only not refuse it, but we should run to meet it! We must bear every kind of trouble from the brethren without being disturbed and without murmuring; because a Monk is only a Monk when, like bast-shoes, he is knocked about and battered by everybody."

"There is no more pernicious sin than to murmur, to judge or to disobey the Superior--that person will perish."

To the Confessor of the Monastery, the Protopresbyter Father Basil Sadovsky, the Saint also said: "Obedience, Father, is superior to fasting and prayer. Remember that and always remind them of it.

The Novice Prochorus

I am always reminding them too." "Afterwards, Father explained to me," wrote Father Basil, "how great, terrible and burdensome for a Monk is the sin of disobedience to the Superior; and still more, criticism of superiors. For the first rule for the Monk (on this the whole of monasticism is based) is obedience and the complete cutting off of the will; as a result of the non-fulfillment of which arose the original sin of the old Adam, which ruined everything. And it was only by obedience that the whole world was saved through a man, the new Adam, our Saviour and Lord Jesus Christ, because He was obedient even to death! Therefore now there can be nothing worse than this sin! He who does so will certainly perish....."

Lord, have mercy on us who are self-willed! In the second place the Saint recommends labour for Novices--no matter what it consisted of. "I order them (that is the Diveyev Sisters), as soon as they rise from sleep, at once to get to work, saying to themselves my little rule of prayer on the way. If they do this, they will be saved." "If there is some handwork," he would afterwards advise a Monk, "busy yourself with that. If you find yourself in a cell without having any handwork, by all means apply yourself to reading, particularly the Psalter. Try to read every section frequently in order to retain it all in the mind." "If you are called to an obedience, go to it." And he himself was never without work, never allowed himself to be idle. If he was free from obediences and prayer, he would silently withdraw to his cell, and there he would undertake some work, either cutting out cypress crosses,

St. Seraphim of Sarov

or reading the Word of God or the works of the Holy Fathers, or the Lives of the Saints. Besides the Bible and the Menology, he had the works of St. Basil the Great, St. Macarius the Egyptian, St. John of the Ladder, the "Marguerite," Philokalia, etc.

He looked upon reading also as a special labour which he called "vigil." The Gospel and the Epistles of the Apostles he read before the Icons and always standing, in the attitude of prayer.

"The soul must be supplied and nourished with the Word of God," he says. "Most of all, we should practice reading the New Testament and Psalter. It ought to be done standing." But he allowed the Psalter sometimes to be read sitting. "From this reading comes the illumination of the mind which is changed by a Divine change."

Besides that, he who reads Holy Scripture "receives within him a warmth which in solitude produces tears. From these tears the person is warmed through and through and filled with spiritual gifts, which delight the mind and heart beyond all description." Above all, this should be done in order to obtain peace of soul, according to the teaching of the Psalmist: *Great peace have they who love Thy law, O Lord* (Ps. 118:165).

Undoubtedly the Saint taught all this from his own experience. And once he even uttered an extraordinary prophetic admonition about reading: "It is very useful...to read through the whole Bible intelligently.

The Novice Prochorus

For this exercise alone, besides other good works, the Lord will not deprive a man of His mercy, but will increase his gift of understanding." He also ordered lay people to read the Word of the Lord. "What am I to read?" a visitor once asked him. "The Gospel," replied the Saint. "Four sections a day from each Evangelist..."

After work and reading the Saint gives Novices instruction about prayer. He says exactly what he heard from the lips of Dositheus, and what he practiced himself. "Those who have truly resolved to serve the Lord God must exercise themselves in the remembrance of God and unceasing prayer to Jesus Christ." "While engaged in handwork, or doing any kind of obedience," he instructs the Monk, "unceasingly make the Prayer: Lord, Jesus Christ have mercy on me, a sinner. In prayer, attend to yourself, that is, gather your mind and unite it with your soul. At first for a day or two, or more, make this prayer with your mind alone, separately, and attend especially to each word. Then, when the Lord warms your heart with the warmth of His grace and unites it within you into one spirit, this prayer will flow within you unceasingly, and will be always with you, delighting and nourishing you...And when you contain this spiritual nourishment within you (that is, conversation with the Lord Himself,) then why go round visiting cells of the brethren, even when called by someone? Truly I will tell you that idle talk is also love of idleness."

Concerning prayer in Church, the Saint would advise:

St. Seraphim of Sarov

"In Church while praying it is useful to stand with closed eyes with inward attention, and to open the eyes only when you grow languid or when sleep oppresses you and makes you drowsy. Then the eyes should be turned to an Icon and the light burning before it."

And he himself stood in Church with closed eyes. He used to come to Divine Service before the others and never left before the end of it. As regards asceticism, during the first years of his monastic life, although he kept himself in the common unceasing and strict temperance, yet he did everything in moderation. And he taught the same thing to others in accordance with the general teaching of the Holy Fathers on the "royal" way.

"We ought not to undertake ascetic labours beyond measure, but to try to make our friend, the flesh, faithful and capable of practicing virtue. We should go by the middle way."

"We should be indulgent with our soul in its infirmities and imperfections, and have patience with its defects, as we have patience with the defects of others." But we must "not be indolent and must urge ourselves to better things."

In particular, with regard to sleep, for instance, the Saint advised a Monk: "Every day, without fail, at night sleep for four hours--the tenth, eleventh and twelfth and an hour after midnight. If feeling feeble it is possible to sleep during the day as well. Keep this

The Novice Prochorus

rule invariably till the end of your life, because it is necessary for the repose of your head. I myself, from early youth, have kept this course too. We always ask the good Lord for rest during the night time. If you take care of yourself in this way, you will not become despondent but healthy and cheerful."

Later, he permitted others more infirm to sleep at night even six hours; and if overtired, he also advised them to rest after dinner a little.

In the same way, the Novice Prochorus observed moderation in food:

"Not everyone can impose upon himself a strict ~Food~ rule of temperance in everything, or deprive himself of all that would serve to relieve his weaknesses. Otherwise, in exhausting the body, the soul becomes ~Fasts~ feeble too." In particular: "On Fridays and Wednesdays, and especially during the four fasts," he said, "food should be taken once a day, and the Angel of the Lord will stick close to you." For other days he recommended the following rule: "At dinner eat sufficient; at supper be moderate." "Gluttony is not a monastic work." But to the Diveyev Sisters he generally gave indulgent instructions that they should eat without uneasiness, whenever and as much as they wanted, even at night, if need be, provided that they were obedient and never lived alone, either in the cells or on the road. Moreover, he considered that women, on account of their weakness, are less capable or adapted for the severe labours of temperance. But apart from that, he did not want to impose an extra

45

weight of sin on anyone's soul in the event of not carrying out strict fasting or vows. "If anyone can, let him do it." Even with regard to Wednesday and Friday he said to a certain Monk: "If you are able, eat but once a day." "But a body that is exhausted by penances and sickness should be strengthened by moderate sleep, food, and drink, regardless even of time. After raising the daughter of Jairus from death, Jesus Christ at once ordered her to eat" (Lk. 8:55).

But instead, the Saint earnestly advised that "peace of soul" should be maintained at all costs, and he paid special attention to this himself: "By all means, we should try to preserve peace of soul, and not be disturbed by offenses from others." "Nothing is better than peace in Christ." *Peace*

"The Holy Fathers always had a peaceful spirit and, being blessed with the grace of God, they lived long." "Acquire peace," he says later on, "and thousands around you will be saved. When a person is in a peaceful state of mind, he can from himself give out to others the light of the illumination of the reason." "This peace, like some priceless treasure, our Lord Jesus Christ left to His disciples before His death" (John 14:27). The Apostle also says of it: *And the peace of God, which passes all understanding, shall guard your hearts and thoughts in Jesus Christ* (Phil. 4:7). For this reason above all he advised: "Immerse your mind within yourself and have activity in your heart," "then the peace of God overshadows it, and it is in a peaceful state." Then one must accustom oneself "to bear offense from others calmly as though their insults do not concern us but others. Such a practice can obtain peace for the human heart and make it the abode of God Himself!"

If it is impossible not to be disturbed, then at least it is necessary to try to control the tongue according to the Psalmist: *I was troubled and spoke not* (Ps. 76:4). "For the preservation of peace of soul, it is also necessary by all means to avoid criticizing others"..."And in order to deliver oneself from criticism, it is necessary to attend to oneself and to ask: 'Where am I?'" Especially for peace of soul "one must avoid despondency"[4] and try to have a joyful spirit, and not a sad one. As Sirach says: *Sadness hath killed many, and there is no profit in it*" (30:25).

It is worth while stopping for a moment to pay special attention to this "joyful spirit" in the life of the Saint. It was his characteristic property, especially later on. But even this grace-given gift was not attained by him without a struggle, although it was so salutary for the suffering souls of those who flocked to him later. There is reason to think that the devil of despondency attacked him in the beginning of his monastic life. "It is hard," he says, "to avoid this disease for a person who has just begun the monastic life, because it is the first one to assail him. Therefore, before everything else, one must beware of it."

"It sometimes happens that a person in this state of spirit thinks to himself that it would be easier for him

---

4 Or, "accidie."

to be destroyed, or to be without any feeling and consciousness, than to remain any longer in this unaccountably tormenting state of mind. One should try to get out of it as quickly as possible. Beware the spirit of despondency, for it gives birth to every evil." "A thousand temptations come from it: agitation, rage, blame, complaint at one's fate, profligate thoughts, constant change of place." "One's place of residence becomes unbearable, and the brethren too." Then "the devil of boredom suggests thoughts to the Monk to leave his cell and talk to someone." "And the Monk becomes like a dry cloud,[5] driven about by the wind." But sometimes, on the contrary, "the evil spirit of sorrow" "possesses the soul" and "deprives it of meekness and kindness in regard to the brethren, and gives birth to repulsion from all conversation." "The soul then avoids people, believing them to be the cause of its trouble, and does not understand that the cause of its illness is within itself."

"The soul filled with sorrow and becoming as if insane and out of its mind is incapable of quietly accepting good advice or of meekly answering questions put to it."

We may think that this evil spirit of despondency (*accidie*) attacked even the Saint. But he immediately and resolutely found a way out of it. The first "medicine" "with the help of which a person soon finds consolation in his soul" is "meekness of heart," as St. Isaac the Syrian teaches. Another cure he found

---

[5] Or, "cloud without water." o.p. Jude 12.

The Novice Prochorus

in work and struggles: "This illness is treated with prayer, abstinence from idle talk, handwork according to one's strength, reading of the Word of God, and patience; because it is born of cowardice, idleness and idle talk."

Both these ways lead above all to the simple, unmurmuring fulfillment of obedience. Here is both humility and struggle. "Above all," said the Saint, "one must fight despondency (*accidie*)" by means of strict and unquestioning fulfillment of all the duties laid upon the Novice. "When your occupations get into real order, then boredom will find no place in your heart. Bored people are those whose life is not in order. And so, obedience is the best remedy against this dangerous illness." And all this taken together leads to the last cure of spiritual sicknesses--dispassion. "Whoever has conquered his passions has conquered dejection too."

And if the Saint himself was always peaceful and joyous, it is a true sign that he gradually attained dispassion and "scorn of the world" with its desires (I John 2:16). And being able to overcome temptation in himself, the Saint could from experience help others too, pouring into them the spirit of divine joy.

A Monk of Sarov had succumbed to a similar temptation. Wishing to find some kind of relief, he shared his sorrow with another Brother. After Vespers they went out of the Monastery and, walking round the enclosure, came to the horse yard. Suddenly, they saw the Saint. Deeply venerating him, they fell at his

St. Seraphim of Sarov

feet. With unusual kindness the Saint blessed them, and seeing through the Brother's despondency (*accidie*), began to sing: "Fill my heart with joy and banish sinful sadness, O Virgin, who receivedest the Fullness of Joy" (Troparion from the Canon to the Mother of God).

Then stamping his foot the holy Elder said with vigour and rapture: "We have no need to despond; for Christ has vanquished everything, raised Adam, released Eve, and slain death!"

His joy was transmitted to the despondent Brother; the temptation instantly vanished, and in a peaceful and cheerful spirit the Monks returned to the Monastery.

The Nun Kapitolina (Xenia Vasilievna) in her notes, has left us a testimonial regarding the Saint's view of despondency (*accidie*) and joy generally: "Cheerfulness is not a sin, Mother. It drives away weariness; and it is from weariness that despondency (*accidie*) comes, and there is nothing worse than that. It brings with it everything. When I entered the Monastery I sang in the choir; and I was so cheerful, my joy![6] Sometimes when I came to the choir, the brethren had got tired and had been attacked by despondency (*accidie*) and were singing without fervour, while others were not singing at all. All gather together, and I cheer them up; they no longer feel weary! To say or do evil is bad, and should certainly

---

[6] St. Seraphim often used to call people "my joy."

not be done in God's Temple. But to say a kind or friendly or cheering word, in order that everyone may be cheerful in the presence of God, and not in a despondent mood, is not sinful at all, Mother."

This spirit of Christ's peace and joy grew more and more in the Saint, later reaching a constant paschal joy. For this reason he often called his interlocutors: "my joy!" Or he welcomed people with the greeting: "Christ is risen!"

As regards Prochorus' struggle with the movements of the flesh, this is unknown to us. True, in his instructions he says: "Is it possible for a person in his early youth to be on fire and not to be disturbed by thoughts of the flesh?"

Consequently, even he was not free from these assaults of nature. But there is no doubt whatever that these passions had no material in him. Pure from his youth he had no difficulty in overcoming the thoughts that came to him and even turned these temptations of the enemy to good account by resisting them. "If we do not agree with the evil thoughts suggested by the devil, we do good."

In these attacks, he taught, one should immediately turn in prayer to "the Lord God, that the spark of vicious passions may be put out at the very start. Then the flame of the passions will not increase." This "impure spirit can have a strong influence only on passionate people, while those that have purified themselves from their passions it attacks only from the side or exteriorly." That exactly describes it; it was only "exteriorly" that it attacked him personally. It was unable to find any food in the holy Novice and was scorched by his prayer in its first tempting assaults. And later he would boldly say of himself to the Confessor of the Diveyev Convent, Father Sadovsky:

"Like myself, a virgin, Father! Only virgins will live within the moat" (surrounding the Convent).

And to N. A. Motovilov he explained that virgin-Nuns should live separately from widows, by order of the Mother of God Herself.

"As I am myself a virgin, Father, so the Queen of Heaven gave her blessing that only virgins should live in my Convent."

"Widows will come to visit us, and bring girls with them," he said to Sister Matrona of Diveyev. "But we have special feelings unlike widows, Mother. In many ways they are very different from us (virgins). A virgin is delighted only by the Sweetest Jesus, contemplates Him in His sufferings and being completely free, she serves the Lord in spirit. But a widow has many memories of the world. 'How good was our late husband! What a kind person he was!' they say."

Therefore, he assigned to the virgins a special part of the Convent with a windmill, which was later named the "Mill-Virgin" Convent. This personal testimony of the Saint vouches for his purity more truly than all other proofs. But in order to purify thor-

The Novice Prochorus

oughly even the remains of the movements of nature, God sent him in the very beginning of his monastic life a serious illness. "The body is the slave, the soul is the queen," he taught afterwards, "and therefore it is God's mercy when the body is exhausted by illnesses; for in this way the passions weaken, and a person becomes normal." But "bodily sickness itself is sometimes born from the passions." "Take away sin, and sickness will go."

Two years after entering the Monastery, Prochorus became seriously ill with dropsy. He became all swollen and spent most of his time lying motionless in his cell. The sickness went on for about three years. The Abbot Pachomius and Father Joseph, who had a burning love for the obedient Monk, tended him with great devotion. But not seeing any improvement, and fearing that the illness might prove fatal, Father Pachomius offered to call a physician. But Prochorus meekly answered him: "I have surrendered myself, holy Father, to the true Physician of souls and bodies, our Lord Jesus Christ and His Immaculate Mother; but if your love thinks fit, supply me, for the Lord's sake, with the heavenly remedy" (Holy Communion).

Father Joseph zealously served the Vigil and Liturgy for the health of the patient, confessed him and communicated him in his cell. After this Prochorus quickly recovered.

Later, he himself told many that after Holy Communion, the Holy Mother of God appeared to him in an ineffable light with the Apostles Peter and

St. Seraphim of Sarov

John the Theologian, and turning her face to the Apostle John, she said, indicating the patient:

"This is one of our kind!" that is to say, one of the heavenly family or race, a heavenly man. Then (his words are recorded by the Nun Kapitolina), "'Her right hand, my joy, she put on my head, while in her left hand she held a scepter; and with this very scepter, my joy, she touched poor Seraphim--on that place, on the right hip--and a hollow was formed, Mother; and all the water in it ran out. And the Heavenly Queen saved poor Seraphim. But the wound was very big; till now there is a cavity, Mother. Look, give me your hand.' And Father himself took my hand and put it into the cavity; and it was tremendous--the whole fist went in."

Thus Prochorus was miraculously healed. But others, especially worldly people, he allowed to be treated by doctors. To a certain Bogdanov, who asked him about it, he gave the following advice:

"Sickness purifies sins. However, do as you like--go by the middle way. Do not take upon yourself what is beyond your power; you will succumb, and the devil will mock you. If you are young, restrain yourself" from high ascetic undertakings. "Once a devil suggested to a Saint to jump into a pit. He was about to consent, but St. George restrained him."[7]

sickness purifies sin

[7] From the Life of St. Theodore Syceotes, 22 April.

The Novice Prochorus

In the following year after his recovery, on the place of this cell a hospital was erected. And the place of the apparition of the Mother of God came to be exactly under the Sanctuary of the Chapel. The Saint himself made the cypress altar, and until his very death, made his Communion there, thankfully remembering the mercy of the Mother of God. For the building of this Church money had to be collected, and the healed Prochorus, with special zeal, undertook his new obedience, that of money-collector. As he went round the towns and villages, he reached as far as Kursk. There, once again he met his mother, his brother Alexis and other relations; from them he received a zealous mite for the holy work, and returned to his (spiritually) native Sarov.

In that mortal illness, all that was merely human in Prochorus died. Henceforth he was not of earthly but of heavenly "race." Here below the Saint lived in outward appearance; he even visited his home as though passing by, only to forget about it completely afterwards. During the eight years of his novitiate, he had clung with all his soul to the world above. That was truly his native land. It only remained to seal it by religious profession. The Novice was ripe for monastic rebirth.

The Ladder of Divine Ascent
Icon of the Moscow School, 16th century, based on the classic
ascetical work by St. John Climacus. St. John is shown at the
bottom guiding Monks as they pass through many attempts of the
demons to pull them off. They are assisted by the angels and,
eventually some reach the Kingdom of Heaven where they are
received by Christ.

CHAPTER IV

In the Angelic Habit

Towards the end of the fast of the Dormition, on the 13th of August 1786, Abbot Pachomius professed the Novice Prochorus as a Monk. In his place there was born to a new spiritual life in "the angelic order" the Monk Seraphim, which means in Hebrew both "flaming" and "warming." And this name, given him no doubt for his burning spirit, he fully justified by his flaming love for God and the Mother of God, and by his warm affection for all. Easily and with trembling joy the new Monk bowed his head under the scissors of the Abbot who professed him; not a single thought of separation from the world darkened his soul at the moment of her spiritual marriage with the Heavenly Bridegroom. As a ripe fruit he gave himself up into the hands of God. With the cutting of his hair, his past life was also finally cut off. Henceforth, having put his hand to the plough, he would never look back (Lk. 6:62). He afterwards told Sister Praskovia of the Diveyev Convent: "I have gone through the whole monastic life, Mother, and have never, even in thought, gone out of the Monastery."

Now his whole future lies ahead of him. And if every Monk knows from experience with what joy and zeal divine grace fires the soul of the newly professed, with what fire must St. Seraphim's flaming spirit have blazed! We do not know this from his words; we can only imagine it. He did not like to broadcast the secrets of his inner life; neither did he afterwards advise it to others. "One should not without necessity open one's heart to people. You may find only one in a thousand who will keep your secret." It is even better

talkativeness quenches the fire of divine love

St. Seraphim of Sarov

"by all means to try to conceal within oneself the treasure of gifts. Otherwise you will lose it and will not find it." "It is most pitiful that through this unguardedness and talkativeness that fire which our Lord Jesus Christ came to send on the earth of the heart may be quenched;" for as the Saint said in the words of St. Isaac the Syrian, "nothing so quenches the fire which has been breathed into the heart of a Monk by the Holy Spirit after the sanctification of his soul as intercourse with people, and much speaking and talking."

And therefore, if even before, during his novitiate, he was inclined to solitude and silence, now he retired altogether into the cell of his soul (Mat. 6:6-7). Later in his instructions he taught:

"Above all one must adorn oneself with silence. For St. Ambrose of Milan says: 'I saw many saved by silence, but by much speaking not a single one.' And again one of the Fathers says that silence is the mystery of the future age, whereas words are but the weapons of this world" (Philokalia, V. The Monks Callistus and Ignatius). "From solitude and silence are born contrition and meekness." "While dwelling in the cell in silence, exercise in prayer and meditation makes a man pious; only remain in your cell in attention and silence, and try by all means to get nearer to the Lord; and the Lord is ready to make a man into an Angel." "But if it is not always possible to remain in solitude and silence, while living in a Monastery and occupied with the obediences imposed by the Abbot, one ought at least to devote to it some of the time left

58

In the Angelic Habit

over from obedience;" "and for this small offering the Lord God will not fail to send down His gracious mercy."

But especially St. Seraphim observed "that we should not pay attention to other people's affairs, or think or speak of them, according to the Psalmist: *My mouth may not speak of the works of men* (Ps. 16:4), but that we should pray to the Lord: *Cleanse me from my secret sins* (18:13).

Even in his outward demeanour a Monk should behave himself in a collected and detached manner: "On meeting Elders or the brethren" they should be "shown respect by bows, having your eyes always under guard."

Even "sitting at table do not look" at any one, "and do not judge what people eat; but attend to yourself and feed your soul with prayer."

And only two exceptions does the Saint make; firstly in conversation with "the children of the Divine Mysteries," that is with truly spiritual and like-minded persons; and secondly, when a Brother is sad, "One should try to cheer the spirit of a troubled or despondent man with a loving word." But here too one must have discernment; an inexperienced person had better keep quiet even here, especially if he has not yet gained self-knowledge. "If you do not understand yourself, can you judge anything or teach others?" said the Saint to a Monk. "Be quiet, constantly be quiet, always remember the presence of God and His

St. Seraphim of Sarov

Name. Do not enter into conversation with anybody, but by all means beware of condemning those who speak or laugh much. Be in this case deaf and dumb." Undoubtedly he acted in this way himself, especially at the beginning of his life as a Monk, for:

"We must pay attention to the beginning and end of our life; but in the middle, both in the case of fortune or adversity, we must be indifferent."

In particular the Saint insistently advised a Monk strictly to "guard himself from intercourse with the female sex; for just as a wax candle, even though not lighted, will melt if put among burning candles; so the heart of a Monk will be imperceptibly weakened through intercourse with the female sex."

And even in his old age he gave the following advice to a seminarist, who became subsequently the Abbot of a Monastery, Archimandrite Nikon:

"Fear like the fire of Gehenna the painted crows (women), for they often turn the King's soldiers into slaves of Satan." And he himself, as we shall presently see, was extremely cautious and reserved at the beginning of his monastic life.

One could further add to this hidden period of the first days of the Saint's Monkhood an undoubted increase in the labour of prayer; and then an urge to complete solitude which usually draws the hearts of ardent souls. But this will be realized somewhat later; for the moment he is faced with ministry among the

In the Angelic Habit

brethren and collaboration with his spiritual Fathers, the Abbot Pachomius and the Elder Isaiah, who had been given to him as spiritual Fathers at his profession, to both of whom he entrusted himself with child-like obedience in response to their strong love for him.

Shortly after his profession he was nominated for Ordination to the order of Deacon, and on the 27th October of this same year 1786, that is after only two months and a half, he was ordained by Bishop Victor of Vladimir, for at that time Sarov belonged to that diocese. By promoting the newly professed Monk so quickly, the holy Fathers evinced thereby the deep esteem which the man of God already enjoyed during his novitiate. To him can be applied the word of Scripture: *Honourable old age is not measured by the number of years, but wisdom is grey hair to men and a spotless life is old age* (Wisdom 4:8-9). He who serves the Lord is loved by God and by men in spite of his youth. *Being made perfect in a short space, he fulfilled long years; for his soul was pleasing to the Lord* (Wisdom 4:13-14). And the Father Abbot, who was usually strict in keeping the rules and Church regulations, in this case deemed the young Monk worthy of high honour, and showed in this too his special love for him. "Our Fathers of blessed memory, the Abbot Pachomius and the treasurer Isaiah," said the servant of God later, "both saintly men, loved me as their own souls. And they hid nothing from me; and they cared for the things which were profitable for their souls and for myself." And "when Father

St. Seraphim of Sarov

Pachomius served[8], he rarely did so without me, poor Seraphim."

And even when he went out of the Monastery to some place, especially for a Service he used to take with him no other than Hierodeacon Seraphim "and hid nothing from him," he so loved and esteemed him.

But Divine Providence had in view another, better and higher aim in the new obedience--to develop and perfect in His ardent servant the burning of love for God and the spirit of prayer, which transports one into the world above. And nothing so assists this as participation in the celebration of the Divine Liturgy. Meanwhile, had the Saint remained in the usual monastic obediences, they would have diverted him from the way of the contemplative life which had been appointed to him by God. But now, for six years and ten months the Saint very often celebrated Liturgies, and was carried away to another world, which in fact was already his own. For had not his heavenly Lady said: "This is one of our kind"?

How he prepared for the celebration of the heavenly Sacrament may be seen from the fact that on the eve of Sundays and holidays the Saint spent whole nights in prayer. And at the end of the Liturgy, he would linger in Church, putting the vessels in order, folding the vestments, caring for the tidiness of the Church. How highly he esteemed the glory of the sacred ministry may be seen from his instructions to the

---

[8] i.e. celebrated the Liturgy.

In the Angelic Habit

Sisters of Diveyev who assisted in Church: "All the Church duties," noted the Nun Kapitolina, "must be performed only by virgins. This is the will of the Heavenly Queen! Remember this and keep it as a sacred trust and pass it on to others!"

"Never and on no account should unprofessed Sisters be allowed to enter the sanctuary."

"Never, God forbid, not for anything, not for anyone should one speak in the Sanctuary, even if one were to have to suffer for it"; for "the Lord Himself is present there! And in fear and trembling all the Cherubim and Seraphim and all the Powers of God stand before Him. Who then will speak before His face!" said the Saint.

Even when wiping the dust and sweeping the dirt from the Temple of God, one should not throw it carelessly anywhere: "Even the dust of the Temple of God is sacred." And the water ought also to be poured into a special, clean place."

And in general Father Seraphim taught thus about the Church: "There is no higher obedience than a Church obedience! And were it only to wipe the floor of the house of the Lord with a cloth, this will be counted higher than any other action by God! There is no higher obedience than a Church obedience. And all that is done there, and how you go in and out, all ought to be performed with fear and trembling and with unceasing prayer." "And Whom are we to fear in it! And where are we so to rejoice in spirit, in heart

St. Seraphim of Sarov

and in our whole mind if not in Church, where our
Lord and Master Himself is always present with us!"

"And one should never speak in Church about
anything else except strictly necessary Church matters
and about the Church. And what is more beautiful,
higher and more glorious than the Church!"

So he felt, and so he himself acted till his very
death. One of his visitors was deemed worthy to visit
him ten days before his death.

"I came," he wrote, "into the hospital Church to the
early Liturgy, even before the beginning of the
Service. And I saw that Father Seraphim was sitting
on the floor in the right choir. I went up to him at
once for his blessing; and after blessing me, he hurriedly went into the Sanctuary, answering my request
to talk to him with the words: "Afterwards, afterwards!"

What an unearthly life he lived in Church and especially at the Liturgy one can only guess to a certain
extent from his saying that when in Church he forgot
about rest, and food, and drink; and on leaving
Church he only said with regret: "Why cannot man,
like the Angels, unceasingly serve the Lord!" And he
contemplated them more than once during the celebration of the Liturgy.

"Their appearance," said Father Seraphim, "was
like lightning. Their garments were white as snow or

woven with gold; as to their singing, it is impossible to describe it."

An ineffable rapture then seized the Saint: "*My heart was like wax from unutterable joy* (Ps. 21:15)," he said. "And I remembered nothing for the joy of it. I only remembered how I went into the holy Church and went out of it."

And once, during the Liturgy, he was granted such a vision as has been granted to only a few Saints, and only to the greatest of them.

"Once I happened to be serving as Deacon on Holy and Great Thursday. The Divine Liturgy began at two o'clock in the afternoon and, as usual, was preceded by Vespers. After the little entry and the readings I, poor sinner that I am, exclaimed in the royal doors: 'O Lord, save the pious, and hear us,' and entering the royal doors and holding up my stole to the people, I finished: 'And to the ages of ages,' when suddenly I was struck by a ray as of sunlight. Glancing at this radiance, I saw our Lord and God Jesus Christ, in the image of the Son of Man, shining with glory and unutterable light, surrounded by heavenly Powers, Angels and Archangels, Cherubim and Seraphim, as if by a swarm of bees, and proceeding through the air from the western doors of the Church. On reaching the ambon, the Lord raised His most pure hands and blessed the Clergy and the congregation: and then stepping into His holy local Icon, which is to the right of the royal gates, He was transfigured, surrounded by choirs of Angels who shone with unutterable light all

St. Seraphim of Sarov

through the Church. And I, who am dust and ashes, by meeting the Lord Jesus then in the air, was granted a special blessing from Him; my heart felt pure, enlightened joy in the sweetness of love for the Lord!"

St. Seraphim's appearance changed and, struck by the divine vision, he could not even move from his place by the royal gates. When Father Pachomius noticed this, he sent two other Hierodeacons, who took him under his arms and led him into the Sanctuary. But he continued to stand there motionless for about three hours in ecstasy. And only his face constantly changed; now it would become white as snow, now a flush would spread all over it.

After the Service the Elders asked him what happened. And Father Seraphim, who hid nothing from his spiritual Fathers, told them everything. They gave him the commandment to enclose himself in silence and to immerse himself still more deeply in humility, and to beware of arrogance from such an unusual vision. The Saint accepted their instructions with whole-hearted meekness and remained silent for the time being.

As to what the Saint experienced in the Holy Sacrament of Communion, this is fully known only to himself. From his instructions we know what a tremendous significance he gave to the Holy Eucharist.

When he was asked how often one should approach the heavenly Sacrament, he answered:

In the Angelic Habit

"The oftener, the better."

In particular he gave the Sisters of Diveyev the following rule, as noted by Sister Kapitolina:

"One should not lose an opportunity of using as often as possible the grace granted through the Communion of Christ's Holy Mysteries[9]. While trying as far as possible to concentrate on the humble realization of one's utter sinfulness, one should approach the Holy Sacrament which redeems everything and everyone with hope and firm faith in the unutterable mercy of God, saying with contrition: I have sinned, O Lord, with my soul, with my heart, in word, in thought and with all my senses."

Especially remarkable is St. Seraphim's order about this to the Confessor of the Diveyev Convent, Father Basil:

"I command them, Father, to partake of Christ's holy and life-giving Sacrament in all the four fasts and on the twelve festivals; I even order them to do so on the great feast days: the oftener, the better." "As their spiritual Father, do not oppose them, I tell you; for the grace given us through Communion is so great that however unworthy and sinful a man may be, as long as he approaches the Lord who redeems us all (in the humble realization of his all-sinfulness), though we be covered from head to foot with the wounds of sins, he will be cleansed, Father, by the grace of

---

[9] Holy Communion--ed.

St. Seraphim of Sarov

Christ, and become more and more enlightened, and will be quite illumined and saved. You, Father, are their spiritual director, and I tell you all this that you may know."

"Besides," writes Father Basil, "he always instructed me as the spiritual Father of the Sisters of the Convent, bidding me to be as indulgent as possible at Confession. In the past many have rebuked and condemned me for that, and have even been angry with me; and even till now they still judge me: but I strictly keep his commandment and have kept it all my life. The servant of God used to say:

'Remember, you are only a witness, Father, but it is God Who is the judge! And how much, how much, and such awful sins as it is impossible even to utter, did not our bountiful Lord and Saviour forgive us. How then are we men to judge a man! We are mere witnesses, mere witnesses, Father. Always remember that: merely witnesses, Father!"

To a layman he gave this commandment: "Communicate four times. Once is also good. As God deems you worthy. He who communicates, will be saved; but he who does not, I think will not. *Where the Master is, there shall also the servant be*" (Jn. 12:26). On another occasion the Saint proclaimed a deep mystery, namely that the Communion of one is also beneficial for others.

"He who reverently partakes of Holy Communion and that not only once a year, will be saved, prosper-

In the Angelic Habit

ous and live long on this earth. I believe," he added, "that according to the great goodness of God, His grace will be manifested in the family of the communicant also. In the Lord's sight one who does His will is more than a legion of transgressors."

What a wonderful, comforting and instructive revelation!

At the same time the Father used to quieten those who were afraid to approach the Sacrament owing to a sense of their unworthiness. We have seen it from his commandment to Father Basil; but it appeared especially forcibly in the case of the Novice John.

Once, on the eve of one of the twelve feasts, when they were to have Holy Communion, John took some food after the Evening Service, which was not in accordance with the rules of the Monastery. To this was added a general consciousness of his unworthiness; and the Novice began to be downcast. And the more he thought the more he despaired: "A legion of terrifying thoughts, one after another, crowded my head. Instead of hope in the merits of Christ the Saviour Who covers all our sins, I imagined that according to God's judgement, on account of my unworthiness, I should be either burnt by fire or swallowed up by the earth alive, as soon as I approached the Holy Chalice."

Wishing to set his conscience at rest, the Novice confessed, but even this brought no peace to his soul; and, standing in the sanctuary, he continued to suffer. St. Seraphim, perceiving this, called him and said

St. Seraphim of Sarov

these wonderful words: "Had we filled the ocean with our tears, even then we should not have been able to satisfy the Lord for what He gives us free, nourishing us with His most pure Flesh and Blood, which wash, cleanse, vivify and raise us up. Ands so, draw near without a doubt, and do not be troubled; only believe that this is the true Body and Blood of our Lord Jesus Christ, which has been given to heal all our sins."

The Novice, now at peace, took the Holy Sacrament with faith and humility.

But another time the Saint uttered an awful word about unworthy communicants. A young widow, Anna Petrovna Eropkina, having lived in marriage only three months, was talking about St. Seraphim, and among other things, noted the following: When her beloved husband suddenly fell ill, she "feared to suggest to him that he should take Christ's Holy Sacrament" being afraid of frightening him; "and though he also was very devout, he feared to grieve his wife by inviting a Priest." And so he died without Communion. His wife was greatly distressed about it.

"Especially to die without the Viaticum seemed to me God's punishment for my sins and those of my husband; I thought that my husband would be for ever alienated from the divine life." "After the burial... at times I was in despair and would have perhaps done away with my life, if I had not been strictly watched."

So the widow remained in anguish for ten months. Then upon the advice of her uncle, she went the five

In the Angelic Habit

hundred versts[10] to distant Sarov. There she found complete peace with the Saint; and as regards her husband's death, the Father told her this: "Do not distress yourself about it my joy; I do not think that for this alone his soul will perish. God only can judge as to whom He will either reward or punish and in what away."

And further he added: "This is what sometimes happens: here in this world people take Holy Communion; but according to the Lord's judgement, they remain uncommunicated."

How awful this is! How enlightening! And then the Saint continued:

"Another may want to communicate; but his wish is not fulfilled, quite independently of himself. To such a one Holy Communion may be granted in an invisible way through an Angel of God." The widow was comforted.

But sometimes the Lord punishes visibly those who unworthily approach the Sacrament. A Priest of the town of Spassk, Father Peter Theoktistov, described the following case. A Deacon, having been convicted of bad conduct by his Priest, in his turn accused the Priest before the Bishop through witnesses who swore a false oath in his favour. The Deacon was promoted. From his village he was transferred to the town to serve with Father Peter. He continued to serve

---

[10] About 330 miles.

there without being troubled by his conscience. Soon the Deacon came to Sarov and went to Father Seraphim. Seeing him, the seer went out of his cell to meet him, immediately turned him back and said with anger: "Go, go away from me; this is not my business!"

The Deacon did not know what to do further. A certain Monk advised him to confess first. But neither did this help; St. Seraphim drove him away for the second time: "Go, go, you perjurer, and do not serve!"[11]

The Deacon returned home and told his people what had happened; but he did not think of repenting of his sin of perjury. Then God punished him. When before the Liturgy the Priest said the appointed prayer with him: "O Lord, open my lips and my mouth shall declare Thy praise," suddenly the Deacon instead of saying according to the rubric: "It is time to act for the Lord. Master, give the blessing," he became dumb. And he even had to leave the Church and go home. There the power of speech was restored to him. But as soon as he reentered the Church, he lost it again. The divine punishment lasted three years until the unworthy minister was brought to full repentance. On the day of the Lord's Ascension, at Matins, after the Magnification they sang this verse of the Psalm: *O clap your hands, all you people; shout to God with the voice of rejoicing* (Ps 46:1)

---

[11] i.e. minister in the Church.

In the Angelic Habit

The Deacon, as he related afterwards, was suddenly struck with terror by these words and began to pray for mercy. And suddenly his tongue was loosed from its dumbness.

Overjoyed by his healing and still more by the mercy of God, the Deacon there and then openly repented of everything, recounted the miracle which had been accomplished and praised the spiritual insight of his accuser, Father Seraphim. So "God," taught the Father, "discloses to us His love for men, saving us in every way, not only when we do good, but also when we offend Him and anger Him. How patiently He bears our transgressions! And when He punishes us, how mercifully He punishes!"

"Therefore," says St. Seraphim in the words of St. Isaac the Syrian, "do not call God just, for His justice is not seen in our works (i.e. God's mercy to us in the face of the multitude of our sins), and His Son has shown us that He is rather good and merciful. Where is His justice? We are sinners and Christ died for us" (Rom. 5:8).

But let us return to the life of the Saint himself. At this period of his life as a Hierodeacon, we must mention an event which afterwards bound him for ever with his spiritual creation--the Diveyev Convent.

In 1789, at the beginning of June, Father Pachomius with the bursar, Father Isaiah, went to the village of Lemet for the burial of a benefactor of the Monastery, the landowner Alexander Solovtzov. As

St. Seraphim of Sarov

was his custom, the Abbot took with him Hierodeacon Seraphim. On the way they called at Diveyev in order to visit the foundress of the community, the blessed Agathia Semenovna Melgounova, in monasticism-- Alexandra. She had received from the Lord the news of her near end and had asked the Fathers to anoint her. On taking leave of them, Mother Alexandra began to beseech Father Pachomius not to deprive her orphans of his care. The Elder answered prophetically: "Mother! I do not refuse to serve the Heavenly Queen according to my strength and your commandment. But how to undertake it, I do not know. Shall I live till that day? But here is Hierodeacon Seraphim. His spirituality is known to you, and he is young. He will live till that day. Entrust him with this great task."

Mother Agathia answered that she was only making a request, and "the Heavenly Queen would then instruct him herself."

The Elders left. On their way back, on the 13th of June, they were just in time for her burial. Having celebrated the Liturgy and the Burial Service of the deceased Abbess, they had intended to go to Sarov. But it was raining heavily. Father Pachomius was delayed. As for the Deacon Seraphim, out of chastity and scrupulous spiritual carefulness, he did not even stay for the funeral dinner in a community of Nuns; but immediately after the burial--surely with the blessing of the Fathers who know his spiritual strictness--he walked back to his Monastery in the rain.

In the Angelic Habit

How wonderful and out of the ordinary are God's Saints! Who else would have acted in this way? What strength and decision! What carefulness! And this in such an angelic man as St. Seraphim.

But only few know another still more striking and edifying fact: this Saint who, one may say, spiritually gave birth to the Diveyev Convent and its Nuns, had never been there except on this single occasion! But he built and directed everything from Sarov, eight miles distant, a fact simply incomprehensible and impossible for others!

No, it is not so simple for people to become "Saints." Even to speak of them is difficult and embarrassing for us sinners. As for imitating them--our strength would fail us, and it is quite impossible even to imagine their labours fully. They are extraordinary people. They are heavenly giants, giants of the spirit. They are not of us, who are earthly, sinful, weak.

Almost seven years of monastic life as a Deacon had passed for St. Seraphim. Father Pachomius was already approaching death. And while still in this life he wanted to see his beloved co-labourer invested with the full grace of the Priesthood.

Together with the senior brethren who had also seen the labours and holy life of the young Monk, the Abbot handed to Theophilus, Bishop of Tambov (to whose diocese the Sarov Monastery had just been transferred), a request for his Ordination to the Priesthood. And on the 2nd September 1793, the

St. Seraphim of Sarov

flaming Seraphim received a new grace from the hands of this Bishop, and was ordained Priest.

It would seem that now a wider field of ministry to the Monastery, as well as to the brethren and pilgrims, was opened to him. But a soul which has been fired with a strong flame of love for God cannot find rest and stop half way.

"God is a fire," said the Saint, "warming and firing the thoughts and feelings."[12]

"He who has acquired perfect love exists in this life as if he did not exist; for he considers himself alien to the visible, and patiently waits for the invisible. He has been completely transformed into love for God and has forgotten all other love."

"He who truly loves God considers himself a pilgrim and a stranger on this earth; for in his striving towards God, he contemplates Him alone with his soul and mind."

Seven years of monastic life spent mostly at God's Altar, had aroused in St. Seraphim a thirst for holy solitude in the wilderness. Moreover his friends, one by one, departed for the other life, and this drew his thoughts all the more to a realization of the vanity of this transient world. Father Joseph, his first director, had long since died; Father Pachomius was now

---

[12] Literally: "the heart and reins." But we trust that we have translated the words correctly, from a psychological point of view, into the modern equivalents.

In the Angelic Habit

preparing for his departure; there remained a third director, who also ardently loved the Saint, the bursar, Father Isaiah, the future Abbot of the Monastery. And so Father Seraphim decided to use his authority for the accomplishment of his desire to go into the solitude for which his soul had so long been striving. For even as a Novice he had sometimes gone to the forest with the permission of the Abbot and the blessing of his Elder, Father Joseph, urged by his spirit and inspired by the example of Abbot Nazarius, Mark the Silent, Dorotheus the hermit. There, in a secret place, he had made a small hut for himself and spent some time in contemplation and prayer. There he performed the short but frequently repeated rule "which an Angel of the Lord had given to the great Pachomius of Egypt."[13] But all the rest of his time was also spent by Prochorus in the "remembrance of God" and unceasing prayer, which had become to him the breath of his soul.

Then he had also combined with contemplation a special fast: he ate only once a day, and then only bread and water; while on Wednesdays and Fridays he completely abstained from food and drink. (

---

[13] It consists of the usual initial prayers from the Trisagion to Our Father; then, Lord have mercy (12); Glory; Now and ever; Come, let us worship (3); Psalm 50; the Creed; 100 Jesus Prayers; It is truly meet; Dismissal. These prayers had to be performed 12 times during the day and 12 during the night, i.e. every hour, They took the place of all other services for the hermits. From this was derived later Father Seraphim's "little rule."

St. Seraphim of Sarov

But these labours had been only the beginning and the first tests of the young spirit in his flights into the upper regions. During the sixteen years of his unceasing struggles in the Monastery his spiritual wings had grown strong, and the "heavenly man" flew away to solitude "for God's sake."

Moreover, we have reason to believe that there was also another cause for it. One must not think that Monasteries, even good and well organized ones, are a peaceful abode of angelic men. No, they are places of repentance, labours and struggle. And nowhere does the devil so trouble souls as among striving Monks. And therefore side by side with noble aspirations and spiritual gifts we always see in Monasteries the wiles of the enemy and human passions. And for the pure soul of Father Seraphim it became difficult to live in this school of strife. We do not know for certain whether he suffered personal affronts from the brethren, who sometimes may have envied his ascetic labours, his holiness, his life in solitude and the love his Elders and especially the Abbot showed him. But this is what he once said himself to another Monk who came to ask his advice as to life in solitude:

"Father," asked this Monk, "people say that retirement from a community into solitude is pharisaism and that such a change of life means disparagement of the brethren or else their condemnation."

To this Father Seraphim replied: "It is not our business to condemn others. And we leave the Brotherhood not out of hatred for them, but chiefly

In the Angelic Habit

because we have accepted and wear the habit of Angels, for whom it is unbearable to be where the Lord God is offended by word and by deed. And therefore when we separate ourselves from the Brotherhood, we only avoid hearing and seeing what is repugnant to God's commandments which may happen in a multitude of brethren. We do not run away from men who are of the same nature as we are and who bear the same name of Christ, but from the sins which they commit. As it was said to the Great Arsenius: 'Flee from men, and thou wilt be saved.'"

The outward cause of his solitude was illness. From much standing at prayer both in Church and in his cell, the Saint's legs had become swollen and ulcerated; and it became difficult for him to carry out his monastic obediences. Officially this was given as the first reason. But the chief inner foundation was spiritual: "according to his zeal...exclusively for the sake of spiritual peace, for God's sake."

Urged by all these circumstances--but rather guided by the Holy Spirit Himself--Father Seraphim undoubtedly even during Father Pachomius' lifetime had asked his blessing to live a life in solitude. Now the time had come. The Abbot was passing his last days. The Saint was constantly with him and served him with ardent zeal, remembering with what love the Abbot had nursed him during his three years of illness. At this time the care of Diveyev was entrusted to him.

St. Seraphim of Sarov

Once Father Seraphim saw on Father Pachomius' face an expression of unusual worry and sadness.

"What makes you so sad, holy Father?" he asked the Elder.

"I am anxious about the Sisters of the Diveyev community," answered the sick man. "Who is going to care for them after me?"

Then the Saint, who was usually so humble and especially cautious concerning the female sex, promised the dying man to continue his work. It was an inspiration of the Holy Spirit and the will of the Heavenly Queen. Father Pachomius was cheered, and gratefully kissed Father Seraphim. And then he soon peacefully fell asleep in God (6th November 1794). Father Isaiah was chosen in his place. Having bitterly lamented and buried his Father, benefactor and friend in the Lord, the Saint received the permission and blessing to live a life in solitude from his Elder, the new Abbot.

It was again the eve of the Presentation of the Mother of God, the 20th November. Sixteen years ago, on that same day the young Prochorus had entered the gates of the Monastery. Now the spiritually flaming Seraphim goes out through them not into the world, but still farther from it, into the depths of the wilderness. The Mother of God leads her beloved servant and suppliant within the tabernacle into the holy of holies, nearer to herself and to God.

In the Angelic Habit

The monastic cell had been for him the threshold to true monasticism--to completely solitary communion with God, to interior prayer."[14]

"Merely exterior prayer is not sufficient," he instructed a future Monk. "God attends to the mind. And therefore those Monks who do not combine exterior prayer with interior, are not Monks, but merely charred logs."

As for the flaming Seraphim, his interior burning had become so strong that he wanted full scope for his spirit in silence.

"I love you," said Arsenius the Great to the brethren on leaving the community for the desert, "but I love God more. And I cannot be with God and with men."

"The hesychast[15] is an earthly Angel." This was the natural outcome of Saint Seraphim's years of novitiate and monasticism in "the angelic order."

---

[14] "The bearer of this," it is said in the ticket of leave from the Monastery, 20th November 1794, "Hieromonk Seraphim of the Sarov Monastery, is given leave to remain in solitude in his (i.e. the Monastery's) summer-house, on account of his unfitness for life in community, owing to his illness, and in accordance with his zeal, after a trial of many years in the monastery; and he is allowed to go into solitude solely for the sake of peace of spirit, for God's sake, and with a rule given to him according to the regulations of the Holy Fathers; and in the future let no one hinder him from remaining in that place; and this I confirm. (signed) Hieromonk Isaiah." "In witness of which, I hereby affix a seal."
[15] Hesychast: one practicing quiet and silence.

Above: The distant hermitage, the "desert" to which St. Seraphim retired to struggle and to be in communion with God. *Below:* The near hermitage, where later in life the Saint prayed and ministered to the Pilgrims.

Chapter V

The Distant Hermitage

Five versts[16] from the Monastery, on the bank of the River Sarovka, in a dense pine forest on a high hill stood a wooden shack or cell consisting of one room with a tiny anteroom and a porch. There the holy solitary went to live. An Icon of the Mother of God in one corner, a stove in the other, a stump which served as both table and chair, an earthen pot for keeping dry bread--this was all the furniture the "distant hermitage" contained. Under the floor of the cell a small cellar had been made, perhaps for storing vegetables. But Father Seraphim used it for solitary prayer and for hiding from visitors, and in summer he used to rest there from the heat. Round the hermitage the Saint cultivated a small kitchen garden in which he planted potatoes, cabbages, onions, beet-roots and such like. For some time he even kept bees, but later he gave up this occupation, probably because it drew him away from the interior life. Here the ascetic also spent nearly sixteen years until he rose to a higher degree. Sixteen years! It is easy to say it. But who can say what was going on all through those long years in his soul, his strong, determined, ecstatic soul? "He who has tasted of the divine sweetness strives for quiet," says St. John of the Ladder, "in order to be insatiably satisfied with it without any hindrance."

St. Seraphim loved to quote the words of St. Basil the Great: "The desert is a paradise of sweetness, where the fragrant flowers of love (for God) now

---

[16] A verst is almost two thirds of a mile.

St. Seraphim of Sarov

flame with fiery blossoms, now shine with snow-white purity; with them is peace and tranquillity...There is the incense of perfect mortification not only of the flesh, but also, which is even more glorious, of the will itself; there is the incense of unceasing prayer constantly kindled by the fire of divine love; there the flowers of virtue glistening with various adornments blossom with the grace of unfading beauty."

And St. Seraphim was satisfied and delighted with the beauty of this sweet paradise. His soul lived by interior prayer, which had long since become an ever-flowing fountain of living water to him. Now in the wilderness his life consisted chiefly of prayer. He usually said the Divine Office in the customary order, namely: after midnight he read the rule of St. Pachomius, then the Morning Prayers, Nocturns, Matins and so on till Compline inclusive. But sometimes he replaced the regular offices by prostrations with the Prayer of Jesus. Thus, instead of the Evening Rule, he made a thousand prostrations. But besides that, he was always in the constant "remembrance of God" and contemplation. Often he was found in ecstasy. Sometimes, while busy with some work in the garden, he would suddenly drop the hoe from his hands and his spirit would be immersed in the heavenly world; or he would chop off one, two, three bits of wood and, dropping his axe would stiffen in the contemplation of the mystery of the Most Holy Trinity, and would be rapt in prayer to Him. At such times people who visited him did not disturb the

The Distant Hermitage

Saint, and waited till he returned to a normal state. But sometimes his rapture would last so long that they did not wait till the end and quietly left the hermitage in order not to disturb the grace-given illuminations of the Saint; and they were just as edified and comforted by what they had seen as if they had waited to hear his teaching. How little we have said! Yet in reality there is little more to say; because the whole of those sixteen years in solitude was chiefly spent in such contemplative life, in unceasing converse with God.

The soul is a great mystery; and its life in the case of ascetics is all hidden in God. Not for nothing did Father Seraphim, even while at work, always sing of the heavenly world. "Solitaries have an incessant divine desire. Those who are outside this vain world," that is those who have renounced the world have a constant desire for God. Or an irmos of the third tone: "O Thou Who hast produced everything from nothing, creating by the Word, perfecting by the Spirit, supreme All-Ruler, establish me in Thy love"... "Establish, strengthen me in love for Thee." Or the wonderful dogmatic to the Mother of God: "Let us sing the praises of Mary the Virgin, Door of Heaven, Glory of all the world..For she revealed herself as Heaven and the Temple of the Godhead... Courage, then, courage, people of God, for He, the All-Powerful, will vanquish your foes."

Living in His heavenly world, the Saint even gave to the surrounding places names which reminded him of heavenly citizens or holy events. He had his own

St. Seraphim of Sarov

city of Jerusalem, Golgotha, Bethlehem, Nazareth, Tabor, Jordan, Kedron and so on. He called his hill Athos. When he visited those places, he usually said there some suitable prayers: at Bethlehem, Matins; at Nazareth, an Akathist to the Mother of God; at Golgotha, the Ninth Hour; and so on.

The reading of the Word of God took, as before, much of his time; but it served him merely as another means of leading to the only goal---the vision of the other world. "One should read Holy Scripture," he said afterwards, "in order to give the spirit the freedom to rise to the heavenly mansions and be fed through sweetest converse with the Lord."

Father Seraphim spent the remaining time in bodily labours, without which the monastic life is unthinkable even in the desert. He was either busy in his garden, or he would gather moss, prepare logs for fuel, or prop up the bank of the river. Later he began to carry on his back a bag heavily filled with sand and stones, in which lay the Holy Gospel. When he was asked why he did that, the Saint answered in the two words of St. Ephrem the Syrian: "I oppress him who oppressed me," that is the enemy who assaults ascetics. To the same end, in order to achieve complete mortification of the old man, he sometimes resorted to drastic measures. Stripped to the waist, he would work near a marsh; or sitting by his cell, he would give himself up to mosquitoes; and they stung him so fiercely that blood trickled down his face, and his body became swollen, blue and clotted with blood. The Saint never went to a bath-house. Neither did he

The Distant Hermitage

wear warm clothes. A smock of white linen, a felt cap, leather mits, birch shoes or leather boots--these were his clothes the year round. On his chest always hung a copper cross, his mother's blessing. His food was of the plainest, and even that was limited in quantity. "Bread and water are sufficient. It was even so before the flood," he said to a layman.

May non-fast food be eaten in Lent if lenten fare does not agree with a person and the doctors order him to stop fasting?

St. Seraphim replied: "Bread and water harm no one. And how did people live to be a hundred? *Man shall not live by bread only, but by every word that proceeds out of the mouth of God* (Deut. 8:3). Keep what the Church has appointed in the seven Ecumenical Councils. Woe to the man who takes away or adds one word thereto. What do the doctors say about Saints who healed septic ulcers by a single touch, and about Moses' staff through which God brought water out of a rock?"

And Father Seraphim knew it himself better than anyone else. At first his food was bread, and that stale, which he took from the Monastery once a week. He also took vegetables from his kitchen-garden; but afterwards, with his blessing of his Elder, the Abbot Isaiah, he stopped taking bread from the Monastery entirely so as not to burden the community, but to take food after the example of the Apostle Paul, *working with our own hands* (Cor.4:12).

St. Seraphim of Sarov

That is how the hermit spent his time on ordinary days. But on the eve of Sundays and festivals, he went to the Monastery and attended the Evening Service; then he confessed, and in the morning he partook of the Holy Mysteries at the early Liturgy in the hospital Church of Saints Zosimus and Sabbatius. And he remained in the Monastery until Vespers. During this time he received the brethren and pilgrims who came to him for comfort and advice. When the brethren went to the Evening Service, Father Seraphim took his ration of bread for the week and went away unobtrusively to his beloved hermitage.

Throughout the first week of the great fast he remained all the time in the Monastery without taking food until Communion on Saturday.

His Confessor was still his Elder, Father Isaiah. And so little by little Father Seraphim went from strength to strength. But in order to strengthen His servant in the spirit of prayer, the All-wise Lord permitted him to have a temptation. The Holy Fathers even uttered a strange saying: if there were no devils, there would be no Saints; that is, if there were no temptations, there would be fewer motives for the ascetic labours of Saints; and there would also be fewer crowns. And he who wants more grace, must prepare himself better for temptations. So teaches St. Isaac the Syrian, that greatest of ascetics.

The following circumstances served as a motive. The Sarov Monastery was already famous in his time for its strong rule and for the austere life of the

The Distant Hermitage

Monks. Therefore people used to apply there for administrators and Abbots for communities in other dioceses. Among others the famous restorer of the Valaam Monastery, Abbot Nazarius, had been professed in Sarov; and here he also ended his days as a hermit during the lifetime of the Saint.

The flaming Seraphim could still less be hidden from human sight. Therefore, barely two years after his retirement into solitude, in 1796, he was offered the post of Abbot of the Alateer Monastery in the province of Samara with a promotion to the rank of Archimandrite. The holy recluse declined this offer, and begged Father Isaiah to refuse it. In his stead was sent the Monk Abraham.

But soon after this the enemy assailed the Saint with hellish malice and raised within him a storm of "mental conflict" and despondency[17].

We have already seen how terrible the Saint considered the spirit of despondency, when a man does not even want to live. But he also knew the way to victory--namely, through prayer.

---

[17] There is a legend that Father Seraphim, having refused promotion, for a moment succumbed to temptation and regretted it. But the Saints did not only fight sinful actions; they also considered the mere desires a no lesser evil (Matt. 5:22-28). Perceiving within himself this shadow of egoism, the Saint decided to uproot every attachment to this world; for "he who is sick with passion and aims at quiet" runs a risk of destroying all his labour (Bishop Theophan). That is why he undertook an extraordinary labour in order to beseech God's forgiveness and conquer the temptation of the enemy.

St. Seraphim of Sarov

In the forest, about halfway between his cell and the Monastery, beside the road, lay a huge granite boulder. Every night Father Seraphim went there; and, either standing or kneeling, with hands raised to heaven, he incessantly cried: "God, be merciful to me, a sinner!" And the Saint dragged another stone into his cell and prayed there by day, so as not to be seen by people. In such tremendous labour he remained for a thousand days and a thousand nights, interrupting it only for necessary rest and for strengthening himself with food. A thousand days and a thousand nights! We have read and heard about it. But have we stopped to think what it means? And is it possible to understand that which we have not experimentally lived through and which we cannot even imagine properly? This is a feat which exceeds human strength. Let us stand in thought near the ascetic and secretly watch him.

It is a dark night. Ordinary people would be scared. But the kneeling hermit thinks of nothing; he only unceasingly raises to heaven a cry for mercy: "God, be merciful, be merciful to me, a sinner!" Wild beasts approach. Death threatens him. But he is not afraid. Perhaps even he would wish to be torn to pieces for the expiation of his sins. But the beasts go away from a man who does not even pay attention to them. And he continues to sigh: "God, be merciful to me a sinner...a sinner...a sinner." Autumn has come, and with it rains, mud, cold. The forest rustles. He is wet through. Who would not wish for a warm corner? But the Saint raises his wet hands and warms his soul with

The Distant Hermitage

the warmth of his repentance: "God, be merciful! Have mercy! I have sinned: forgive! Punish me, but have mercy. I have angered Thee: restore Thy mercy! I have defiled my soul; cleanse me! Without purity, I do not see Thee!"

Now it is winter, with bitter frost. The pine trees are cracking. Hands and feet are numb. The bones ache from the intense cold. But he may not, he has no right, to step down from the stone of repentance. And he still cries to God: "Have mercy on me, O God! Have mercy on me!" Sleep, weariness seize his whole being. A freezing man always especially wants to sleep. But the ascetic overcomes this law of nature and he stretches his hands still harder; he gets up from his knees and cries still louder: "God, be merciful to me a sinner!"

And what horrors did not come from the devils? Could the devil leave his adversary at such a time? Of course not. But what were his threats and terrors beside the torturing thought of the Saint whose one fear was that the Lord should abandon him on account of his sins!

His legs ache. They are covered with wounds. His bloodless hands are numb. But he must plead for mercy: he has sinned.

This is difficult to imagine. But then what was it in reality? And so it went on a thousand nights. And in the cell for a thousand days. It is inconceivable!

St. Seraphim of Sarov

The Saint was silent about this labour. But still rumors of it reached the Bishop of Tambov, and later on he asked Abbot Niphont for information. The latter replied: "We know about the labours and life of Father Seraphim; but as to any secret actions or about his standing one thousand days and nights on a stone, nobody knows."

Before his end the Saint himself told some of the brethren about his temptation and contest. One of them said in astonishment: "This is above human strength." St. Seraphim replied: "St. Simeon the Stylite stood for forty-seven years on a pillar. Are my labours comparable to this?" His interlocutor observed that probably he was helped by grace. "Yes," answered the Elder, "otherwise human strength would not have been sufficient." Then he added: "When there is contrition in the heart, then God is also with us." By this labour and by grace-given contrition the Saint overcame the devil of vanity and despondency and ascended to an extraordinary height of the spirit of prayer. And so the Lord turned evil itself into good for his sake, according to the word of Scripture: *All things work together for good to those who love God* (Rom. 8:28)

Not long before his end the holy Elder entrusted the Novice John with the errand of finding this stone in the forest, telling him the special marks of the place. Only with great difficulty did he find it. Leaves and dust had covered it up. Later the admirers of Father Seraphim began to chop off small bits of it and carried them away not only as mementoes of his con-

The Distant Hermitage

test, but also for miraculous help. And in this way these bits spread all over Russia, and can be found even abroad. We kiss them in the same way as we do an Icon. And sometimes they are put into water which is afterwards drunk for healing purposes. The remains of the forest stone were kept in Sarov and Diveyev. And the day--or cell--stone was transferred whole to the Diveyev Convent.

Having overcome and conquered the temptation and having received from God a token of pardon, St. Seraphim returned again to his former ordinary spiritual life, though interiorly it became still more intense.

But now for all the rest of his life his health became noticeably weaker. He felt especially pain in his legs. And perhaps this was an outward motive for the ascetic to stop the thousand days of prayer on the stones; the Saint saw that his enfeebled "friend," the body, would be completely exhausted and would refuse to serve the spirit.

Nevertheless the temptation of promotion was renewed again after the great struggle. St. Seraphim was offered a second time the position of Superior in the Krasno Slobodsky Spassky Monastery. But he who has once been tempted becomes experienced (James 1:3,4). And the Saint declined the new offer calmly and decisively, as though it did not concern him at all. Then the enemy turned to other means of assault.

St. Seraphim of Sarov

The common monastic temptation through people, especially through women, St. Seraphim set aside simply and easily. In general he received almost nobody in his hermitage; even very few of the Monks came to him: only Mark the Silent, Father Isaiah, Hierodeacon Alexander, and later Father Tikhon. As to the brethren, he talked to them only on feast days, receiving them in the Monastery between the Liturgy and Vespers. Knowing this custom of his in accordance with the blessing of the Abbot, the Monks did not trouble him in the forest. But lay people, and especially women, drawn by rumours about the hermit and urged by their sorrows, soon found the way to him, and began to infringe upon his solitude for the sake of which "exclusively" he had left the Monastery. In order to protect himself from them, Father Seraphim decide to receive nobody at all, and especially women. But at first he fervently prayed to the Lord and to the Most Holy Mother of God, whether it were the will of God that people should be left without edification and comfort. To be quite sure, he audaciously asked for a sign: if this decision were pleasing to God, let the trees bar the way to his cell.

Just at that time a feast was approaching. Father Seraphim went according to his custom to the Monastery. And at the descent of his Mount Athos (where, as is well-known, women are not allowed at all) he saw that some pine trees were bent and were blocking the path. Father Seraphim fell on his knees in gratitude to God for the wonderful sign and hastened to the Monastery to the Liturgy. Father Isaiah

The Distant Hermitage

was celebrating with other Priests. Father Seraphim stood in the Sanctuary.

After the song of the Cherubim he reverently went up to his spiritual Father: "Father Abbot," said he meekly, "give your blessing that women should not be allowed to come to the mountain on which I now live."

Father Isaiah, who was just preparing to read the secret prayer of oblation, answered in a tone of displeasure, "At such a moment and with such a request have you come, Father Seraphim!"

"Even now bless me, Father," continued the Saint, not in the least offended.

"But how can I, at a distance of five versts, see that women are not allowed to come?" retorted Father Isaiah.

"Only bless me, Father," St. Seraphim insisted humbly but firmly, "and not one of them will go up my mountain."

Then the Abbot ordered him to be given the Icon of the Mother of God "the Blessed Womb," and blessing him, said: "I bless you not to allow women to visit your mountain; but guard it yourself!"

Father Seraphim kissed the holy Icon and returned to his place. After partaking of the Holy Mysteries, he went back to the hermitage and barricaded the path

St. Seraphim of Sarov

with tree stumps. Now the way to him was closed; but Father Seraphim still received men from time to time. Defeated here, the tempter assailed him in other ways. When even to a layman Father Seraphim said, "The enemy is everywhere with you!" how could he leave him free of his wiles. He said to some Monks that brethren who lived in a Monastery were fighting with the evil powers as with doves, but that those who lived in solitude fought as with lions and leopards.

A layman in the simplicity of his heart put the following question to Father Seraphim: "Father, have you seen evil spirits?"

The Elder answered with a smile: "They are foul! As it is impossible for a sinner to gaze upon the light of an Angel, so it is awful to see devils, for they are foul."

"He led me through the forest," Sister Aquilina Malyshev later related, "past his stone and the place where Mark the hermit lived and told me everything: how the foes tempted him here, how he fought with them there." But we have little detailed information about this conflict. This is what the author of the Diveyev chronicle writes about the temptations of the enemy: "According to his cunning he begins with the lightest temptations and at first assails the ascetic with fears. So, according to the narrative of a Hieromonk of the Sarov hermitage, who lived to a venerable old age, he once suddenly heard during prayer behind the walls of his cell the howling of a beast; then it was just as if a crowd of people began to break the door of

The Distant Hermitage

his cell; they battered the frame of the door and threw at the feet of the praying Monk a huge beam, which was afterwards carried away with great difficulty by eight men."

"At other times, by day, and especially at night, while standing at prayer suddenly it seemed to him that his cell was tumbling down in four directions and that from all sides frightful beasts were rushing at him with an angry and wild roar."

"Sometimes there would suddenly appear before him an open coffin, from which a dead man would rise."

"As the Elder did not succumb to fear, the devil raised against him the most cruel assaults. So, by God's permission, he would lift him into the air and from there would hurl him with such force to the ground that if his Angel Guardian had not been present, his very bones would have been broken from such blows. But even in this way he could not overcome the Elder."

"All visions, temptations and assaults of the enemy" Father Seraphim "conquered by the power of the Holy Cross and by prayers. Thereafter he would long remain peacefully in his hermitage, thanking the Lord." "The temptations of the devil," he boldly said afterwards, "are like a cobweb; there is only need to blow at it, and it will be destroyed; so it is with the devilish foe. There is only need to shield oneself with

St. Seraphim of Sarov

the sign of the Holy Cross, and all his wiles will completely disappear."

But the wily enemy is inexhaustible in his malicious plans against ascetics. As he had not overcome the holy combatant by inner temptations and fears, he assailed him outwardly. This happened after ten years of life in solitude on the 12th of September 1804.

Once Father Seraphim was cutting wood in the forest. Three unknown peasants went up to him and began arrogantly to ask for money: "Lay people come to you and bring you money!"

"I do not take anything from anyone," answered the Elder. But they did not believe him and assaulted him. Father Seraphim possessed great bodily strength, and besides he had an axe and could defend himself. This thought, as he afterwards said, even flashed through his mind, but he at once remembered the words of the Saviour: *All who take the sword will perish by the sword* (Mat. 26:52). And the holy ascetic calmly put down the axe and said: "Do what you want." Then one of the robbers raised his own axe and with the shaft gave the hermit a blow on the head. The blood poured from Father Seraphim's mouth and ears, and he fell unconscious to the ground. But the evildoers went on beating him and dragged him to his cell, hoping he would there regain consciousness and show them the money himself. In the anteroom they bound him hand and foot and began to search the hermitage; they even broke the stove. They broke the

The Distant Hermitage

floor and found nothing. Suddenly they were assailed by fear and ran away in terror.

Father Seraphim regained consciousness and untied himself with difficulty. First of all he thanked God for granting him to bear sufferings, though innocent, and prayed for the forgiveness of the criminals. On the next day he reached the Monastery with tremendous effort. The Liturgy was being celebrated. The brethren were terrified at the dreadful appearance of the Saint. His clothes and both his head and beard were covered with blood and dust; his face and hands bore numerous wounds; blood had clotted in his ears and mouth; his teeth had been partly broken. On being questioned by the Monks Father Seraphim remained silent. But after the Service he revealed everything to Father Isaiah and the Confessor of the Monastery. He was kept in the Monastery. For eight days the patient suffered unbearably, without sleeping or taking either food or drink.

The Father Superior, fearing for his life, sent to Arzamas for medical help; three doctors and three assistants arrived. Having examined the patient they found the following: his head was broken, his ribs smashed, his chest stamped in, the body also bore some mortal wounds. They were astonished that a man could remain alive after all that. At the beginning of the examination Father Seraphim was conscious, but towards the end of it he fell into a coma and was granted a wonderful vision.

St. Seraphim of Sarov

At the right side of his bed appeared the Most Holy Mother of God with the same Apostles Peter and John as on her first visit. Pointing with the finger of her right hand at the sufferer, she turned to the side where the doctors stood and said: "Why do you trouble yourselves?" Then she looked at St. Seraphim and again repeated to the Apostles her previous words: "This is one of our kind."

The vision ended. At that moment the Father Superior entered. The doctor proposed to him and to the patient "to let blood," to wash the wounds with alcohol and apply plasters. But Father Seraphim declined all this, surrendering himself to the will of God and the Most Holy Mother of God. And he was suddenly filled with unutterable joy which lasted for about four hours. Towards evening he rose from his bed to the amazement of all, and at the ninth hour he asked for some bread and salt cabbage and strengthened himself. And he gradually began to recover. But the traces of this onslaught remained on his body for life. Even before he used to stoop, having been crushed while cutting down a tree, but now he was quite bent. And from that time Father Seraphim walked leaning upon an axe or a hoe.

The ascetic spent five months in the Monastery. Father Isaiah and the brethren advised him to stay for good, but he obtained the blessing to return again to his beloved solitude. Soon after this the evil-doers were found: they turned out to be peasants (serfs) from the village of Kremenky (Ardatovsky district). They were to have been tried; but learning this, Father

The Distant Hermitage

Seraphim begged their master, the landowner Tatischeff, and Father Isaiah, to forgive them.

"Otherwise," he declared to the Superior, "I shall leave the Sarov Monastery and go to another place."

His request was granted. But God punished the evil-doers Himself: their houses were burnt. Then they came to the Saint and offered repentance with tears, asking for his forgiveness and prayers.

Father Seraphim forgave them and took up again the life of a hermit. But it was not spent only in labours and sufferings. Not only did the Saint grow spiritually and attain to dispassion--that aim of hesychasm; but at the same time the Lord rewarded His servant with unutterable consolations, and also glorified him with extraordinary miracles.

Meanwhile let us here give a brief account of the wonderful subjection in which he held wild beasts and reptiles.

Having fallen from God, man has been deprived of his royal sovereignty over the world; but when he returns to his original state, he receives again power over creatures. And so it happened to Saint Seraphim. There is a legend that to his cell, as to the cell of St. Blasius, various beasts came at night, and snakes crept near; and he came out to them and fed them from his meager fare. One of the brethren who was more intimate with him and visited his hermitage, the Hierodeacon Alexander, once even asked how the

St. Seraphim of Sarov

bread sufficed for the animals. The holy Elder replied that he always found in the sieve as much as was needed for them.

But the most noteworthy and touching records are those of how the Saint fed bears. Who has not heard of this amazing miracle? Its certainty has been testified by many eyewitnesses. It was related by this same Hieromonk Alexander, by the Monk Peter, by a person who afterwards became Mother Matrona of Diveyev, by the Superior of the Lyskov Community, Alexandra, by Mother Anna and others. This is the account of the Sarov Monk Peter. "Bound with ties of affection to Father Seraphim, I once went to his distant hermitage in order to profit by the soul-saving counsels of the man of God. As I drew near, I saw that Father Seraphim was sitting on the trunk of a tree and feeding a bear that was standing in front of him with dry bread, which he took from his cell. Struck by this wonderful and strange sight, I stopped behind a big tree and began to pray mentally to Father Seraphim that he might deliver me from fear. And I saw at once that the bear left the Elder and went into the forest in the opposite direction to me. Then I plucked up courage and approached Father Seraphim. The Elder welcomed me joyfully and said that since I had been deemed worthy to see this wild beast near him, I should keep it secret until his death. After this I have always marveled at the purity of soul and at the faith of this righteous Elder, whom even the dumb animals obeyed, while we were scared at the very sight of them."

The Distant Hermitage

Further on we shall hear of still more touching and edifying occurrences.

Thus twelve years of his life as a hermit went by. Father Isaiah gave up his post as Superior owing to his failing strength and retired to rest, wishing to prepare himself for his departure to the other life. The brethren decided to elect Father Seraphim in his place.

This was the third offer made to him. Besides Alateer, they had also wanted to make him the Superior of the Krassno-Slobodsky Spassky Monastery. But after his feat on the stone, the hermit now firmly and calmly rejected such offers.

Then they chose the bursar of the Monastery, Father Niphont, as the Superior of Sarov.

Father Isaiah, who had a deep love and esteem for Father Seraphim, formerly used to visit him, as he delighted in his conversations and was benefited by the spiritual experience of his own spiritual son in religion. But now he had grown weak; and so the brethren used to take him in a small cart to the distant hermitage. Thus the teacher had become the pupil. To what heights the hermit had attained! Consequently, what great profit he derived from solitude!

The next year (1807) Father Isaiah peacefully departed. Father Seraphim held him all his life in deep esteem as well as his other Elders and friends whom he regarded as men pleasing to God.

St. Seraphim of Sarov

"When you come to me," he afterwards instructed the Superior of the Ardatov Community, Mother Evdoxia, and many others, "visit the graves, make three bows and pray to God that the souls of His servants Isaiah, Pachomius, Mark and others, may rest in peace; and then fall down before the grave and say mentally: 'Forgive me, holy Fathers, and pray for me.' They are 'fiery pillars from earth to heaven.'" And he himself, when he went to the Monastery, used to go first to the graves of his beloved Fathers.

And so his close friends departed to eternity. He felt like an orphan. The new Superior was spiritually distant from him. They were quite unlike one another in spirit.

Father Seraphim wanted to profit by the death of Father Isaiah, as he had profited by the death of Father Pachomius. Then he had retired from the Monastery into the wilderness; now he chose a new, further penance--silence after the example of St. Arsenius the Great and John the Silent.

He stopped going out altogether even to receive those few visitors who still occasionally made their way to him. And if he happened to meet anyone in the forest, the Saint fell prone on the ground and silently lay there until the person went away. He also began to turn up less frequently at the Monastery; he did not always go there even on feasts days.

Food was brought to him once a week from the Monastery. Stepping into the anteroom, the Novice

The Distant Hermitage

would say the customary monastic prayer: "By the prayers of our holy Fathers, O Lord Jesus Christ our God, have mercy on us." The Elder would say: "Amen" from within and open his cell. With hands crossed on his breast and face cast downwards he stood at the door without even blessing the caller. The Novice bowed down to him and put the food on the table in the anteroom. And the Saint put there some bread or cabbage, which was meant to indicate what he needed further. The Brother again bowed down to him, asked him for his prayers and went away without having heard a single word except "Amen."

Father Seraphim remained in this penance for three years. This silence was for him only the culmination of his solitude. Therefore all that had hitherto constituted the Saint's interior life was now only strengthened and deepened. He went completely within himself and away from the world.

"Silence is the sacrament of the future life," he used to say in the words of the Fathers. Therefore let us also venerate this penance of his by our silence; let us not dare to enter within the tabernacle of his soul with our inexperienced minds and our impure thoughts; that is a place only for the Most Pure Spirit of God. Let us only repeat from his instructions the words of St. Barsanuphius the Great:

"Perfect silence is a cross on which a man must crucify himself with all his passions and lusts. But think how many rebukes and offenses did Christ our Master suffer first, and only then did He ascend the

St. Seraphim of Sarov

Cross. So neither can we attain perfect silence and hope for holy perfection unless we suffer with Christ. For, as the Apostle says: *If we suffer with Him, we shall also be glorified with Him* (Rom. 8:17). There is no other way." And this was the way chosen by the great Saint of our time, and he followed it to the end.

Glorification awaits him ahead; but he will still carry the cross of silence, only in another place and under other, more difficult conditions--as a recluse in the Monastery. Sixteen years previously he had gone away to the wilderness; now by Divine Providence he came back again to the Monastery.

The cycle of his labours in the wilderness had been completed.

Chapter VI

Reclusion

The term "reclusion" frequently conveys the idea that Father Seraphim rose to the highest degree of asceticism--solitude. But one may think otherwise. His solitude or life as a hermit really ended with his apparent reclusion; the Saint's ministry to the world had already begun. Even though he spent the first years of this penance still in silence, they were rather a preparation for his new obedience--the salvation of men.

In fact, his abandonment of the wilderness and return to a crowded Monastery, even though into reclusion, is already a kind of intercourse with the world. And his life there was a living, visible sermon both to Monks and pilgrims. By his reclusion and silence Father Seraphim taught them the way of salvation, penance and love of God no less than by words. In any case, his example here, in sight of all, was more effectual and edifying than in the far hermitage, where he was cut off from intercourse with people with few exceptions. And after another five years the spiritually mature Seraphim would leave his solitude for good and openly commence his apostolic labour of ministry to people. And so, with his life in the distant hermitage the second period of his life also came to an end; the first, the worldly period, lasted until his pilgrimage to Kiev, the second--the monastic period-- from Dositheus' cell to his leaving the hermitage; and the third--the apostolic period--from his reclusion till his death.

St. Seraphim of Sarov

The Saint himself in his humility would not have dared to have left his hermitage and go forth as a preacher, teacher and minister. He would not have wanted to give up the sweet silence of the wilderness so beloved by him. But God's providence guides His Saints.

"I know a man," said a great solitary of ancient times, Macarius the Great, probably speaking of himself, "who would like nothing better than to sit in a corner of his cave and delight in blessed contemplation. But God Himself abandons him from time to time in order that at least in this way he should come back to his ordinary state and still minister to his brethren."

That is what happened with Saint Seraphim; the ripe fruit of the wilderness was plucked from the tree of solitude and placed before the eyes of men. But even there it was given some time to mature completely in order that it should be quite mellow and attain its utmost sweetness, so as to be wholly pleasing to the Lord and pleasant to men.

Thus reclusion was in one sense the climax of his solitude; yet still more it was the preparation and the beginning of a new period of life, the second half of his monasticism. But in order that the transition from solitude to service should not be too sudden, the Lord led His lover of silence from the wilderness into the Monastery, where for some time he apparently still continued his former life, but in reality he began his new ministry.

Reclusion

This is how it happened. As we have seen, after his retirement into solitude Father Seraphim began to visit the Monastery less and less frequently, and seldom even partook of the Holy Mysteries.

To one who knows the life of solitaries, there is nothing astonishing in this. Many of them acted in a similar manner. Saint Mary of Egypt did not even once communicate during the forty-seven years of her life in solitude, after she had left the Jordan Monastery of St. John the Baptist; and it was only one hour before her death that she was granted the favour of receiving the life-giving Sacrament from the Elder Zosimus.

Whether it is that the Lord grants them the saving sweetness of communion with Himself through prayer and contemplation, or whether in a certain "invisible manner they are granted Communion through an Angel of God," as Father Seraphim said to the widow Eropkina, this is beyond our ordinary knowledge and experience.

And so, it is not surprising that the brethren of the Monastery began to be offended. People are often perplexed and even indignant when others do not act just as they do. The new Abbot Niphont also sided with the brethren. It has already been mentioned that he was of quite a different spirit from Father Seraphim. He was remarkable for his administrative abilities and his experience in money matters. He insisted on the strict observance of the rules and rubrics; during his life-time the memorial lists of the living

St. Seraphim of Sarov

and departed were read unremittingly at the proskomidia before the reading of the hours. He is remembered as an able builder and decorator of the Monastery. He kept the fasts strictly. He was industrious, unselfish, genial with visitors to the Monastery, well-read, eloquent.

Yet certain facts lead us to think that he was not of one mind with Father Seraphim. Nor was he alone. The well-known pilgrim and writer Muravyov who visited Sarov soon after the death of the Saint, reverently asked the Brothers about him. What was his amazement when he was told with levity and impudence:

"Here we are all Seraphims."

In order to understand this, it is necessary to acquire a deep knowledge of the teaching of the Saint-- or rather of the Church or the Holy Spirit Himself--as to the essence of Christianity and the meaning not only of ascetic labours, but also of the virtues, and to put this teaching into practice. And the reader will see it for himself in the wonderful, illuminating conversation between Father Seraphim and N. A. Motovilov.

Possibly, also, the demon of envy was troubling the Abbot. He had come to the Monastery twenty years after the Saint (1787) and had been chosen Superior only after Father Seraphim had refused that office. God knows! Certainly Father Niphont shows no joy at being in contact with the wonder of Sarov, and even of the whole world--for that is what St.

Reclusion

Seraphim was. Not one kindness, not a single loving word or act showing his sympathy has been recorded.

And this is not due to chance. His predecessor, Father Isaiah, so tenderly loved the Saint and reverenced him, that he was even brought in a cart to see the man of God. But here we see something quite different. And yet the Saint lived twenty-five years (1807-1832) under his rule, and those were the years of his most glorious labours, his miracles, his spiritual insight. His fame was already spreading all over Russia; yet in his own home--according to the word of Scripture--few considered him a prophet (Mat. 13:57).[18]

But the Lord makes *all things work together for good to those who love God* (Rom. 8:28). That is what happened here. The strict and law-abiding Abbot took counsel with the senior brethren of the Monastery concerning the extraordinary life of the hermit, and they decide to offer Father Seraphim, if he were healthy and strong on his legs, to come as before on Sundays and holidays and partake of Holy Communion, but if his legs refused to serve him, to return to the Monastery and live in his cell.

---

[18] Later, Father Niphont spread his opinion further. Metropolitan Philaret of Moscow wrote to his friend and spiritual Father, Archimandrite Antony, a former pupil of Father Seraphim: "The Abbot of Sarov evidently sinned, when he wrote to Metropolitan Jonah his dark thoughts" about the Saint. And Metropolitan Philaret was an extremely discreet judge.

St. Seraphim of Sarov

The Brother who used to take him his food had to transmit that decision on his first visit to the hermitage. Father Seraphim listened to him in silence and then dismissed him without uttering a single word. The decision of the council of the Monastery was so unexpected that it took the solitary unawares. He was used to obedience; but was this the will of God? Was he to give up holy silence, when he had undertaken it with the blessing of his spiritual Fathers--Joseph, Pachomius, Isaiah? It was no easy thing for him now, after sixteen years, to tear himself away from sweet solitude and return to the community.

"He who has developed a 'drawing within' and 'rapture to God'," writes the later solitary and recluse Bishop Theophan, "and especially he in whom perfect surrender to God and ceaseless prayer have begun to act, cannot be kept in a community in intercourse with others."

"Those who have come to love blessed silence pass to the activity of the holy Angels and imitate their mode of life. They never weary of praising the Creator, even to all eternity. So too he who has ascended to the heaven of solitude will not weary of hymning the Creator." "Therefore the whole occupation of the solitary is to be with the Lord alone with Whom he converses face to face, just as the favourites of a king speak into his ear."

Reclusion

At the same time such an interior silent "activity is kept and guarded by another one--the keeping of the thoughts undisturbed."[19]

And so now Father Seraphim was offered to leave this "blessed solitude." They wanted to force him to return to "intercourse with others." He was to be placed again amid the noise of a crowded Monastery which was visited by thousands of pilgrims.

What a crisis in his life! This was an even more important and decisive step than leaving his home and beloved mother thirty-two years previously. Then all that was bright and attractive lay ahead; now it seems he is to be drawn back to a lower state through which he had passed and which he had almost forgotten after his sixteen years of solitude. What was he to do?

The behaviour of the holy solitary is now easy to understand. He silently listened to the Brother's message, and he silently dismissed him without uttering a single word. It meant that there was not as yet any word of response in his soul.

The Novice went away in perplexity. And the Elder undoubtedly had recourse to God "face to face, just as the favourites of a king speak into his ear." A whole week passed in this way.

To one accustomed as he was to complete obedience, disobedience was out of the question. But still

---

[19] Theophan: "Way to Salvation."

113

less could St. Seraphim abandon "blessed quietude." Like St. Gregory the Theologian, he found the solution in choosing the middle way. He decided to live in the Monastery as in a hermitage--to be with people bodily, but to be quiet in spirit. In this way he combined outward obedience with inward solitude. This would only make his toil all the harder, for it would be more difficult to preserve quiet of spirit in the Monastery, even though in reclusion.

"There is an exterior quietude," says one writer, "when a man cuts himself off from everyone and lives alone; and there is an interior quietude, when a man remains alone with God in spirit, but without exertion, as freely as the chest breathes and the eye sees." "The cell of the solitary is the confines of his body, and his interior is a shrine of knowledge" (Ladder of Paradise, 27:12).

"Solitude," says Bishop Theophan the Recluse, "is not always a solitary mode of life; but it is essentially a state in which the spirit is collected and immersed within, and by the fire of the Divine Spirit it is raised to seraphic purity and ardour for God and in God."

Father Seraphim had already reached that state; and therefore he could safely return to the Monastery and go further along the way of living communion with God. And it seemed as if no fundamental change had been made. But God had planned something better.

Reclusion

The Brother related how the Saint had received him. Perhaps the Father Superior saw in this silence a sign of self-will, and he told the Novice to repeat the decision of the council on the following Sunday. This time Father Seraphim blessed the Brother and returned to the Monastery with him. This was the 8th of May 1810, on the day of the Seer and Apostle of love, St. John the Divine, and on the eve of the great Wonder-worker St. Nikolas. The former united the loftiest contemplation with the most tender love for his "little children" (Jn. 2:1; 4:4, 21). As for St. Nikolas, when he wanted to go away into the desert, he heard the voice of God saying: "Go into the world and thou wilt save thy soul."

Without going to his cell, Father Seraphim directed his steps to the hospital; and when the bells rang for the all-night Vigil, he went to Church.

The news quickly spread among the brethren. They were surprised, and at the same time they were glad that Father Seraphim had decided to live among them once more.

On the following day the Saint, according to his custom partook of Holy Communion in the hospital Church; and then he went to Father Niphont and received his blessing to live as a recluse in his cell in the Monastery.

So he started on his new monastic labour--a third period which also lasted nearly sixteen years. The first five years of this period were spent in reclusion in the

St. Seraphim of Sarov

full sense of the word; and then Father Seraphim gradually relaxed in order to minister to people.

Outwardly and inwardly he led about the same life as in the hermitage. The only difference was that he received absolutely no one, and spoke to no one. Also he could no longer do physical work in the same way and he allowed very little time for it. And so, he gave himself up wholly and unreservedly to prayer, contemplation, reading the Word of God and the works of the Holy Fathers, having freed himself from all other cares and solicitude.

"A small hair disturbs the eye, and a small care destroys silence," says one of the Holy Fathers. And this "care-freedom" was granted to the recluse. In his cell there was nothing but an Icon and the stump of a tree. He did not even use fire for himself. His only drink was water. For food he used oatmeal and salted cabbage. This was brought to him by a Monk who lived in the next cell, Father Paul.

"The recluse," writes the author of the Diveyev Chronicle, "covered himself with a big cloth, so that no one should see him; then he took the plate kneeling as if receiving the food from the hands of God, and carried it into his cell. There, having strengthened himself with food, he would put the plate back in its place, again hiding his face under the cloth." The veil thrown over the face is explained by the examples of the ancient desert dwellers who hid their face with a hood so as to keep their eyes *from beholding vanity* (Ps. 118:37). Sometimes the Elder would not appear

Reclusion

at all to the Brother, and he would have to take the food back to the kitchen. On such days the Saint would go without food entirely.

Subsequently, when Father Seraphim somewhat relaxed from the strictness of reclusion and sometimes even secretly went to the forest, he at times lived only on herbs, as he related later, after his reclusion, to the Diveyev Sister Praskovia Ivanovna, who after her profession became Mother Seraphima.

Having only just come to the Convent, she received on the 2nd of February, on the day of the "Presentation"[20] of Our Lord in the Temple, her first obedience from Father Seraphim: to come to him twice in one day from Diveyev to Sarov and back. This was about fifty versts (1 verst=almost two-thirds of an English mile). The Sister was at first troubled; but on being urged by the Elder, she acted according to his order. Meeting her for the first time after the early Liturgy, the Elder joyfully opened his door to her with the words: "My joy." Then he made her sit down, strengthened her with bits of prosphora and holy water, and sent her back with a big bag of oatmeal and dried bread for the Convent. She came for the second time at Vespers.

"Come in, come in, my joy!" Father Seraphim enthusiastically welcomed her. "See, I will feed you with my own food."

---

[20] Literally, "Meeting."

St. Seraphim of Sarov

And he put before her a big dish of stewed cabbage with the juice. When she began to eat, she found it uncommonly tasty. On another occasion he told her to work in the wood and gather fuel.

About three o'clock, as is told in the Chronicle, he wanted to eat himself and said:

"Go to the hermitage, Mother. There I have a piece of bread hanging on a string; bring it." The Sister brought it. Father Seraphim salted the bread, soaked it in cold water and began to eat. He left a share for Sister Praskovia; but she could not manage to chew it --it was so dry and stale. And she thought: "What privations Father puts up with!" But he read her thoughts and said:

"This is at least daily bread, Mother! But when I lived in reclusion, I fed on herbs. I poured some hot water over a kind of herb called sneet and ate it like that. That is desert food. You shall eat it too."

Not long before his death the Saint gave further details about his fasting.

"I prepared my own food from sneet. I gathered it, and put it in a little pot. I used to pour some water over it and put it in the oven. It turned out to be a glorious meal."

I asked him whether what he had told me about sneet was to be taken as a parable or reality. He replied:

Reclusion

"What kind of a person are you? Don't you know the herb sneet? I am telling you about myself. I used to prepare this dish for myself."

I asked him how he ate it in winter and where he got it from. He replied:

"What kind of a person are you? I dried sneet for the winter and lived only on that. The Brothers used to wonder what I lived on. But I was eating sneet. But I did not tell the brethren, though I have told you."

The Saint also bore other penances. He slept but little. How long he slept exactly, we do not know; but certainly not more than was necessary so as not to harm his "friend" the flesh in its service of the spirit. If he said that even at the beginning of his monastic life he slept only four hours at night (from 10 p.m. to 2 a.m.), he now surely gave still less time to sleep, just enough so as "not to injure his head." All this is, unfortunately, wrapt in mystery.

Whether the Saint practiced any other extraordinary kinds of privations and mortifications of the body is unknown. There is a legend which is related in the Diveyev edition of his "Life," according to which he secretly wore chains of twenty pounds on his chest and of eight pounds on his back, and an iron belt, which still further bent his stooping figure. And apparently during the frosty period he used to put a sock or a piece of rag under the iron.

St. Seraphim of Sarov

But this has not been verified. No such chains have been found. According to the Sarov Elders, Father Seraphim wore on his chest a big cross nine inches long on a cord. Probably this led people to talk about chains. Anyway, it is certain that subsequently he did not advise others to practice excessive exterior labours. In their stead he commanded a spiritual struggle with oneself and with one's passions.

Once--this was many years later--a bare-footed pilgrim from Kiev, accompanied by a Sarov Novice came to the Saint. The Elder was at the moment reaping reed-grass with his bare hands. He at once ordered the pilgrim to be brought to him. Having blessed him and made him sit down, the clairvoyant at once began to advise his bare-footed visitor to give up the way he had chosen: to abandon pilgrimage, put on shoes and take off his chains, which however could not be seen at all under the pilgrim's clothes. And he should go home; his wife, mother and children were anxiously waiting for him there.

"I think," added Father Seraphim, "that it would be very good to be a grain-dealer. I even know a merchant in Yeletz. You need only to go to him, greet him and say that you have been sent to him by poor Seraphim, and he will take you as a clerk."

Having given further advice to the pilgrim, the Saint dismissed him lovingly.

On his way back to the Monastery the pilgrim revealed to the Novice that everything was exactly as

Reclusion

the clairvoyant Elder had said. Formerly he had been in the grain trade; then, out of love for God, but without a blessing, he decided to leave his family, managed to obtain a passport for a year, put on chains, took off his shoes and began to travel barefoot from one Monastery to another, thinking to please God in this way. Now he had clearly seen his error and was going to obey the directions of the holy Elder.

The Novice John (Tikhonov) said that he had long dreamt of wearing chains and a hair-shirt for the mortification of his body, and that at last he got them; but first he went to Father Seraphim. The great Elder, on seeing him, read the vainglorious intention of the inexperienced book-worm, whose head was crammed with lives of Saints; and before the Novice could open his mouth he said smilingly:

"Look here! The Diveyev infants come to me and ask my advice and my blessing, one to wear chains and others hair-shirts. Now what do you think: is their way the right way? Tell me!"

The Novice could not understand what he was driving at, and replied:

"I do not know, Father."

Father Seraphim repeated the question. Only then did the Novice guess that the clairvoyant was referring to him; and he asked his blessing to wear chains.

St. Seraphim of Sarov

"How is it you don't understand? This is just what I am talking to you about," said Father Seraphim. And he further explained to him the folly and futility of wearing chains for such undisciplined people as he. Then, all of a sudden, the Elder struck at the Novice with his right hand, as if he were going to hit him in the face with all his strength. But he did not hit him; he only touched him lightly on the ear and said:

"Look, if anyone gives you a box on the ears like that--that is the spiritual and heaviest kind of chain."

Then, collecting saliva in his mouth, he made a movement as if he were going to blind him with it, and said:

"And if anyone spits in your eyes like that--that is the spiritual and most salutary hair-shirt. Only you must wear[21] them with gratitude. These spiritual chains and hair-shirts are higher than the ones you are thinking of and wish to wear. True, many of the Holy Fathers wore chains and a hair-shirt; but they were wise and perfect men, and they did it all out of love for God, in order to mortify their flesh and passions completely and make them subservient to their spirit. But it cannot be done by babes in whose bodies the passions reign and oppose the will of God and His law. What if we put on chains and a hair-shirt, but sleep and drink and eat as much as we like? We cannot bear the least offense from a Brother patiently. A word or a rebuke from a Superior casts us into utter

---

[21] The Russian word means "to wear" or "to bear, carry".

Reclusion

despondency and despair, so that we even think of
going to another Monastery; and as we point with
envy at some other brethren who enjoy the favour and
trust of the Superior, we accept all his orders as
wrongs or injuries due to oversight and animosity towards us. From this you can judge for yourself how
little (if any) foundation for monastic life there is in
us! And all this is because we hardly ever think of it
or attend to it."

Thus rebuked, the Novice gave up the idea of
wearing chains; but nevertheless he left the Sarov
Monastery afterwards. There proved to be no founda-
tion--that is, no obedience.

Yet we know of a case when Father Seraphim
blessed the anchoress Anastasia Logatchev, in religion
Athanasia, to wear chains in order to subdue fleshly
lust, when she was hardly twenty-three years old. She
afterwards became the foundress of the Kurihina
Sisterhood in the Province of Nizny-Novgorod.

But usually Father Seraphim advised his clients,
instead of exterior penances, to force themselves to
and to train themselves in good deeds.

This is what he said to a layman who secretly
thought of undertaking a pilgrimage to Kiev:

"If you are rebuked, do not rebuke; if you are persecuted, endure patiently; condemn yourself, so that
God will not condemn you; subdue your will to the
will of God; never flatter; love your neighbour--your

St. Seraphim of Sarov

neighbour is your own flesh. If you live according to the flesh, you will ruin both soul and body; but if you live according to God, you will save both. These are greater works than going to Kiev or even further."

The study of the Word of God during his reclusion was naturally augmented; as it was impossible for him to work, there remained more time free from prayer.

"As for me, poor Seraphim," he afterwards told certain people, "I go through the Gospel daily: on Monday I read Matthew from beginning to end; on Tuesday, Mark; on Wednesday, Luke; on Thursday, John; and I divide the Acts and the Epistles among the last days; and not a single day do I omit reading the daily Gospel and Epistle, as well as those appointed for the Saint of the day. Through this not only my soul, but even my body itself is sweetened and quickened, for I converse with the Lord and keep in my memory His life and passion. And day and night I glorify, praise and give thanks to my Redeemer for all His mercies poured out on the human race and on me, unworthy as I am." He subsequently also kept this rule.

When reading the Holy Scriptures, Father Seraphim sometimes commented aloud on the Gospel and the Epistles. He could even be heard through the door; and then the brethren and the pilgrims would come and listen delightedly to his expositions.

But sometimes there would be a sudden silence; not even the turning over of pages could be heard.

Reclusion

The holy recluse had become immersed in the contemplation of what he had read.

It was on an occasion of this kind that he was granted an extraordinary rapture, exactly like the one described by the Apostle Paul (II Cor. 12:1-5). Father Seraphim told several people about this grace. This is how it was recorded by the Novice John (Tikhonov).

At first the Saint spoke at length about the holy Prophets, Apostles, Martyrs and Saints, about their faith, ascetic labours, cross-bearing and miracles, and of how they had obtained the grace of the Holy Spirit through carrying out the commandments.

"And the fulfilling of Christ's commandments," he said, "is an easy burden, as our Saviour said Himself; it is only necessary to keep them always in memory; and to this end we must have in our mind and on our lips the Prayer of Jesus, and meditate upon the life and passion of our Lord Jesus Christ, Who out of love for the human race suffered even death on a Cross. At the same time it is necessary to cleanse our conscience through the confession of our sins and through the Communion of the most pure Mysteries of the Body and Blood of Christ."

Then he turned to his hearer and, wishing to prepare his spirit to accept this miracle, he said to him:

"My joy! I implore you to acquire a peaceful spirit!"

St. Seraphim of Sarov

And he went on to explain that to acquire peace of soul, we must bring ourselves to such a state of detachment from earthly things and creatures generally that nothing can disturb us. We must be like a dead man, completely deaf and blind to all troubles, calumnies, scandals and persecutions which are the inevitable lot of all who wish to follow Christ, and that *through many sufferings we must enter the Kingdom of God* (Acts 14:22). And he further explains that, in order to give our spirit freedom and enable it to rise from the earth and be strengthened by sweet converse with the Lord, we must humble ourselves by constant vigils, prayer and the remembrance of God. And he related how, in order to do this, he read through the whole New Testament every week, and that not only his spirit but even his body was invigorated and received fresh vitality in this way and shared his soul's delight "that I converse with the Lord, hold in my memory His life and sufferings, and day and night glorify, praise and thank my Redeemer for all His mercies lavished upon the human race and upon me, unworthy as I am." Then he said:

"My joy! I implore you, acquire a peaceful spirit, and then thousands of souls will be saved around you."

Then he advised him to bear sorrows for the sake of the Heavenly Kingdom. "Without sorrows there is no salvation," he used to say. "On the other hand, the Kingdom of God awaits those who have patiently endured. And all the glory of the world is nothing in

Reclusion

comparison." And again he repeated: "My joy! I implore you, acquire a peaceful spirit."

Thereupon, with inexpressible joy the Saint told Brother John of his wonderful vision.

"Listen! I am going to tell you something about poor Seraphim! Once,"--one may think that it happened at the period of his reclusion--"while I was reading in the Gospel of St. John the words of the Saviour, *In My Father's house are many mansions* (14:2), I, poor creature as I am, stayed my thought on them and desired to see those heavenly dwellings. Five days and nights I spent in vigil and prayer, asking the Lord for the grace of that vision. And indeed the Lord, in His great mercy, did not deprive me of consolation according to my faith; for He showed me those eternal mansions where I, poor earthly pilgrim, was caught up for a moment (whether in the body or out of the body, I do not know) and saw the unutterable heavenly beauty and those who dwell there: the Lord's Great Forerunner and Baptist John, the Apostles, Holy Hierarchs, Martyrs and our Holy Fathers--Antony the Great, Paul of Thebes, St. Sabbas, Onuphrius the Great, Mark of Thrace and all the Saints shining with unspeakable glory and joy, which *eye has not seen nor ear heard, neither has entered into the heart of man* (Is. 64:4; I Cor. 2:9), but *which God has prepared for them that love Him.*"

"With these words," writes Tikhonov, "Father Seraphim became silent. At the same time he leaned forward a little, his head (with closed eyes) bent

St. Seraphim of Sarov

down, and with the extended palm of his right hand he evenly (rhythmically) and gently stroked over his heart. His face gradually changed and gave out a wonderful light, and at last it became so radiant that it was impossible to look at him. His mouth and his whole appearance expressed such joy and such heavenly ecstasy that at this moment he might have been truly called an earthly Angel and a heavenly man. During his mysterious silence, he seemed to be contemplating something with tender emotion and to be listening to something with wonder. But what it was exactly that enraptured and delighted the soul of that just man, God alone knows.

"After rather a long silence Father Seraphim spoke again. Sighing from the depth of his heart, he said to me with a feeling of unutterable joy:

"'Oh! If only you knew what joy, what sweetness awaits the just soul in heaven, you would resolve to bear thankfully in this temporal life all manner of sorrows, persecutions and slander. And even though this very cell of ours were full of worms and though these worms were to eat our flesh during the whole of this temporal life, we ought to consent to it with the utmost longing, so as not to lose that heavenly joy which God has prepared for those who love Him. There is no pain, no sorrow, no sighing there; there all is unutterable sweetness and joy; there the just will shine like the sun. But if that heavenly glory and joy could not be described even by our dear little Father the Apostle Paul, what other human tongue can describe the beauty of the heavenly city, where the souls of the righteous dwell?

"'As for you, my joy,' continued the Elder, 'for the sake of such future happiness, you and your brethren must acquire chastity and guard your virginity, for the virgin who keeps his virginity for the sake of the love of Christ has a part with the Angels, and his soul is the bride of Christ. Christ is her bridegroom who leads her into His heavenly palace. But the soul who remains in sin is like the idle widow who in her lust is *dead while alive* (I Tim. 5:6, 15).'"

He told the same thing to Mrs. A. P. Eropkin, reminding her of the holy women martyrs, of the beauty of St. Fevronia and many others who are shining in unutterable glory.

"Ah, my joy," he would then exclaim, "there is such beatitude there as it is impossible to describe."

"His face," as she afterwards wrote, "was extraordinary. The light of grace shone through his skin. While in his eyes there was an expression at once of peace and of a special kind of spiritual rapture." Even during the description of his visions "he was probably outside the visible world--in the heavenly mansions."

This wonderful and supernatural ecstasy was only the summit of his lights or illuminations. But to a lesser degree he experienced this elevation of the spirit to God not merely frequently, but almost continually.

St. Seraphim of Sarov

His greatest consolation was Holy Communion. On all Sundays and feast days the Holy Mysteries were brought to him after the early Liturgy by the ministering Priest from the Hospital Church to his cell so as not to interrupt his reclusion. Then the Saint put on his mantle (mantia) over his usual white smock, a linen stole (epitrachelion) and cuffs. On the appearance of the Holy Mysteries, he fell down and communicated with tremulous joy.

On the other days they brought him a piece of antidoron which had been set aside especially for him.

The hermit also devoted some of his time to work. In the cell it was replaced by prostrations, and God alone knows how many he made. But sometimes he allowed himself to go out of his cell secretly at night in order to work in the fresh air.

Once a Brother who had the obedience to wake the Monks, having risen before Matins, was walking near the Cathedral, where the remains of the Fathers and hermits of Sarov rest. And from there he saw in the dark a man who was quickly moving to and fro. Making the Sign of the Cross, the Brother went in that direction and saw the hermit himself. Saying the Prayer of Jesus under his breath he was quietly but quickly carrying logs from one place to another, near his cell. Overjoyed at the sight of the holy Elder, the Novice threw himself at his feet and, kissing them, asked for a blessing.

Reclusion

"Protect yourself with silence and attend to yourself!" said the Saint. And having blessed the happy observer, he hid himself in his cell.

Father Seraphim also prepared for himself with his own hands a coffin with a lid. He cut it out of a whole oak. And it always stood in his ante-room in order to remind him and others of the hour of death. The Saint would often pray before it, especially just before his death. And after his reclusion he would often ask the Monks:

"When I am dead I beg you, brethren, to bury me in my coffin!"

This was actually done afterwards.

In such strict reclusion St. Seraphim spent five years, without receiving people or talking to anyone; he opened his cell only to receive the Bread of Heaven and--though not always--earthly food.

Towards the end of this period Bishop Jonah, who later became Exarch of Georgia, came to the Monastery for the Dormition of the Mother of God which was the dedication feast of the Monastery Church. Wishing to see the hermit whose fame had reached his distant episcopal palace of Tambov, he went to the cell of Father Seraphim with Father Niphont and some others. They knocked at the door, but as usual there was no response. They told him through the door that Vladyka[22] wanted to see the Elder; but Father Seraphim remained silent as usual.

Then Father Niphont offered to take the door from its hinges and in this way see the hermit against his will. But the Bishop thought it better to give up his wish, and added with fear:

"Beware lest we should sin!"

And leaving the Elder in peace, the visitors took their departure from the Monastery.

Fearing man-pleasing (Gal. 1:10), the hermit did not modify his vow even for a Bishop. And perhaps his insight saw the defects in the Bishop's character and a lack of faith in the grace of God. [23]

But how wonderful are the works of God! Only a few days later the same door was to open, not to Monks at first, but to lay people. The hermit is to undertake a higher labour, higher than which there is nothing on earth--the labour of love (I Cor. 13).

---

[22] Monseigneur (Lit. "Master" or "Lord", although the term in Russian is more affectionate--ed.)

[23] Apparently Bishop Jonah had not much confidence in the sanctity of Father Seraphim. It is well known, for instance, that when he was a member of the Synod, he opposed the edition of the first Life of Saint Seraphim in spite of the fact that it was advocated by Metropolitan Philaret of Moscow himself (See his letters to Archimandrite Antony, part I, page 383--in Russian).

Chapter VII

The Height of Perfection

The fruit of such long and excessive labours as the Saint had practiced was dispassion, which in its turn is the way that leads to the indwelling of the Holy Spirit in the heart.

"He who has been granted this disposition, that is dispassion," says Bishop Theophan the Recluse of Vishensky, "though he be still clad with corruptible flesh, has become the Temple of the living God, Who guides and instructs him in all his words, deeds and thoughts; and on account of this inner enlightenment, he will know the will of the Lord as if he were hearing some voice."

"Communion with God and the indwelling of God, the final aim of the human spirit, has been attained when the man is in God and God in him. At last the will of God has been fulfilled as well as His prayer that, just as He is in the Father and the Father in Him, so may every believer be one in Him (Jn. 17:21). Such souls are the *temple of God* (I Cor. 3:16), and the *Spirit of God dwells in them*" (Rom. 8:9).

"Those who have reached this are mystics of God and their state is the same as the state of the Apostles."

The manifestation of God is the source of a multitude of other gifts of grace, and first of all "flaming love which makes them boldly say: *Who shall separate us* from God?" (Rom. 8:35).

St. Seraphim of Sarov

"And love is the source of prophecies, the cause of miracles, a depth of enlightenment, the fountain of divine fire."

"Since such a state is the fruit of quietude if it is practiced with discernment, not all solitaries remain in solitude forever. Those who have attained dispassion through quietude and have been granted thereby the most intimate communion with God and the indwelling of God, are led out from this state for the service of those who seek salvation and they minister to them by enlightening them, guiding them and working miracles. As to John in the desert, so to Antony the Great came a voice in his solitude which led him out to the labour of directing others in the way of salvation; and the fruits of their labours are known to all. And it has been the same with many others."

This we shall also see realised in the case of St. Seraphim. As we read these words of the recluse, we seem to see a vivid portrait of the Saint himself, and yet they have been taken from the works of the great ascetics: St. John of the Ladder (Ch. 29 and 30), St. Isaac the Syrian and the Philokalia.

This wonderful unity is not only an evident testimony of the One Most Holy Spirit of God Who inspires the Saints, but it is also a clear proof that Father Seraphim's spiritual way was right.

The Height of Perfection

"We do not know anything on earth higher than this Apostolic state. This is the highest degree of the spiritual life."

"Father" was now called to this final degree of perfection. And it is clear why from this period the sweet and tender name of "Father", of a true and loving father, was specially applied to him. His paternal spiritual direction had begun.

The doors of his hermitage were opened for the first time almost immediately after the Saint's refusal to receive Bishop Jonah.

The Bishop may not have had time to return to his episcopal city of Tambov, when the governor of the province, Alexander Mikhailovitch Bezobrazov, set out from the same town with his wife for Sarov.

It was in September 1813. On their arrival at the Monastery and after a prayer in the Church, husband and wife went to the cell of the Saint. The Monks who accompanied the governor and his wife had no hope of their seeing the Elder, as they were lay people. Had he not lately given a silent refusal to a Monk, his Bishop? But now the unexpected happened. When the visitors came to Father Seraphim's cell, he opened the door to them himself and silently blessed them.

The period of strict reclusion was over. Why the Saint behaved in this way remains a mystery. It is certain only that he acted in this way according to the will of God which he discerned with his inner sight.

135

St. Seraphim of Sarov

"Those who have reached perfection," says Bishop Theophan the Recluse, "hear the voice of God clearly in their soul. In them the word of the Lord begins to be fulfilled: *When He, the Spirit of Truth, comes, He will guide you into all truth* (Jn. 16:13). And the Apostle John also writes: *The anointing* (of the Spirit) *remains in you, and you do not need any man to teach you: but as His anointing teaches you about everything, and is true and is no lie, so remain in Him as it has taught you* (I Jn. 2:27)."

However, in the Diveyev edition of the Life of the Saint it is said that on this occasion also the Mother of God appeared to Father Seraphim accompanied by St. Onuphrius the Great and St. Peter of Athos, and that she commanded him not to hide any longer, but to minister to people. From this time the doors of the recluse were open to all. His activity as an Elder had begun.

Unfortunately most of the written records date from 1825 when he had quite given up reclusion. But it is not a matter of great importance, and we shall make a selection from his most valuable instructions given by him at different times and in different places.

But first of all let us describe from the evidence of eyewitnesses the interior of his cell and his manner of receiving visitors. Here is a piece of information from General Otrostchenkoff who visited the Saint on his way to Moscow.

The Height of Perfection

"In accordance with a reverent frame of mind, partly out of curiosity, and especially at the urgent request of my wife, Natalia Mikhailovna, I decided" to call at Sarov and pay my respects "to the holy recluse." After the early Liturgy he and his wife, accompanied by a Monk, went to Father Seraphim's cell.

"The key of the common door (of the corridor) was with the Monk who guided us, for the recluse never went anywhere out of his room, not even to Church. Having opened that door, our guide went to the door of the recluse and said the greeting prayer; then he repeated it twice and added that some travelers wanted to see Father Seraphim. But again he got no answer. Then he said: 'Would you like to speak yourself?'

"I replied that I did not know what to say. 'Say simply: Christ is risen, Father Seraphim!' (It was then the week of the Holy Resurrection). I went up to the door and said this greeting: but neither did I get any response. I turned to my wife who was holding some gifts in her hands (candles, oil, and red wine) and trembling with awe, coughing violently at the same time (she was in the first half of her pregnancy). She said loudly: 'Well, my friend, we must have been very naughty, since the holy man will not receive us. Let us leave our gift and regretfully continue our journey.'

"We were about to go when suddenly the door of the recluse opened and he stood in a white cassock and beckoned to us with his finger to come in.

137

St. Seraphim of Sarov

"From my first glance at him I was seized with a feeling of reverence for him. He seemed to me an Angel, a heavenly man; his face was white like clear wax, his eyes blue as the sky, his hair was white and hung down to his shoulders. We came into his cell and he closed the door at once with a hook. At the entrance, on the left side stood a jug and bottles of various sizes, some empty, some with oil and wine; there was also a big pewter cup with a spoon of the same metal. On the left side near the wall were heaped up stones of different sizes; on the right side were logs of wood, and above them on a peg hung all kinds of old rags. In the front corner on a wooden shelf stood an Icon of the Mother of God,[24] and before it burned a lamp. The two windows were double ones and filled with rubbish up to the top casements.

"In spite of the crowdedness and untidiness, the air in this small room was perfectly pure. From the door to the Icon there was only a small passage. The place where the recluse slept was not to be seen.[25]

"He closed the door and said to us: 'Pray to God! And you,' addressing my wife, 'light a candle and put it before the Icon,' But she was trembling so much that she could not make the candle stick.

"'Leave it then; I'll do it myself.'

---

[24] "Our Lady of Compunction" (or "Tender Feeling"--ed) whose feast is on the 28th of July, the day of his patron Saint, Prochorus.
[25] He slept on the stones; he also slept sitting or kneeling on the floor.

The Height of Perfection

"After this Father Seraphim took from under a bench a bottle of wine, poured some into the cup, then poured in some water, put some dry bread into it, took a spoon and said: 'Repeat after me.' He said the prayer before Confession, and began to feed us in turns from the spoon. The wine was so sour that the water did not temper the acidity.

"My wife whispered to me that she could not take it because it was very sour." The husband transmitted her words, adding:

"She is not well."

"I know," replied the Elder, "that is why I am giving it her--to make her well."

"After giving us some three times, he said: 'Kiss one another.' We did so. Then he turned to me and said: 'You are in difficult circumstances, you are sad. But pray to God and don't grieve; He will soon comfort you.' Then he wrapped up some dry bread in a piece of paper and gave it to me. But I said to him: 'Holy Father! I have many friends who know you from hearsay; and they will be very glad if I take them some of the dry bread I have received.' He smiled and added some more dry bread. Then he thanked us for having visited him, and dismissed us with a blessing.

"What he had said to me and my wife came to pass. On the same day her coughing and vomiting stopped; and on reaching the town of Riazan I received 5,000

St. Seraphim of Sarov

rubles which the Emperor Alexander I granted me for a military review near the town of Penza."

Here is another record, this time by General Galkin-Vrassky, with new and touching details.

"When I was an officer I visited the Sarov Monastery and after the example of the other pilgrims I went to receive a blessing from the holy Father Seraphim. In the corridor outside his cell the cold was intense, and I shivered with cold in my thin military coat. His neighbour told me that there was a Monk with Father Seraphim and that he was talking to him. Standing in the corridor, I prayed to the Most Holy Mother of God. The door opened; the Monk went out. And a few minutes later Father Seraphim opened his door and said: "What joy God gives me!" He led me into his cell, but as it was crowded with different things, he made me sit on the threshold of his cell, while he himself sat on the floor before me holding my hand; and he talked to me caressingly and even kissed my hand repeatedly. Such was his love for his neighbour. I sat opposite him in a kind of extraordinary rapture."

After a long talk the visitor mentioned his illness-- a disease of the lungs. Father Seraphim gave him some oil from his lamp to drink. The illness was cured for ever.

Here is another example. A landowner of Simbirsk, Elizabeth Nikolaievna Pasuhin, called on Father Seraphim and wanted him to hear her Confes-

The Height of Perfection

sion, but a Monk called Damascene told her that it was impossible on account of the crowds of visitors. Nevertheless she prepared herself all night for Confession with the Saint and asked God to grant it.

"In the morning on the following day," she writes, "I went to him. And when my servant opened the door of his anteroom, I saw the Elder near his coffin. Seeing me, he rose and led me into his cell. He commanded me to make the Sign of the Cross and three times gave me holy water to drink, putting the cup to my lips himself. Then he asked for my handkerchief. I gave him a corner of the shawl I was wearing and he poured in a handful of dry bread. Then with fear and reverence lest I should offend the righteous Elder, I ventured to tell him of my wish to confess with him, and said: 'Holy Father, allow me to say one word to you.' He answered: 'Please do, mother.' And suddenly to my unutterable surprise and amazement, as well as to my unspeakable joy, he took me by both hands and began to read the prayer: 'O God, absolve, remit and pardon me my sins which I have committed' etc. I repeated this prayer after him, sobbing loudly; then I fell on my knees. And he knelt beside me, and all through the prayer he held my hands. After the absolution and dismissal he gave me his copper cross to kiss, and taking my right hand, he said: 'The grace of our Lord Jesus Christ and the love of God the Father and the communion of the Holy Spirit be with you all your life, at your end and after your death!' I was beside myself with joy and kissed his hands."

141

St. Seraphim of Sarov

The events described are to be referred to a later period. At the beginning, especially during the first three years, the Saint still continued his silence, though his door was open. Everyone could enter and look at him, but he behaved as if there were no one with him. The visitors would be deeply impressed by such dispassion, would ask for his blessing and depart in silence. But gradually the Saint began to give instructions, advice, and absolution of sins; he would anoint with the oil from his lamp, and give dry bread and so on.

The pilgrims brought him gifts: candles, oil, sometimes wine which he gave his visitors from a spoon. He put the candles before the Icons for those who had brought them. N. A. Motovilov was once wondering what good there was in lighting those candles and lamps. The Saint read his doubt and said to him:

"I have many people who are devoted to me and are benefactors to my mill orphans (the Diveyev Nuns). They bring me oil and candles, and ask me to pray for them. So when I read my rule, I remember them at first one by one. But on account of the great number of names I cannot repeat them at every place in the rule, as it is required, for then I should have no time for my rule, and so I put all these candles for them as an offering to God--a candle for each one. For some I put collectively one big candle, for others I always keep a lamp burning, and where it is necessary to remember their names in the rule, I say: 'Lord, remember all these people, Thy servants, for whose souls I have lighted these candles and lamps.' It is also

The Height of Perfection

said in the Bible that Moses heard the voice of the Lord saying to him: 'Moses, Moses! Tell thy brother Aaron to light a lamp before me by day and by night; this is pleasing in My sight and it is an acceptable offering to Me.'"[26]

At the same time the Saint observed how the candles burned.

"If anyone has faith in me, poor Seraphim," he said, "I keep a candle burning for that person before the holy Icon. And if the candle fell, it was a sign to me that that person had fallen into mortal sin. Then I bow my knees for him before God's compassion."

In such reclusion the Saint spent fifteen and a half years. The memorable feast of the Presentation of the Mother of God had passed for the forty-eighth time for the Saint in Sarov. It was the 25th of November 1825, the last day or "octave" of the feast. With this octave or end of the festival his reclusion also ended. The Mother of God appeared in a dream to St. Seraphim together with St. Clement, Pope of Rome, and St. Peter, Archbishop of Alexandria, who are commemorated on that day, and allowed him to give up reclusion completely.

Such was God's will now. With the octave of the Presentation the Saint had completed the circle of his salvation, and he now had to please God through ministering to others. But monastic conditions are not

---

[26] We do not know to what passage St. Seraphim is alluding.

always quite congenial to it. Every Monastery lives according to its fixed rule which is most suitable for the majority of ordinary Monks. And every exception, every infringement of the rules and customs usually creates a disturbance not only in the exterior life of the Monastery, but also in the interior spirit of the Monks. Meanwhile, since the door of the recluse was open, Father Seraphim's visitors increased more and more; sometimes there were as many as from one thousand to two thousand daily. All the courtyard of the Monastery was full of people eager just to look at the holy Elder or to receive a blessing from him; to have a talk with him was considered a special piece of luck.

This is how N. Aksakova describes the scene on Father Seraphim's leaving Church after an early Liturgy.

"All of us, rich and poor, were waiting for him, crowding at the entrance of the Church. When he appeared at the Church door, everyone's eyes were fixed on him. He slowly came down the steps of the porch and in spite of having a slight limp and being somewhat hunch-backed, he seemed and was supremely beautiful.

"He walked in silence, and appeared to take no notice of anyone. The crowds of people standing like two walls hardly left him room to pass in complete silence, wishing to have just a look at his gracious face. And only then began the reception of people in his cell."

The Height of Perfection

Another visitor who was afterwards his devoted spiritual daughter and whose name has already been mentioned, A. P. Eropkina, describes what happened there.

Arriving for the first time in the Monastery, she was struck by the crowd of pilgrims who moved between the Cathedral of the Dormition and the house where Father Seraphim's cell was.

"I mixed," she afterwards wrote, "with a crowd of people of both sexes and of all ages and callings. I worked my way through it to the porch where all were converging. With the greatest difficulty I wriggled into the anteroom and got through the open door into the cell itself. Father Seraphim was thronged by a dense crowd of worshippers. I tried to approach him as the others did and reached out my hand for his blessing. On giving me his blessing and some bits of dry bread he said:

"'The servant of God Anna partakes of the grace of God.'

"What was my amazement when I heard my name mentioned in an unknown place! But when I looked Father Seraphim straight in the face, I recognized in him that same Elder who had warned me in my dream against my unhappy marriage. But one could not stop near him even for a minute, for the people behind me pushed me away in order to get a blessing themselves and hear something from his lips. I was hustled out into the anteroom where with my feet I felt a few logs near the wall; scrambling on to them, I began to gaze at Father Seraphim over the heads of the people. I soon noticed that he apparently wanted to end the reception; for he began to dismiss everyone, saying meekly: 'Go in peace.' At the same time he made his way towards the open door near which I was standing. He took hold of the padlock with one hand and, unexpectedly for myself, he took my hand with the other and led me into his cell; and without asking anything, he at once started talking to me.

"'Why have you come to a poor sinner like me, my treasure? I know! Your sorrow is very great; but the Lord will help to bear it.' After these and other consoling words he commanded me to prepare for Holy Communion with them, to confess with Father Hilarion, the Confessor of the Monastery, and to partake of the Holy Mysteries."

And this went on day after day, from the early Liturgy till 8 o'clock, and then until midnight.

The Abbot Niphont once said in doubt and perplexity:

"When Father Seraphim lived in the desert, he barred all access to himself with trees, so that the people should not come; but now he has begun to receive everyone, so that it is impossible for me to shut the gates of the Monastery until midnight."

And one can understand that the Superior of the Monastery was disturbed by the increasing crowds of

The Height of Perfection

people; for he was responsible not only for the outward discipline but also for the inner peace of the brethren. Meanwhile, many of them began to be offended. Some were disturbed by the vanity and idle talk of the lay people; others were vexed by the presence of women who constantly crowded the courtyard and the corridor of the Monastery. Others were perplexed by the behaviour of the recluse who did not go to Church, but was in his cell with the people. Some were irritated by the teaching itself, and perhaps were jealous of the Saint.

A Monk said to Father Seraphim: "You are worried by people of both sexes; and you let them all in without distinction."

In his answer to him the humble Elder referred to the example of St. Hilarion the Great who ordered the gates to be kept open for the sake of the pilgrims, and he added: "Suppose I close the door of my cell. Those who come in need of a word of comfort will beg me to open the door for God's sake and on receiving no answer from me will go home in sadness. What justification shall I then offer to God at His awful judgement?"

Formerly the hermit had solved this doubt in quite a different way, when he had asked Father Isaiah's blessing to forbid women access to his "Mount Athos." But then he had been still on his way of ascension to dispassion. Now the time had come to radiate the grace he had acquired. But what was clear to the Saint could not be easily understood and accepted

St. Seraphim of Sarov

by ordinary Monks who had come to the Monastery on purpose to renounce the world. And now the world itself was rushing after Father Seraphim into the desert.

"Some are offended because of you," they said to him.

"I am not offended if many derive benefit and others are offended," calmly replied the Elder.

He was even rebuked for anointing with oil from a lamp. To such the Saint would say: "We read in Scripture that the Apostles anointed with oil, and many sick people were healed by it. Who are we to follow if not the Apostles?"

But people became especially offended by Father Seraphim when he took on himself the care of the Diveyev Convent. They even began to track him. The Nun Eupraxia relates the following:

"Everyone knows how the Sarov Monks disliked Father Seraphim on account of us; they even harassed him and persecuted him continually for our sakes and caused him a lot of annoyance and trouble! But he, our own Father, bore everything serenely. He even laughed; and knowing it, he would often play a trick on us. Once I came to Father. During his life he fed us and provided for us himself and always asked us with a fatherly solicitude: 'Have you everything? Don't you need anything?' With me and with Xenia Vassilievna (Mother Kapitolina) he would send honey, linen, oil,

The Height of Perfection

candles, incense and red wine for the Service. And so it was this time. I came. He had filled a big bag, such a load he could hardly lift it himself from the coffin. He even grunted as he picked it up, and said: 'There, carry it, Mother, and go straight through the holy gate. Don't be afraid of anyone!' At that time there were soldiers in Sarov and they always stood on guard at the gate. The Abbot of Sarov and the bursar with the brethren were extremely angry with Father Seraphim for always giving or sending us things. And they ordered the soldiers to be always on the look-out for us and to catch us; I had been especially pointed out to them. And so I approached the gate and said the Prayer. Two soldiers immediately took me and brought me to the Abbot who was in his anteroom. His name was Niphont and he was very strict; he did not like Father Seraphim, and he liked us still less. He ordered me harshly to untie the bag. I did so, but my hands were shaking, shaking uncontrollably while he looked on. At last I untied it and began to take out everything. But there were only old birch shoes, broken bread crusts, bits of wood and stones of different kinds. It was all firmly pressed down.

'Oh! Seraphim, Seraphim!' cried Niphont. 'Just look at it. What a person he is! Not only does he torment himself, but he torments the Diveyev Sisters as well.' And he let me go."

Once even the Father Abbot deemed it expedient to speak openly to the Saint concerning these scandals. This is how it happened. As the Saint was going from his hermitage to the Monastery, he was met by Father

149

St. Seraphim of Sarov

Niphont who began to tell him that he was a cause of offense to the brethren. "They are especially offended at your loving care of the Diveyev orphans."

On hearing this Father Seraphim fell at his feet, and then said to him humbly though with authority: "You are a pastor. Do not allow everyone to disturb you and your companions on the way to eternity by vain talk. For your word is powerful and your staff[27] is terrible as a whip."

Father Niphont kept silent and left things as they were. However, later on, following some slanderous reports against the Saint, the consistory of Tambov ordered an investigation of the case to be made. It was intrusted to the then bursar who later became the Abbot of the Monastery, Father Isaiah II. Of course they could not find anything criminal. But they could not understand the Saint's lofty dispassion. We, sinners, cannot rise to such heights.

"He who is dispassionate towards all the objects which rouse our passions," writes Bishop Theophan the Recluse, "has become so impassible (lit. insensible) that they do not exert any influence on him, even though they are before his eyes. This is because he is completely united to God. Even if he enters a brothel, he will not only not feel the stir of passion, but will even lead a sinner to a pure and ascetic life."

---

[27] Meaning probably his abbatial authority.

The Height of Perfection

How are we to understand this, we who are passionate? Everyone looks out of the window of his own sinful nature and he sees in others what he experiences himself.

The peasant Euphemius Vassiliev of Likhatchovo worked in Sarov. Once, as he was approaching the hermitage, he saw Father Seraphim talking to a well-dressed sixteen year old girl and thought: "What has the Father to say to her? What kind of instruction does one so young need?"

When he came nearer, the clairvoyant calmly said to him: "I am dead to all; and what are you thinking?"

The tempted peasant fell at his feet and asked forgiveness.

"Be at peace," said the Father, "and don't do it again."

He was already truly dead, but the living could not realize it. Father Seraphim understood this and, in accordance with the direction of the Mother of God, he decided to abandon reclusion so as to be free to work for the salvation of souls, and in particular for the organization of "Our Lady's Heritage"--Diveyev. Besides, he needed the hermitage himself as a resting place from the countless visitors and for solitary prayer.

In the morning of the 25th November 1825, Father Seraphim left his cell and went to the Abbot for a

St. Seraphim of Sarov

blessing to go away as in former times to his distant hermitage. Father Niphont blessed him, and the Elder directed his steps toward the forest.

About two versts from the Monastery there was a spring called the "Theologian's Spring" after St. John the Theologian whose Icon stood over it. And a quarter of an hour's walk from it stood the cell of the hermit Dorotheus who had died, but two months previously. On the way there, St. Seraphim had a wonderful vision which has been related in Motovilov's diary.

"On the 25th November 1825--as Father Seraphim himself told me, as well as many others--he was threading his way to the hermitage through a thicket along the bank of the river Sarovka when he saw the Mother of God who appeared to him below the Theologian's Spring almost by the bank of the river Sarovka. Behind her on a hillock stood two Apostles, St. Peter and St. John the Evangelist. And the Mother of God struck the ground with her staff so that a spring spurted out from the earth--a fountain of clear water." And then she gave him instructions regarding the organization of the Diveyev Convent, which will be related further on.

On the place "where her most pure feet had stood and where a healing spring spurted out upon her striking the ground with her staff, as a memorial for future generations," Father Seraphim decided to dig a well. He returned to the Monastery, fetched the necessary tools and for two weeks was engaged in digging the ground, building the walls and consolidating them

The Height of Perfection

with stones. That is why this well is called "Seraphim's well."

Afterwards the Saint himself told the Monk Anastasius that he had prayed that "the water of this well should have the property of healing diseases. And the Mother of God," he added, "promised to give these waters a greater blessing than that which had rested on the pool of Bethesda in Jerusalem."

Actually a great number of miracles were performed by means of this holy water. The first cure was two weeks later, on December 6th. On that day Father Seraphim was visited by two Sisters from Diveyev--Paraskeva Stepanovna and Maria Semyonovna who was still a child. He went with them to the distant hermitage. On the way the Saint explained to them that he had already abandoned reclusion twelve years previously for the sake of the people who came to him, but he had not yet visited the places dear to him. They came to the well and "Father" told them its history. Paraskeva Stepanovna was ill and kept coughing.

"Why are you coughing? Stop! It's unnecessary."

"I can't help it, Father!" she replied.

Then Father Seraphim dipped up some water with his leathern glove and gave the Sister to drink. The disease vanished at once and forever.

St. Seraphim of Sarov

Then they went on to the distant hermitage. But unfortunately it was too far away for the weak and varicose legs of the very old man, and so he settled down at first in the vacant cell of Father Dorotheus. In the spring of 1829 he resumed his work in the kitchen garden near the "Theologian's Well." A small wooden hut had been built for him there, 2 1/3 yards high, 2 1/3 yards long and 1 1/2 yards wide. It had neither windows nor doors, so that one had to climb through a hole in the ground under the wall. There the Saint took refuge from people and bad weather. A year later a new cell was built for him with a door but without windows. There was a stove inside. Between the stove and the wall there was a narrow space with standing room only for one person. In a corner of the cell and behind the stove hung Icons with lamps which illumined the darkness. This was the "near hermitage" of the Saint which became his chief trysting-place with visitors.

At about four in the morning, and sometimes as early as two at night, Father Seraphim left the Monastery and went to his new dwelling place, where he spent his time till 7-8 in the evening, when he returned to the Monastery. On Sundays and holidays he still had Holy Communion in his cell in the Monastery, so that he was thus in semi-reclusion. But he soon had to give it up altogether.

The brethren were scandalized. They wanted to know why the recluse received people both in his cell and in his hermitage, but would not visit their Church even to receive Holy Communion. They wrote to

The Height of Perfection

Bishop Athanasius of Tambov about it all, and he ordered that St. Seraphim should in future receive the Holy Sacrament in Church. The Saint submitted to this order unquestioningly, merely remarking:

"Even if I had to crawl on my knees to fulfill my obedience, still I would not give up communicating of the life giving Mysteries of the Body and Blood of Christ."

Thus the Providence of God was bringing him into closer touch with the people who needed his word, his blessing, his comfort and even just a look at his holy face.

Now the pilgrims could see him every holiday in the Church of Saints Zossimus and Sabbatius and thence they could accompany him to his cell.

But when he spent his time in the near hermitage, the people rushed to him there. Only the place was changed; the crowds were almost as bad as at the Monastery, only there were fewer people. Sometimes though the Elder vanished completely.

"At the hermitage in the forest," writes a pilgrim, "the Saint received people sitting on a bench adjoining his log cabin. He took some people into his cell and prayed there with them before the Icon of the Mother of God. He also prayed in the forest before an Icon of the Mother of God which he had fixed on an aged pine tree. All the pilgrims knelt down to pray

St. Seraphim of Sarov

with Father Seraphim. What a wonderful picture it was!"

"Standing in front of the door of his forest hut," says N. Aksakova, "the Elder slowly crossed himself while continuing his prayer, his unceasing prayer...People did not disturb him, just as his constant conversation with God could not be disturbed either by wood-cutting or haymaking, heat or cold, day or night. The people prayed too."

Here is what another pilgrim who came with his wife writes:

"We found the Elder at work; he was loosening the earth with a hoe. When we approached him and bowed down to him, he blessed us and, putting his hand on my head, read the troparion for the Dormition of the Mother of God: 'In giving birth thou didst preserve thy virginity.' Then he sat down on a border and bade us sit down too; but we involuntarily knelt down before him, and in that position we listened to his talk."

Sometimes the Saint went to his former distant hermitage in quest of greater solitude, but people found him there too. Yet he sometimes told people to come to that very place. It was at this time that he especially began to take in hand the organization of the Diveyev Convent. So often one could meet some of the Sisters in his hermitage. They often worked for him. In some cases they even stayed overnight in his

The Height of Perfection

hermitage, as he used to go to the Monastery. This was also a source of scandal to weak souls.

"Though Father Seraphim was ever so holy, a Saint of God," said the old Nun Xenia Kuzminishna, "still he had to suffer persecution. Once we came to Father, a group of seven Sisters. We worked at his place the whole day, and as we were tired we stayed for the night at the hermitage. About 10 o'clock the Sister in charge of us saw from the window that people were coming down the path with three lanterns straight towards us. We guessed that it was the bursar Isaiah and we hastened to open the door to him. They came in, but they did not scold us. No, they only looked at us searchingly, and silently began to look for something. Then they ordered us to dress and to go away at once."

The Sisters went to Sarov, to the hostel of the Monastery.

"As soon as the bell rang for Matins at two o'clock, the Sister in charge went to Father's cell and told him everything. Father knew it all himself, but he did not show it, and seemed even displeased with us.

"'This happened because you do not behave properly', he said.

"And he sent us there and then to the Convent (Diveyev). But though Father tried to exonerate them (the Sarov Monks), everyone knew that he had to suffer a great deal on all sides for being kind to us."

157

St. Seraphim of Sarov

But notwithstanding all this, people kept coming to him in increasing numbers from all directions. His fame had already spread throughout Russia, and pilgrims of all conditions and callings flocked to Sarov and to the hermitages, rich and poor, learned and simple, Monks and Priests, grown-ups and children--all were attracted by the holy Priest. In 1825 he received among other visitors the Grand-Duke Michael Pavlovitch. According to tradition he also received about that time the visit of the Emperor Alexander I on his way to Siberia. He came as a simple pilgrim and asked the Saint's blessing to live a life of secret penance incognito, in which he continued till death under the name of "Theodore Kuzmitch."

But Father Seraphim maintained the closest relations with his "orphans," the Diveyev Sisters. Moreover, it was they who had the privilege of witnessing the wonderful spectacle of the holy Elder with the bear.

"Once," said the old Nun Matrona Plescheyev, "I was in a state of great perplexity and despondency owing to bad health and to a temptation from the devil. My obedience (she worked in the kitchen) seemed to me so difficult and unbearable that I decided to leave the Convent for good secretly and without a blessing."

Father Seraphim saw her temptation with his spirit and sent for her to come to the Monastery.

The Height of Perfection

"In obedience to his command I went to him after lunch, and wept all the way. It was on the third day after St. Peter's feast."

Father Seraphim took her by the hand and led her into his cell, saying: "There my joy, I have been waiting for you all day."

"Then he wiped my tears with his handkerchief saying: 'Mother, your tears do not fall on the ground in vain.' And then he led me to the Icon of the Heavenly Queen of Tenderness, and said: 'Kiss her, Mother; the Heavenly Queen will comfort you.'

"I kissed the Icon, and my soul was filled with such joy that I felt quite revived."

"'Well, Mother, now go to the hostel, and tomorrow come to the distant hermitage,' he said to me. I did so. As I approached the hermitage I suddenly saw that Father Seraphim was sitting on a tree trunk near his cell, and beside him stood a huge bear.

"I was paralyzed with fear, and shouting with all my might: 'Father, this is my death!' I fell down.

"On hearing my voice, Father Seraphim hit the bear and waved his hand at him. And the bear, as though he were a rational being, went at once in the direction pointed out to him by the Elder, into a thicket. Seeing all this I was shaking with fear, and even when Father Seraphim came up to me with the words: 'Don't be scared, don't be afraid.' I continued to

St. Seraphim of Sarov

shout as before: 'This is my death!' The Elder said in reply: 'No, Mother, this is not death; death is far from you; this is joy.'

"And then he led me to the same tree trunk and, having prayed, made me sit down, and he sat down himself. We had hardly had time to sit down when that same bear came out of the thicket and lay down at St. Seraphim's feet. Finding myself close to such a terrible beast I was at first trembling with terror, but afterwards seeing that Father Seraphim treated him as a gentle lamb without any fear and even fed him with his own hands with bread which he had brought in his bag, little by little my confidence revived. Then the face of the great Elder seemed to me especially wonderful; it was as joyful and radiant as an Angel's. At last, when I had grown quite calm and most of the bread had been eaten, the Elder gave me the remaining bit and bade me feed the bear myself. But I replied: 'I am afraid, Father, he will bite off my hand too,' and at the same time I felt glad as I thought: 'If he bites off my hand, I shall not be able to cook then.'

"Father Seraphim looked at me, smiled and said: 'No, Mother, I believe that he won't bite off your hand.'

"Then I took the bread he gave me, and the feeding gave me such pleasure that I wished I could feed him longer, for the beast was gentle even with me a sinner. Seeing me quiet, Father Seraphim said to me: 'Do you remember, Mother, how a lion served St. Gerasimus on the Jordan? As for poor Seraphim, a bear serves

The Height of Perfection

him. You see, even the beasts obey us! And you, Mother, feel despondent. Why should we be despondent? If I had taken a pair of scissors with me, I would have cut off some of his hair as a proof. I beg you in the Name of God, Mother, never and on no account lose hope, but always imitate the humility of St. Isidora. In her Convent she was last in the eyes of all, but with God she was first, because she loathed no obedience.'

"I was just thinking: Now I am going to tell the Sisters about this amazing miracle!

"But Father Seraphim answered my thought: 'No, Mother, tell no one until eleven years after my death; and then God's will will make it clear to you whom to tell.'"

In course of time, exactly eleven years later, Sister Matrona told this for the first time to the peasant Euphemius Vassiliev who at the time was already engaged in painting a portrait of Father Seraphim.

Another time the Abbess Alexandra with a Sister named Anna witnessed a similar miracle.

"Without stopping at the Monastery," she writes, "we went straight to the distant hermitage, and on approaching it we saw Father sitting on a log. Suddenly an enormous bear walked out of the wood on its hind legs. Our hands became clammy, our eyes grew dim.

St. Seraphim of Sarov

"Then Father said: 'Misha[28] why do you frighten my orphans? Better go back and bring us some kind of consolation, as I have nothing to offer them.'

The bear turned round and went off into the forest. About two hours had passed in sweet converse with Father Seraphim in his cell when that same bear suddenly appeared again, scrambled clumsily into the cell and roared. The Elder went up to it.

"'Well, well, Misha, show me what you have brought us.' The bear rose on its hind legs and gave Father Seraphim something wrapped up in leaves and somehow tangled together. The contents of the parcel proved to be a fresh honeycomb of pure honey. The Elder took the honey and silently pointed at the door. The beast seemed to make a bow and the Elder, taking a bit of bread out of his bag, gave it to him. Then the bear went off into the forest."

The Sisters were also witnesses of other events.

"Great was the Sisters' faith in the power of Father Seraphim's prayers," says the author of the Chronicle, "and many contemporaries were astonished at it. The sick Mother Callista reported the following case. They once went to the Sarov mill. All at once the horse stumbled, fell and dislocated its leg, so that it could not get up. The Sisters were afraid; they did not know what to do with the cart and how to return home. They

---

[28] Misha (i pronounced as in "machine") in Russian is the diminutive form of Michael.

The Height of Perfection

started to weep and to cry: 'Father Seraphim, help us!' Hearing their weeping and crying, some Monks came and one of them struck the horse; it jumped up, its leg cracked, the joint came into its place, and in a second all had passed. Another Monk who had seen what happened said: 'Well, brethren, we have not such faith as the Nuns have. As soon as they cried: 'Father Seraphim, help us!' he worked a miracle and helped them according to their faith.'"

Much that is extraordinary, striking, almost incredible to the human mind happened through the man of God during the organization of the Diveyev Convent. But we shall relate it further on. And now let us only mention the short but very important information of the Diveyev Sister Barbara which bears witness to the perfection and holiness of the Saint.

"Once I came to Father Seraphim in his hermitage," she relates, "and there were flies on his face, so that blood was trickling down his cheeks. I felt sorry for him and wanted to drive them away, but he said: 'Don't touch them, my joy; let every breath praise the Lord,'[29] He is so patient!"

Yet it was not patience that mattered so much as loving pity for every creature of God which, according to St. Isaac the Syrian, is a sign of perfection.

---

[29] "Let every breath praise the Lord" is the Greek (Septuagint) version of Psalm 150:5.

St. Seraphim of Sarov

However, though he had attained to such heights and such dispassion, the Saint did not cease his labours. On his return from the near hermitage to the Monastery he used to take a little food, but only once a day.

"As to his sleep," writes one of his biographers, "it was always brief, and during the last years of his life Father Seraphim especially struggled against the night's rest. The Monks who came to visit the holy ascetic sometimes found him sleeping either in his cell or in the anteroom in different attitudes: sometimes he slept on the floor with his back against the wall and with outstretched feet; sometimes he leaned his head on a log or a stone; at other times he stretched himself out on the logs and bags with bricks and sand which were in his cell. As death drew near, the Saint began to sleep in such an inconvenient attitude that it is terrible even to think of it, and it was impossible to witness it without awe: he knelt down and slept with his face and elbows on the floor, supporting his head with his hands. One cannot but feel amazed at such extraordinary asceticism."

St. Seraphim "tormented the tormentor" even when his human powers were failing.

The Height of Perfection

God's Saints are truly amazing and incomprehensible! One can only wonder and worship and glorify God Who gives such abundant grace to men.[30]

---

[30] We have already mentioned more than once the regrettable attitude which was adopted towards the Saint by some of the Sarov Brothers and by Abbot Niphont himself. Intentionally we have not hushed up these temptations which are unavoidable in a Saint's career.

However, we did not write about this to censure those who were tempted. Such misgivings are easy to understand. On the contrary, the Saints themselves cannot be grasped by our mind. Long after Father Seraphim's death, rumours of the incompatibility and misunderstandings between the Sarov people and St. Seraphim were still a floating tradition. In 1848 the famous pilgrim and author A. N. Muravyov visited the Monastery. He was astonished to learn of this, and applied to the then Abbot Isaiah II for an explanation of the strange attitude towards the Saint. "According to God's permissive will, misunderstandings may occur among the most holy men, as we read in their lives," said the Father Abbot. "But I know that my predecessor (Abbot Niphont) was filled towards him (Father Seraphim) with sincere and deep esteem." It was not quite clear to all at the time that not only esteem but deepest reverence was required with regard to one of God's greatest Saints who was wonderful even among the Saints of the whole world. All this has only gradually been revealed in the course of a whole century. Therefore, let us not judge too strictly those who could not avoid a worldly opinion of their contemporary. Leave it to God. And let us mention their names in our prayers among the names of the fathers, brethren and friends of the Saint: Pachomius, Isaiah II, Joseph, Mark the Silent, his Confessor Hilarion, Bishop Antony of Voronezh, and a host of Diveyev ascetics (both male and female). By their prayers, O Lord, have mercy on us sinners.

St. Seraphim as seen in the Uncreated Light by Motovilov during his famous conversation on the Acquisition of the Holy Spirit.

Chapter VIII

A Wonderful Revelation to the World

But the most wonderful, most striking, truly super-natural instruction--or rather Divine revelation--was given by Father Seraphim in his amazing conversation with N. A. Motovilov.[31]

This revelation is undoubtedly of world-wide significance. True, there is nothing essentially new in it, for the full revelation was given to the Apostles from the very day of Pentecost. But now that people have forgotten the fundamental truths of the Christian religion, and are immersed in the darkness of materialism or the exterior and routine performance of "ascetic labours," Father Seraphim's revelation is truly extraordinary, as indeed he himself regarded it.

"It is not given to you alone to understand this," said Father Seraphim at the end of the revelation, "but through you it is for the whole world!"

---

[31] The very discovery of Motovilov's manuscript is a great miracle. For about seventy years, this most valuable manuscript lay buried in complete oblivion and was in danger of being destroyed, for it had already been thrown away and was lying in a heap of rubbish in an attic under a layer of bird-droppings. Here it was miraculously found by S. A. Nilus, the famous author of the book "Multum in Parvo." Reverently searching for scraps of the great Seraphim's life, Nilus was rummaging among odds and ends in the attic and was already beginning to lose hope of finding anything when an exercise book which was very indistinctly written attracted his attention. This proved to be the memoirs of Motovilov, and that is how they came to be given to the world. The memoirs were found in 1902 and printed in the "Moscow News" in 1903; almost simultaneously the exposition of the relics of St. Seraphim took place.

St. Seraphim of Sarov

Like a flash of lightning this wonderful conversation illumined the whole world which was already immersed in spiritual lethargy and death, less than a century before the struggle against Christianity in Russia and at a time when Christian faith was at a low ebb in the West.

Here God's Saint appears before us as in no way inferior to the great prophets through whom the Holy Spirit Himself spoke.

We record everything word for word without any interpretations of our own.

Conversation of St. Seraphim with N. A. Motovilov

It was Thursday. The day was gloomy. The snow lay eight inches deep on the ground; and dry, crisp snowflakes were falling thickly from the sky when Father Seraphim began his conversation with me in a field adjoining his near hermitage, opposite the River Sarovka, at the foot of the hill which slopes down to the river bank. He sat me on the stump of a tree which he had just felled, and he himself squatted opposite me.

"The Lord has revealed to me," said the great Elder, "that in your childhood you had a great desire to know the aim of our Christian life, and that you continually asked many great spiritual persons about it."

A Wonderful Revelation to the World

I must say here that from the age of twelve this thought had constantly troubled me. I had, in fact, approached many clergy about it; but their answers had not satisfied me. This was not known to the Elder.

"But no one," continued Father Seraphim, "has given you a precise answer. They have said to you: 'Go to Church, pray to God, do the commandments of God, do good---that is the aim of the Christian life.' Some were even indignant with you for being occupied with profane curiosity and said to you: 'Do not seek things that are beyond you.' But they did not speak as they should. And now poor Seraphim will explain to you in what this aim really consists.

"Prayer, fasting, vigil and all other Christian activities, however good they may be in themselves, do not constitute the aim of our Christian life, although they serve as the indispensable means of reaching this end. The true aim of our Christian life consists in the acquisition of the Holy Spirit of God. As for fasts, and vigils, and prayer, and almsgiving, and every good deed done for Christ's sake, they are only means of acquiring the Holy Spirit of God. But mark, my son, only the good deed done for Christ's sake brings us the fruits of the Holy Spirit. All that is not done for Christ's sake, even though it be good, brings neither reward in the future life nor the grace of God in this. That is why our Lord Jesus Christ said: *He who gathers not with Me scatters* (Luke 11:23). Not that a good deed can be called anything but gathering, since even though it is not done for Christ's sake, yet it is good. Scripture says: *In every nation he who fears*

169

St. Seraphim of Sarov

God and works righteousness is acceptable to Him (Acts 10:35).

"As we see from the sacred narrative, the man who works righteousness is so pleasing to God that the Angel of the Lord appeared at the hour of prayer to Cornelius, the God-fearing and righteous centurion, and said: 'Send to Joppa to Simon the Tanner; there shalt thou find Peter and he will tell thee the words of eternal life, whereby thou shalt be saved and all thy house.'[32] Thus the Lord uses all His divine means to give such a man in return for his good works the opportunity not to lose his reward in the future life. But to this end we must begin here with a right faith in our Lord Jesus Christ, the Son of God, Who came into the world to save sinners and Who, through our acquiring for ourselves the grace of the Holy Spirit, brings into our hearts the Kingdom of God and opens the way for us to win the blessings of the future life. But the acceptability to God of good deeds not done for Christ's sake is limited to this: the Creator gives the means to make them living (cp Heb. 6:1). It rests with man to make them living or not. That is why the Lord said to the Jews: *If you had been blind, you would have no sin. But now you say, We see, and your sin remains on you* (Jn. 9:41). If a man like Cornelius enjoys the favour of God for his deeds, though not done for Christ's sake, and then believes in His Son, such deeds will be imputed to him as done for Christ's sake merely for faith in Him. But in the opposite event a

---

[32] St. Seraphim is giving the sense of Acts 10:5ff. and not quoting literally.

170

A Wonderful Revelation to the World

man has no right to complain that his good has been no use. It never is, except when it is done for Christ's sake, since good done for Him not only merits a crown of righteousness in the world to come, but also in this present life fills us with the grace of the Holy Spirit. Moreover, as it is said: *God gives not the Spirit by measure. The Father loves the Son, and has given all things into His hand.* (Jn. 3:34-35).

"That's it, your Godliness.[33] In acquiring this Spirit of God consists the true aim of our Christian life, while prayer, vigil, fasting, almsgiving and other good works[34] done for Christ's sake are merely means for acquiring the Spirit of God."

"What do you mean by acquiring?" I asked Father Seraphim. "Somehow I don't understand that."

"Acquiring is the same as obtaining," he replied. "You understand, of course, what acquiring money means? Acquiring the Spirit of God is exactly the same. You know well enough what it means in a worldly sense, your Godliness, to acquire. The aim in life of ordinary worldly people is to acquire or make money, and for the nobility it is in addition to receive honours, distinctions and other rewards for their services to the government. The acquisition of God's Spirit is also capital, but grace-giving and eternal, and

---

[33] Lit. "Your God-lovingness," corresponding to the English idioms "Your Worship", "Your Excellency", etc.
[34] "Good works." It is one compound word in Russian, and may also be translated "virtue". St. Augustine says: "Wisdom's labours are virtues."

171

St. Seraphim of Sarov

it is obtained in very similar ways, almost the same ways as monetary, social and temporal capital.

"God the Word, the God-Man, our Lord Jesus Christ, compares our life with a market, and the work of our life on earth He calls trading, and says to us all: *Trade till I come* (Lk. 19:13), *redeeming the time, because the days are evil* (Eph. 5:16). That is to say, make the most of your time for getting heavenly blessings through earthly goods. Earthly goods are good works done for Christ's sake and conferring on us the grace of the All-Holy Spirit.

"In the parable of the wise and foolish virgins, when the foolish ones lacked oil, it was said: 'Go and buy in the market.' But when they had bought, the door of the bride-chamber was already shut and they could not get in. Some say that the lack of oil in the lamps of the foolish virgins means a lack of good deeds in their lifetime. Such an interpretation is not quite correct. Why should they be lacking in good deeds if they are called virgins, even though foolish ones? Virginity is the supreme virtue, an angelic state, and it could take the place of all other good works.

"I think that what they were lacking was the grace of the All-Holy Spirit of God. These virgins practiced the virtues, but in their spiritual ignorance they supposed that the Christian life consisted merely in doing good works. By doing a good deed they thought they were doing the work of God, but they little cared whether they acquired thereby the grace of God's Spirit. Such ways of life based merely on doing good

172

A Wonderful Revelation to the World

without carefully testing whether they bring the grace of the Spirit of God, are mentioned in the Patristic books: 'There is another way which is deemed good at the beginning, but it ends at the bottom of hell.'

"Antony the Great in his letters to Monks says of such virgins: 'Many Monks and virgins have no idea of the different kinds of will which act in man, and they do not know that we are influenced by three wills: the first is God's all-perfect and all-saving will: the second is our own human will which, if not destructive, yet neither is it saving; and the third is the devil's will--wholly destructive.' And this third will of the enemy teaches man either not to do any good deeds, or to do them out of vanity, or to do them merely for virtue's sake and not for Christ's sake. The second, our own will, teaches us to do everything to flatter our passions, or else it teaches us like the enemy to do good for the sake of good and not care for the grace which is acquired by it. But the first, God's all-saving will, consists in doing good solely to acquire the Holy Spirit, as an eternal, inexhaustible treasure which cannot be rightly valued. The acquisition of the Holy Spirit is, so to say, the oil which the foolish virgins lacked. They were called foolish just because they had forgotten the necessary fruit of virtue, the grace of the Holy Spirit, without which no one is or can be saved, for: 'Every soul is quickened by the Holy Spirit and exalted by purity and mystically illumined by the Trinal Unity.'

"This is the oil in the lamps of the wise virgins which could burn long and brightly, and these virgins

173

with their burning lamps were able to meet the Bridegroom, Who came at midnight, and could enter the bridechamber of joy with Him. But the foolish ones, though they went to market to buy some oil when they saw their lamps going out, were unable to return in time, for the door was already shut. The market is our life; the door of the bridechamber which was shut and which barred the way to the Bridegroom is human death; the wise and foolish virgins are Christian souls; the oil is not good deeds but the grace of the All-Holy Spirit of God which is obtained through them and which changes souls from one state to another--that is, from corruption to incorruption, from spiritual death to spiritual life, from darkness to light, from the stable of our being (where the passions are tied up like dumb animals and wild beasts) into a Temple of the Divinity, into the shining bridechamber of eternal joy in Christ Jesus our Lord, the Creator and Redeemer and eternal Bridegroom of our souls.

"How great is God's compassion to our misery, that is to say, our inattention to His care for us, when God says: *Behold, I stand at the door and knock* (Rev. 3:20), meaning by 'door' the course of our life which has not yet been closed by death! Oh, how I wish, your Godliness, that in this life you may always be in the Spirit of God! 'In whatsoever I find you, in that will I judge you,'[35] says the Lord.

"Woe to us if He finds us overcharged with the cares and sorrows of this life! For who will be able to

---

[35] St. Justin (Dial. 47) records this "unwritten saying" of Christ.

A Wonderful Revelation to the World

bear His anger, who will withstand the wrath of His countenance? That is why it has been said: *Watch and pray, lest you enter into temptation* (Mk. 14:38), that is lest you be deprived of the Spirit of God, for watching and prayer bring us His grace.

"Of course, every good deed done for Christ's sake gives us the grace of the Holy Spirit, but prayer gives us it most of all, for it is always at hand, so to speak, as an instrument for acquiring the grace of the Spirit. For instance, you would like to go to Church, but there is no Church or the Service is over; you would like to give alms to a beggar, but there isn't one, or you have nothing to give; you would like to preserve your virginity,[36] but you have not the strength to do so because of your temperament, or because of the violence of the wiles of the enemy which on account of your human weakness you cannot withstand; you would like to do some other good deed for Christ's sake, but either you have not the strength or the opportunity is lacking. This certainly does not apply to prayer. Prayer is always possible for everyone, rich and poor, noble and humble, strong and weak, healthy and sick, righteous and sinful.

"You may judge how great the power of prayer is even in a sinful person, when it is offered whole-heartedly, by the following example from Holy Tradition. When at the request of a desperate mother who had been deprived by death of her only son, a harlot whom she chanced to meet, still unclean, from

---

[36] That is, you would like to remain unmarried.

her last sin, and who was touched by the mother's deep sorrow, cried to the Lord: 'Not for the sake of a wretched sinner like me, but for the sake of the tears of a mother sorrowing for her son and firmly trusting in Thy loving kindness and Thy almighty power, Christ God, raise up her son, O Lord!' And the Lord raised him up.

"You see, your Godliness! Great is the power of prayer, and it brings most of all the Spirit of God, and is most easily practiced by everyone. We shall be blessed if the Lord God finds us watchful and filled with the gifts of His Holy Spirit. Then we may boldly hope to *be caught up...in the clouds to meet the Lord in the air* (I Thes. 4:17) Who is coming *with great power and glory* (Mk. 13:26) *to judge the living and the dead* (I Pet. 4:5) and *to reward every man according to his works* (Mat. 16:27).

"Your Godliness deigns to think it a great happiness to talk to poor Seraphim, believing that even he is not bereft of the grace of the Lord. What then shall we say of the Lord Himself, the never-failing source of every kind of blessing, both heavenly and earthly? Truly in prayer we are granted to converse with Him, our all-gracious and life-giving God and Saviour Himself. But even here we must pray only until God the Holy Spirit descends on us in measures of His heavenly grace known to Him. And when He deigns to visit us, we must stop praying. Why should we then pray to Him, 'Come and abide in us and cleanse us from all impurity and save our souls, O Good One,' when He has already come to us to save us who trust

A Wonderful Revelation to the World

in Him and truly call on His Holy Name, that humbly and with love we may receive Him, the Comforter, in the mansions of our souls hungering and thirsting for His coming.

"I will explain this to your Godliness by an example. Imagine that you have invited me to pay you a visit and at your invitation I come to have a talk with you. But you continue to invite me, saying: 'Come in, please. Do come in!' Then I should be obliged to think: 'What is the matter with him? Is he out of his mind?' So it is with regard to our Lord God the Holy Spirit. That is why it is said: *Be still and realize that I am God; I shall be exalted among the heathen, I shall be exalted in the earth* (Ps. 45:10). That is, I shall appear and shall continue to appear to everyone who believes in Me and calls upon Me, and I shall converse with him as I once conversed with Adam in Paradise, with Abraham and Jacob and other servants of Mine, with Moses and Job, and those like them.

"Many explain that this stillness refers only to worldly matters; in other words, that during prayerful converse with God you must 'be still' with regard to worldly affairs. But I will tell you in the name of God that not only is it necessary to be dead[37] to them at prayer, but when by the omnipotent power of faith and prayer our Lord God the Holy Spirit condescends to visit us, and comes to us in the plenitude of His unutterable goodness, we must be dead to prayer too.

---

[37] Lit. "be still."

St. Seraphim of Sarov

"The soul speaks and converses during prayer, but at the descent of the Holy Spirit we must remain in complete silence, in order to hear clearly and intelligibly all the words of eternal life which He will then deign to communicate. Complete soberness of both soul and spirit, and chaste purity of body is required at the same time. The same demands were made at Mount Horeb, when the Israelites were told not even to touch their wives for three days before the appearance of God on Mount Sinai. For our God is a fire which consumes everything unclean, and no one who is defiled in body or spirit can enter into communion with Him."

"Yes, Father, but what about other good deeds done for Christ's sake in order to acquire the grace of the Holy Spirit? You have only been speaking of prayer!"

"Acquire the grace of the Holy Spirit also by practicing all the other virtues for Christ's sake. Trade spiritually with them; trade with those which give you the greatest profit. Accumulate capital from the super-abundance of God's grace, deposit it in God's eternal bank which will bring you immaterial interest, not four or six percent, but one hundred percent for one spiritual ruble, and even infinitely more than that. For example, if prayer and watching give you more of God's grace, watch and pray; if fasting gives you much of the Spirit of God, fast; if almsgiving gives you more, give alms. Weigh every virtue done for Christ's sake in this manner.

A Wonderful Revelation to the World

"Now I will tell you about myself, poor Seraphim. I come of a merchant family in Kursk. So when I was not yet in the Monastery we used to trade with the goods which brought us the greatest profit. Act like that, my son. And just as in business the main point is not merely to trade, but to get as much profit as possible, so in the business of the Christian life the main point is not merely to pray or to do some other good deed. Though the Apostle says: *Pray without ceasing* (I Thess. 5:17), yet, as you remember, he adds: *I would rather speak five words with my understanding than ten thousand words with the tongue* (I Cor. 14:13). And the Lord says: *Not everyone that says unto Me: Lord, Lord,* shall be saved, *but he who does the will of My Father*, that is he who does the work of God and, moreover, does it with reverence, for *cursed is he who does the work of God negligently* (Jer. 48:10). And the work of God is: *Believe in God and in Him Whom He has sent, Jesus Christ* (Jn. 14:1;6:29). If we understand the commandments of Christ and of the Apostles aright, our business as Christians consists not in increasing the number of our good deeds which are only the means of furthering the purpose of our Christian life, but in deriving from them the utmost profit, that is in acquiring the most abundant gifts of the Holy Spirit.

"How I wish, your Godliness, that you yourself may acquire this inexhaustible source of divine grace, and may always ask yourself: Am I in the Spirit of God or not? And if you are in the Spirit, blessed be God!--there is nothing to grieve about. You are ready

St. Seraphim of Sarov

to appear before the awful judgement of Christ immediately. For 'In whatsoever I find you, in that I will
judge you.' But if we are not in the Spirit, we must
discover why and for what reason our Lord God the
Holy Spirit has willed to abandon us; and we must
seek Him again, and must go on searching until our
Lord God the Holy Spirit has been found and is with
us again through His goodness. And we must attack
the enemies that drive us away from Him until even
their dust is no more, as has been said by the Prophet
David: *I shall pursue my enemies and overtake them;
and I shall not turn back till they are destroyed. I
shall harass them, and they will not be able to stand;
they will fall under my feet.* (Ps. 17:37-38).

"That's it, my son. That is how you must spiritually
trade in virtue. Distribute the Holy Spirit's gifts of
grace to those in need of them, just as a lighted candle
burning with earthly fire shines itself and lights other
candles for the illumining of all in other places, without diminishing its own light. And if it is so with regard to earthly fire, what shall we say about the fire of
the grace of the All-Holy Spirit of God? For earthly
riches decrease with distribution, but the more the
heavenly riches of God's grace are distributed, the
more they increase in him who distributes them. Thus
the Lord Himself was pleased to say to the Samaritan
woman: *Whoever drinks of this water will thirst
again. But whoever drinks of the water that I shall
give him will never thirst; but the water that I shall
give him will be in him a well of water springing up
into eternal life* (Jn. 4:13-14).

A Wonderful Revelation to the World

"Father," said I, "you speak all the time of the acquisition of the grace of the Holy Spirit as the aim of the Christian life. But how and where can I see it? Good deeds are visible, but can the Holy Spirit be seen? How am I to know whether He is with me or not?"

"At the present time," the Elder replied, "owing to our almost universal coldness to our holy faith in our Lord Jesus Christ, and our inattention to the working of His Divine Providence in us, and to the communion of man with God, we have gone so far that, one may say, we have almost abandoned the true Christian life. The testimonies of Holy Scripture now seem strange to us, when, for instance, by the lips of Moses the Holy Spirit says: *And Adam saw the Lord walking in paradise* (cp. Gen. 3:10), or when we read the words of the Apostle Paul: 'We went to Achaia, and the Spirit of God went not with us; we returned to Macedonia, and the Spirit of God came with us'. More than once in other passages of Holy Scripture the appearance of God to men is mentioned.

"That is why some people say: 'These passages are incomprehensible. Is it really possible for people to see God so openly?' But there is nothing incomprehensible here. This failure to understand has come about because we have departed from the simplicity of the original Christian knowledge. Under the pretext of education, we have reached such a darkness of ignorance that what the ancients understood so clearly seems to us almost inconceivable. Even in ordinary conversation, the idea of God's appearance among

St. Seraphim of Sarov

men did not seem strange to them. Thus, when his friends rebuked him for blaspheming God, Job answered them: *How can that be when I feel the Spirit of God in my nostrils?* (cp. Job 27:3). That is, 'How can I blaspheme God when the Holy Spirit abides with me? If I had blasphemed God, the Holy Spirit would have withdrawn from me; but lo, I feel His breath in my nostrils.'

"In exactly the same way it is said of Abraham and Jacob that they saw the Lord and conversed with Him, and that Jacob even wrestled with Him. Moses and all the people with him saw God when he was granted to receive from God the tables of the law on Mount Sinai. A pillar of cloud and a pillar of fire, or, in other words, the evident grace of the Holy Spirit, served as guides to the people of God in the desert. People saw God and the grace of His Holy Spirit, not in sleep or in dreams, or in the excitement of a disordered imagination, but truly and openly.

"We have become so inattentive to the work of our salvation that we misinterpret many other words in Holy Scripture as well, all because we do not seek the grace of God and in the pride of our minds do not allow it to dwell in our souls. That is why we are without true enlightenment from the Lord, which He sends into the hearts of men who hunger and thirst wholeheartedly for God's righteousness.

"Many explain that when it says in the Bible: 'God breathed the breath of life into the face of Adam the first-created, who was created by Him from the dust

182

of the ground,' it must mean that until then there was neither human soul nor spirit in Adam, but only the flesh created from the dust of the ground. This interpretation is wrong, for the Lord God created Adam from the dust of the ground with the constitution which our dear little Father, the holy Apostle Paul describes: *May your spirit and soul and body be preserved blameless at the coming of our Lord Jesus Christ* (I Thess. 5:23). And all these three parts of our nature were created from the dust of the ground, and Adam was not created dead, but an active living being like all the other animate creatures of God living on earth. The point is that if the Lord God had not breathed afterwards into his face this breath of life (that is, the grace of our Lord God the Holy Spirit Who proceeds from the Father and rests in the Son and is sent into the world for the Son's sake), Adam would have remained without having within him the Holy Spirit Who raises him to Godlike dignity. However perfect he had been created and superior to all the other creatures of God, as the crown of creation on earth, he would have been just like all the other creatures which, though they have a body, soul and spirit each according to its kind, yet have not the Holy Spirit within them. But when the Lord God breathed into Adam's face the breath of life, then, according to Moses' word, *Adam became a living soul* (Gen. 2:7), that is, completely and in every way like God, and, like Him, for ever immortal. Adam was immune to the action of the elements to such a degree that water could not drown him, fire could not burn him, the earth could not swallow him in its abysses, and the air

183

could not harm him by any kind of action whatever. Everything was subject to him as the beloved of God, as the king and lord of creation, and everything looked up to him, as the perfect crown of God's creatures. Adam was made so wise by this breath of life which was breathed into his face from the creative lips of God, the Creator and Ruler of all, that there never has been a man on earth wiser or more intelligent than he, and it is hardly likely that there ever will be. When the Lord commanded him to give names to all the creatures, he gave every creature a name which completely expressed all the qualities, powers and properties given to it by God at its creation.

"Owing to this very gift of the supernatural grace of God which was infused into him by the breath of life, Adam could see and understand the Lord walking in paradise, and comprehend His words, and the conversation of the holy Angels, and the language of all beasts, birds and reptiles and all that is now hidden from us fallen and sinful creatures, but was so clear to Adam before his fall. To Eve also the Lord God gave the same wisdom, strength and unlimited power, and all the other good and holy qualities. And He created her not from the dust of the ground but from Adam's rib in the Eden of delight, in the Paradise which He had planted in the midst of the earth.

"In order that they might always easily maintain within themselves the immortal, divine[38] and perfect properties of this breath of life, God planted in the

---

[38] Lit. "God-gracious" or "Divine-grace-given."

A Wonderful Revelation to the World

midst of the garden the tree of life and endowed its fruits with all the essence and fullness of His divine breath. If they had not sinned, Adam and Eve themselves as well as all their posterity could have always eaten of the fruit of the tree of life and so would have eternally maintained the quickening power of divine grace.

"They could have also maintained to all eternity the full powers of their body, soul and spirit in a state of immortality and everlasting youth, and they could have continued in this immortal and blessed state of theirs for ever. At the present time, however, it is difficult for us even to imagine such grace.

"But when through the tasting of the tree of the knowledge of good and evil--which was premature and contrary to the commandment of God--they learnt the difference between good and evil and were subjected to all the afflictions which followed the transgression of the commandment of God, then they lost this priceless gift of the grace of the Spirit of God, so that, until the actual coming into the world of the God-Man Jesus Christ, *the Spirit of God was not yet* in the world *because Jesus was not yet glorified* (Jn. 7:39).

"However, that does not mean that the Spirit of God was not in the world at all, but His presence was not so apparent[39] as in Adam or in us Orthodox

---

[39] Lit. "His abiding (stay, sojourn, dwelling, residence) was not so full-measured."

Christians. It manifested only externally; yet the signs of His presence in the world were known to mankind. Thus, for instance, many mysteries in connection with the future salvation of the human race were revealed to Adam as well as to Eve after the fall. And for Cain, in spite of his impiety and his transgression, it was easy to understand the voice which held gracious and divine though convicting converse with him. Noah conversed with God. Abraham saw God and His day and was glad (cp. Jn. 8:56). The grace of the Holy Spirit acting externally was also reflected in all the Old Testament prophets and Saints of Israel. The Hebrews afterwards established special prophetic schools where the sons of the prophets were taught to discern the signs of the manifestation of God or of Angels, and to distinguish the operations of the Holy Spirit from the ordinary natural phenomena of our graceless earthly life. Simeon who held God in his arms, Christ's grand-parents Joakim and Anna, and countless other servants of God continually had quite openly various divine apparitions, voices and revelations which were justified[40] by evident miraculous events. Though not with the same power as in the people of God, nevertheless, the presence of the Spirit of God also acted in the pagans who did not know the true God, because even among them God found for Himself chosen people. Such, for instance, were the virgin-prophetesses called Sibyls who vowed virginity to an unknown God, but still to God the Creator of the universe, the all-powerful Ruler of the world, as He was conceived by the pagans. Though the pagan

---

[40] Or, "were proved true."

A Wonderful Revelation to the World

philosophers also wandered in the darkness of ignorance of God, yet they sought the truth which is
beloved by God, and on account of this God-pleasing
seeking, they could partake of the Spirit of God, for it
is said that the nations who do not know God practice
by nature the demands of the law and do what is
pleasing to God (cp. Rom. 2:14). The Lord so praises
truth that He says of it Himself by the Holy Spirit:
*Truth has sprung out of the earth, and righteousness
has looked down from heaven* (Ps. 84:11).

"So you see, your Godliness, both in the holy
Hebrew people, a people beloved by God, and in the
pagans who did not know God, there was preserved a
knowledge of God--that is, my son, a clear and rational comprehension of how our Lord God the Holy
Spirit acts in man, and by means of what inner and
outer feelings one can be sure that this is really the
action of our Lord God the Holy Spirit, and not a
delusion of the enemy. That is how it was from
Adam's fall until the coming in the flesh of our Lord
Jesus Christ into the world.

"Without this perceptible realization of the actions
of the Holy Spirit which had always been preserved in
human nature, men could not possibly have known for
certain whether the fruit of the seed of the woman
who had been promised to Adam and Eve had come
into the world to bruise the serpent's head (Gen. 3:15).

"At last the Holy Spirit foretold to St. Simeon, who
was then in his 65th year, the mystery of the virginal
conception and birth of Christ from the most pure

St. Seraphim of Sarov

Ever-Virgin Mary. Afterwards, having lived by the grace of the All-Holy Spirit of God for three hundred years, in the 365th year of his life he said openly in the Temple of the Lord that he knew for certain[41] through the gift of the Holy Spirit that this was that very Christ, the Saviour of the world, Whose supernatural conception and birth from the Holy Spirit had been foretold to him by an Angel three hundred years previously.

"And there was also Saint Anna, a prophetess, the daughter of Phanuel, who from her widowhood had served the Lord God in the Temple of God for eighty years, and who was known to be a righteous widow, a chaste servant of God, from the special gifts of grace she had received. She too announced that He was actually the Messiah Who had been promised to the world, the true Christ, God and Man, the King of Israel, Who had come to save Adam and mankind.

"But when our Lord Jesus Christ condescended to accomplish the whole work of salvation, after His Resurrection, He breathed on the Apostles, restored the breath of life lost by Adam, and gave them the same grace of the All-Holy Spirit of God as Adam had enjoyed. But that was not all. He also told them that it was expedient for them that He should go to the Father, for if He did not go, the Spirit of God would not come into the world. But if He, the Christ, went to the Father, He would send Him into the world, and He, the Comforter, would guide them and all who fol-

---

[41] Lit. "palpably recognized" or "perceptibly realized."

A Wonderful Revelation to the World

lowed their teaching into all truth and would remind them of all that He had said to them when He was still in the world. What was then promised was *grace upon grace* (Jn. 1:16).

"Then on the day of Pentecost He solemnly sent down to them in a tempestuous wind the Holy Spirit in the form of tongues of fire which alighted on each of them and entered within them and filled them with the fiery strength of divine grace which breathes bedewingly and acts gladdeningly in souls which partake of its power and operations (Cp. Acts 2:1-4). And this same fire-infusing grace of the Holy Spirit which is given to us all, the faithful of Christ, in the Sacrament of Holy Baptism, is sealed by the Sacrament of Chrismation on the chief parts of our body as appointed by Holy Church, the eternal keeper of this grace. It is said: 'The seal of the Gift of the Holy Spirit.' On what do we put our seals, your Godliness, if not on vessels containing some very precious treasure? But what on earth can be higher and what can be more precious than the gifts of the Holy Spirit which are sent down to us from above in the Sacrament of Baptism? This Baptismal grace is so great and so indispensable, so vital for man, that even a heretic is not deprived of it until his very death; that is, till the end of the period appointed on high by the Providence of God as a life-long test of man on earth, in order to see what he will be able to achieve (during this period given to him by God) by means of the power of grace granted him from on high.

St. Seraphim of Sarov

"And if we were never to sin after our Baptism, we should remain for ever Saints of God, holy, blameless and free from all impurity of body and spirit. But the trouble is that we increase in stature, but do not increase in grace and in the knowledge of God as our Lord Jesus Christ increased; but on the contrary, we gradually become more and more depraved and lose the grace of the All-Holy Spirit of God and become sinful in various degrees, and most sinful people. But if a man is stirred by the wisdom of God which seeks our salvation and embraces everything, and he is resolved for its sake to devote the early hours to God and to watch in order to find his eternal salvation[42], then, in obedience to its voice, he must hasten to offer true repentance for all his sins and must practice the virtues which are opposite to the sins committed. Then through the virtues practiced for Christ's sake he will acquire the Holy Spirit Who acts within us and establishes in us the Kingdom of God. The word of God does not say in vain: *The Kingdom of God is within you* (Lk. 17:21), and it *suffers violence, and the violent take it by force*[43] (Mat. 11:12). That means that people who, in spite of the bonds of sin which fetter them and (by their violence and by inciting them to new sins) prevent them from coming to Him, our Saviour, with perfect repentance for reckoning with Him, yet force themselves to break their bonds, despising all the strength of the fetters of sin--such

---

[42] Cp. Wisdom 7:27; 6:14-20.
[43] Lit. "The Kingdom of Heaven is forced, and the forceful seize it"; or "the Kingdom of Heaven is stormed, and the stormers capture it." Cp. Luke 16:16; "Everyone forces himself into it."

A Wonderful Revelation to the World

people at last actually appear before the face of God made whiter than snow by His grace. *Come, says the Lord: Though your sins be as purple, I will make them white as snow* (Is. 1:18).

"Such people were once seen by the holy Seer John the Divine *clothed in white robes* (that is, in robes of justification) and *palms in their hands* (as a sign of victory), and they were singing to God a wonderful song: Alleluia. And no one could imitate the beauty of their song. Of them an Angel of God said: *These are they who have come out of great tribulation and have washed their robes, and have made them white in the blood of the Lamb* (Rev. 7:9-14). They were washed with their sufferings and made white in the Communion of the immaculate and life-giving Mysteries of the Body and Blood of the most pure and spotless Lamb--Christ--Who was slain before all ages by His own will for the salvation of the world and Who is continually being slain and divided until now but is never exhausted. Through the Holy Mysteries we are granted our eternal and unfailing salvation as a viaticum to eternal life, as an acceptable answer at His awful judgement and as a precious substitute beyond our comprehension for that fruit of the tree of life of which the enemy of mankind Lucifer who fell from heaven would have liked to deprive our human race. Though the enemy and devil seduced Eve, and Adam fell with her, yet the Lord not only granted them a Redeemer in the fruit of the seed of the woman Who trampled down death by death, but also granted us all in the woman, the Ever-Virgin Mary Mother of God,

191

who crushes the head of the serpent in herself and in all the human race, a constant mediatress with her Son and our God, and an invincible and insistent intercessor even for the most desperate sinners. That is why the Mother of God is called the 'Plague of Demons,' for it is not possible for a devil to destroy a man so long as the man himself has recourse to the help of the Mother of God.

"And I must further explain, your Godliness, the difference between the operations of the Holy Spirit who dwells mystically in the hearts of those who believe in our Lord God and Saviour Jesus Christ and the operations of the darkness of sin which, at the suggestion and instigation of the devil, acts predatorily in us. The Spirit of God reminds us of the words of our Lord Jesus Christ and always acts triumphantly with Him, gladdening our hearts and guiding our steps into the way of peace, while the false diabolic spirit reasons in the opposite way to Christ, and its actions in us are rebellious, stubborn, and full of the lust of the flesh, the lust of the eyes and the pride of life.

"*And whoever lives and believes in Me shall not die for ever* (Jn. 11:26). He who has the grace of the Holy Spirit in reward for right faith in Christ, even if on account of human frailty his soul were to die from some sin or other, yet he will not die for ever, but he will be raised by the grace of our Lord Jesus Christ Who *takes away the sin of the world* (Jn. 1:29) and freely gives grace upon grace. Of this grace, which was manifested to the whole world and to our human race by the God-Man, it is said in the Gospel: *In Him*

A Wonderful Revelation to the World

was life, and the life was the light of men (Jn. 1:4); and further: *And the light shines in the darkness; and the darkness did not over-power it* (Jn. 1:5). This means that the grace of the Holy Spirit which is granted at Baptism in the name of the Father and the Son and the Holy Spirit, in spite of men's falls into sin, in spite of the darkness surrounding our soul, nevertheless shines in the heart with the divine light (which has existed from time immemorial) of the inestimable merits of Christ. In the event of a sinner's impenitence this light of Christ cries to the Father: 'Abba, Father! Be not angry with this impenitence to the end (of his life)'. And then, at the sinner's conversion to the way of repentance, it effaces completely all trace of past sin and clothes the former sinner once more in a robe of incorruption woven from the grace of the Holy Spirit, concerning the acquisition of which, as the aim of the Christian life, I have been speaking so long to your Godliness.

"I will tell you something else, so that you may understand still more clearly what is meant by the grace of God, how to recognize it and how its action is manifested particularly in those who are enlightened by it. The grace of the Holy Spirit is the light which enlightens man. The whole of Sacred Scripture speaks about this. Thus our holy Father David said: *Thy word is a lamp to my feet, and a light to my path* (Ps. 118:105), and: *Unless Thy law had been my meditation I should have died in my humiliation* (Ps. 118:92). In other words, the grace of the Holy Spirit which is expressed in the Law by the words of the

St. Seraphim of Sarov

Lord's commandments is my lamp and light. And if this grace of the Holy Spirit (which I try to acquire so carefully and zealously that I meditate on Thy righteous judgements seven times a day) did not enlighten me amidst the darkness of the cares which are inseparable from the high calling of my royal rank, whence should I get a spark of light to illumine my way on the path of life which is darkened by the ill-will of my enemies?

"And in fact the Lord has frequently demonstrated before many witnesses how the grace of the Holy Spirit acts on people whom He has sanctified and illumined by His great inspiration[44]. Remember Moses after his talk with God on Mount Sinai. He so shone with an extraordinary light that people were unable to look at him. He was even forced to wear a veil when he appeared in public. Remember the Transfiguration of the Lord on Mount Tabor. A great light encircled Him, *and His raiment became shining, exceedingly white like snow* (Mk. 9:3), and His disciples fell on their faces from fear. But when Moses and Elias appeared to Him in that light, a cloud overshadowed them in order to hide the radiance of the light of the divine grace which blinded the eyes of the disciples. Thus the grace of the All-Holy Spirit of God appears in an ineffable light to all to whom God reveals its action."

"But how," I asked Father Seraphim, "can I know that I am in the grace of the Holy Spirit?"

[44.]Lit. "descents." Slavonic *naitie* = επιφοιτησις.

A Wonderful Revelation to the World

"It is very simple, your Godliness," he replied. "That is why the Lord says: 'All things are simple to those who find knowledge.' The trouble is that we do not seek this divine knowledge which does not puff up, for it is not of this world. This knowledge which is full of love for God and for our neighbour builds up every man for his salvation. Of this knowledge the Lord said that God *wills all men to be saved, and to come to the knowledge[45] of the truth* (I Tim. 2:4). And of the lack of this knowledge He said to His Apostles: *Are you also yet without understanding* (Mat. 15:16)? Concerning this understanding,[46] it is said in the Gospel of the Apostles: *Then opened He their understanding[47]* (Lk. 24:45), and the Apostles always perceived whether the Spirit of God was dwelling in them or not; and being filled with understanding, they saw the presence of the Holy Spirit with them and declared positively that their work was holy and entirely pleasing to the Lord God. That explains why in their Epistles they wrote: *It seemed good to the Holy Spirit and to us* (Acts 15:28). Only on these grounds did they offer their Epistles as immutable truth for the benefit of all the faithful. Thus the holy Apostles were consciously aware of the presence in themselves of the Spirit of God. And so you see, your Godliness, how simple it is!"

---

[45] In the Slavonic one word represents three different Greek words.

[46] Same as above.--ed.

[47] Same as above.--ed.

St. Seraphim of Sarov

"Nevertheless," I replied, "I do not understand how I can be certain that I am in the Spirit of God. How can I discern for myself His true manifestation in me?"

Father Seraphim replied: "I have already told you, your Godliness, that it is very simple and I have related in detail how people come to be in the Spirit of God and how we can recognise His presence in us. So what do you want, my son?"

"I want to understand it well," I said.

Then Father Seraphim took me very firmly by the shoulders and said: "We are both in the Spirit of God now, my son. Why don't you look at me?"

I replied: "I cannot look, Father, because your eyes are flashing like lightning. Your face has become brighter than the sun, and my eyes ache with pain."

Father Seraphim said: "Don't be alarmed, your Godliness! Now you yourself have become as bright as I am. You are now in the fulness of the Spirit of God yourself; otherwise you would not be able to see me as I am."

Then, bending his head towards me, he whispered softly in my ear: "Thank the Lord God for His unutterable mercy to us! You saw that I did not even cross myself; and only in my heart I prayed mentally to the Lord God and said within myself: 'Lord, grant him to see clearly with his bodily eyes that descent of

196

A Wonderful Revelation to the World

Thy Spirit which Thou grantest to Thy servants when Thou art pleased to appear in the light of Thy magnificent glory.' And you see, my son, the Lord instantly fulfilled the humble prayer of poor Seraphim. How then shall we not thank Him for this unspeakable gift to us both? Even to the greatest hermits, my son, the Lord God does not always show His mercy in this way. This grace of God, like a loving mother, has been pleased to comfort your contrite heart at the intercession of the Mother of God herself. But why, my son, do you not look me in the eyes? Just look, and don't be afraid! The Lord is with us!"

After these words I glanced at his face and there came over me an even greater reverent awe. Imagine in the center of the sun, in the dazzling light of its midday rays, the face of a man talking to you. You see the movement of his lips and the changing expression of his eyes, you hear his voice, you feel someone holding your shoulders; yet you do not see his hands, you do not even see yourself or his figure, but only a blinding light spreading far around for several yards and illumining with its glaring sheen both the snow-blanket which covered the forest glade and the snow-flakes which besprinkled me and the great Elder. You can imagine the state I was in!

"How do you feel now?" Father Seraphim asked me.

"Extraordinarily well," I said.

St. Seraphim of Sarov

"But in what way? How exactly do you feel well?"

I answered: "I feel such calmness and peace in my soul that no words can express it."

"This, your Godliness," said Father Seraphim, "is that peace of which the Lord said to His disciples: *My peace I give unto you; not as the world gives, give I unto you* (Jn. 14:21). *If you were of the world, the world would love its own; but because I have chosen you out of the world, therefore the world hates you* (Jn. 15:19). *But be of good cheer; I have overcome the world* (Jn. 16:33). And to those people whom this world hates but who are chosen by the Lord, the Lord gives that peace which you now feel within you, the peace which, in the words of the Apostle, *passes all understanding* (Phil. 4:7). The Apostle describes it in this way, because it is impossible to express in words the spiritual well-being which it produces in those into whose hearts the Lord God has infused it. Christ the Saviour calls it a peace which comes from His own generosity and is not of this world, for no temporary earthly prosperity can give it to the human heart; it is granted from on high by the Lord God Himself, and that is why it is called the peace of God. What else do you feel?" Father Seraphim asked me.

"An extraordinary sweetness," I replied.

And he continued: "This is that sweetness of which it is said in Holy Scripture: *They will be inebriated with the fatness of Thy house; and Thou shalt make*

198

A Wonderful Revelation to the World

them drink of the torrent of Thy delight[48] (Ps. 35:8).
And now this sweetness is flooding our hearts and
coursing through our veins with unutterable delight.
From this sweetness our hearts melt as it were, and
both of us are filled with such happiness as tongue
cannot tell. What else do you feel?"

"An extraordinary joy in all my heart."

And Father Seraphim continued: "When the Spirit
of God comes down to man and overshadows him
with the fulness of His inspiration[49], then the human
soul overflows with unspeakable joy, for the Spirit of
God fills with joy whatever He touches. This is that
joy of which the Lord speaks in His Gospel: *A woman
when she is in travail has sorrow, because her hour is
come; but when she is delivered of the child, she
remembers no more the anguish, for joy that a man is
born into the world. In the world you will be
sorrowful*[50] *but when I see you again, your heart shall
rejoice, and your joy no one will take from you* (Jn.
16:21-22). Yet however comforting may be this joy
which you now feel in your heart, it is nothing in
comparison with that of which the Lord Himself by
the mouth of His Apostle said that that joy *eye has not
seen, nor ear heard, nor has it entered into the heart
of man what God has prepared for them that love Him*

---

[48] The same word which in Slavonic means *delight* in Russia
means *sweetness*.

[49] Lit. "descent." Slavonic *naitie* = επιφοιτησις.

[50] "In the world you will be sorrowful." This is the Slavonic for
"In the world you will have tribulation"(Jn.16:33). St. Seraphim
has transposed it to its present context.

St. Seraphim of Sarov

(I Cor. 2:9). Foretastes of that joy are given to us now, and if they fill our souls with such sweetness, well-being and happiness, what shall we say of that joy which has been prepared in heaven for those who weep here on earth? And you, my son, have wept enough in your life on earth; yet see with what joy the Lord consoles you even in this life! Now it is up to us, my son, to add labours to labours in order to *go from strength to strength* (Ps. 83:7), and to come *to the measure of the stature of the fulness of Christ* (Eph. 4:13), so that the words of the Lord may be fulfilled in us: *But they that wait upon the Lord shall renew their strength; they shall grow wings like eagles; and they shall run and not be weary* (Is. 40:31); *they will go from strength to strength, and the God of gods will appear to them in* the *Sion* (Ps. 83:8) of realisation and heavenly visions. Only then will our present joy (which now visits us little and briefly) appear in all its fulness, and no one will take it from us, for we shall be filled to overflowing with inexplicable heavenly delights. What else do you feel, your Godliness?"

I answered: "An extraordinary warmth."

"How can you feel warmth, my son? Look, we are sitting in the forest. It is winter out-of-doors, and snow is underfoot. There is more than an inch of snow on us, and the snowflakes are still falling. What warmth can there be?"

I answered: "Such as there is in a bath-house when the water is poured on the stone and the steam rises in clouds."

A Wonderful Revelation to the World

"And the smell?" he asked me. "Is it the same as in the bath-house?"

"No," I replied. "There is nothing on earth like this fragrance. When in my dear mother's lifetime I was fond of dancing and used to go to balls and parties, my mother would sprinkle me with scent which she bought at the best shops in Kazan. But those scents did not exhale such fragrance."

And Father Seraphim, smiling pleasantly, said: "I know it myself just as well as you do, my son, but I am asking you on purpose to see whether you feel it in the same way. It is absolutely true, your Godliness! The sweetest earthly fragrance cannot be compared with the fragrance which we now feel, for we are now enveloped in the fragrance of the Holy Spirit of God. What on earth can be like it? Mark, your Godliness, you have told me that around us it is warm as in a bath-house; but look, neither on you nor on me does the snow melt, nor does it underfoot; therefore, this warmth is not in the air but in us. It is that very warmth about which the Holy Spirit in the words of prayer makes us cry to the Lord: 'Warm me with the warmth of Thy Holy Spirit!' By it the hermits of both sexes were kept warm and did not fear the winter frost, being clad, as in fur coats, in the grace-given clothing woven by the Holy Spirit. And so it must be in actual fact, for the grace of God must dwell within us, in our heart, because the Lord said: *The Kingdom of God is within you* (Lk. 17:21). By the Kingdom of God the Lord meant the grace of the Holy Spirit. This Kingdom of God is now within us, and the grace of

St. Seraphim of Sarov

the Holy Spirit shines upon us and warms us from without as well. It fills the surrounding air with many fragrant odours, sweetens our senses with heavenly delight and floods our hearts with unutterable joy. Our present state is that of which the Apostle says; *The Kingdom of God is not food and drink, but righteousness and peace and joy in the Holy Spirit* (Rom. 14:17). Our faith consists not in the plausible words of earthly wisdom, but in the demonstration of the Spirit and power (cp. I Cor.2:4). That is just the state that we are in now. Of this state the Lord said: *There are some of those standing here who shall not taste of death till they see the Kingdom of God come in power* (Mk. 9:1). See, my son, what unspeakable joy the Lord God has now granted us! This is what it means to be in the fulness of the Holy Spirit, about which St. Macarius of Egypt writes: 'I myself was in the fulness of the Holy Spirit.' With this fulness of His Holy Spirit the Lord has now filled us poor creatures to overflowing. So there is no need now, your Godliness, to ask how people come to be in the grace of the Holy Spirit. Will you remember this manifestation of God's ineffable mercy which has visited us?"

"I don't know, Father," I said, "whether the Lord will grant me to remember this mercy of God always as vividly and clearly as I feel it now."

"I think," Father Seraphim answered me, "that the Lord will help you to retain it in your memory forever, or His goodness would never have instantly bowed in this way to my humble prayer and so quickly anticipated the request of poor Seraphim; all

202

A Wonderful Revelation to the World

the more so, because it is not given to you alone to understand it, but through you it is for the whole world, in order that you yourself may be confirmed in God's work and may be useful to others. The fact that I am a Monk and you are a layman is utterly beside the point. What God requires is true faith in Himself and His Only-begotten Son. In return for that the grace of the Holy Spirit is granted abundantly from on high. The Lord seeks a heart filled to overflowing with love for God and our neighbour; this is the throne on which He loves to sit and on which He appears in the fulness of His heavenly glory. 'Son, give Me thy heart,' He says, 'and all the rest I Myself will add to thee,'[51] for in the human heart the Kingdom of God can be contained. The Lord commanded His disciples: *Seek first the Kingdom of God and His righteousness, and all these things shall be added to you; for your heavenly Father knows that you need all these things* (Mat. 6:32,33). The Lord does not rebuke us for using earthly goods, for He says Himself that, owing to the conditions of our earthly life, we need all these things; that is, all the things which make our human life more peaceful and make our way to our heavenly home lighter and easier. That is why the holy Apostle Paul said that in his opinion there was nothing better on earth than piety and sufficiency (cp. II Cor.9:8; I Tim.6:6). And Holy Church prays that this may be granted us by the Lord God; and though troubles, misfortunes and various needs are inseparable from our life on earth, yet the Lord God neither willed nor wills that we should have nothing

---

[51] Prov. 23:26; Matt. 6:33.

St. Seraphim of Sarov

but troubles and adversities. Therefore, He commands us through the Apostles to *bear one another's burdens and so fulfill the law of Christ* (Gal. 6:2). The Lord Jesus personally gives us the commandment to love one another, so that, by consoling one another with mutual love, we may lighten the sorrowful and narrow way of our journey to the heavenly country. Why did He descend to us from heaven, if not for the purpose of taking upon Himself our poverty and of making us rich with the riches of His goodness and His unutterable generosity? He did not come to be served by men but to serve them Himself and to give His life for the salvation of many. You do the same, your Godliness, and having seen the mercy of God manifestly shown to you, tell of it to all who desire salvation. *The harvest truly is great*, says the Lord, but *the labourers are few* (Lk. 10:2). The Lord God has led us out to work and has given us the gifts of His grace in order that, by reaping the ears of the salvation of our fellow-men and bringing as many as possible into the Kingdom of God, we may bring Him fruit-- some thirtyfold, some sixtyfold and some a hundredfold. Let us be watchful, my son, in order that we may not be condemned with that wicked and slothful servant who hid his talent in the earth, but let us try to imitate those good and faithful servants of the Lord who brought their Master four talents instead of two, and ten instead of five (Cf. Mat. 25:14-30).

"Of the mercy of the Lord God there is no shadow of doubt. You have seen for yourself, your Godliness, how the words of the Lord spoken through the

A Wonderful Revelation to the World

Prophet have been accomplished in us: *I am not a God far off, but a God near at hand* (cp. Jer. 23:23), and *thy salvation is at thy mouth* (cp. Deut. 30:12-14; Rom. 10:8-13). I had not time even to cross myself, but only wished in my heart that the Lord would grant you to see His goodness in all its fulness, and He was pleased to hasten to realise my wish. I am not boasting when I say this, neither do I say it to show you my importance and lead you to jealousy, or to make you think that I am a Monk and you only a layman. No, no, your Godliness! *The Lord is nigh unto all them that call upon Him in truth* (Ps. 144:18) *and there is no partiality with Him* (Eph. 6:9). For the Father loves the Son and gives everything into His hand (cp. Jn. 3:35). If only we ourselves loved Him, our heavenly Father, in a truly filial way! The Lord listens equally to the Monk and the simple Christian layman provided that both are Orthodox believers, and both love God from the depth of their souls, and both have faith in Him, if only as a grain of mustard seed; and they both shall move mountains. 'One shall move thousands and two tens of thousands' (cp. Deut. 32:30). The Lord Himself says: *All things are possible to him who believes* (Mk. 9:23). And the holy Apostle Paul loudly exclaims: *I can do all things in Christ Who strengthens me* (Phil. 4:13). But does not our Lord Jesus Christ speak even more wonderfully than this of those who believe in Him: *He who believes in Me*, not only *the works that I do*, but even *greater then these shall he do, because I am going to My Father. And I will pray* for you *that your joy may be*

St. Seraphim of Sarov

full. Hitherto you have asked nothing in My name. But now *ask...* (Jn. 14:12,16; 16:24).

"Thus, my son, whatever you ask of the Lord God you will receive, if only it is for the glory of God or for the good of your neighbour, because what we do for the good of our neighbour He refers to His own glory. And therefore He says: "All that you have done unto one of the least of these, you have done unto Me" (cp. Matt. 25:40). And so, have no doubt that the Lord God will fulfil your petitions, if only they concern the glory of God or the benefit and edification of your fellow men. But, even if something is necessary for your own need or use or advantage, just as quickly and graciously will the Lord be pleased to send you even that, provided that extreme need and necessity require it. For the Lord loves those who love Him. The Lord is good to all men; He gives abundantly to those who call upon His Name, and His bounty is in all His works. He will do the will of them that fear Him and He will hear their prayer, and fulfil all their plans. The Lord will fulfil all thy petitions (cp. Ps. 144:19; 19:4,5). Only beware, your Godliness, of asking the Lord for something for which there is no urgent need. The Lord will not refuse you even this in return for your Orthodox faith in Christ the Saviour, for the Lord will not give up the staff of the righteous to the lot of sinners (cp. Ps. 124:3), and He will speedily accomplish the will of His servant David; but He will call him to account for having troubled Him without special need, and for having asked Him for something without which he could have managed very easily.

"And so, your Godliness, I have now told you and given you a practical demonstration of all that the Lord and the Mother of God have been pleased to tell you and show you through me, poor Seraphim. Now go in peace. The Lord and the Mother of God be with you always, now and ever, and to the ages of ages. Amen. Now go in peace."

And during the whole of this time, from the moment when Father Seraphim's face became radiant,[52] this illumination continued; and all that he told me from the beginning of the narrative till now, he said while remaining in one and the same position. The ineffable glow of the light which emanated from him I myself saw with my own eyes. And I am ready to vouch for it with an oath.

---

[52] Or, "became illumined," "began to shine."

The Last Judgement
In the center is Christ seated on a throne flanked by the Mother of
God and St. John the Baptist. To either side are the choirs of the
Saints. At the bottom right (the Judge's left) are the various tor-
ments of hell, at the bottom left the Saints are led into Paradise.

Chapter IX

Are the Torments of Hell a Reality?

Nikolas Alexandrovitch Motovilov, "Seraphim's servant" as he liked to call himself, had been granted a miraculous healing and the further privilege of seeing with his own eyes St. Seraphim's illumination by the light of Tabor or, in other words, by the grace of the Holy Spirit. Being a fervent and sincere man, he wanted to perpetuate Father Seraphim's memory. So he decided to visit Kursk (the Saint's birth-place) personally in order to collect information about his childhood and youth; he also wanted to visit the Kiev-Florovsky Monastery. The journey had very sad consequences for Nikolas Alexandrovitch. Through the permissive will of God, the enemy inflicted upon him an illness in revenge for his literary labours; for his writings served to enhance the fame of one of God's Saints--Father Seraphim--to a very considerable extent.

Certain circumstances which preceded N. A. Motovilov's illness throw light on its origin. Once during a talk with St. Seraphim the question somehow arose as to the reality of diabolic assaults on men. Motovilov who had had a worldly upbringing did not fail, of course, to doubt the existence of the evil power. Then the Saint told him of his terrible fight with the devils for one thousand days and nights, and by the power of his word, by the authority of his holiness which excluded all possibility of even the shadow of a lie or exaggeration, he convinced Motovilov of the existence of devils, not as phantoms or figments of the imagination, but as a stark and bit-

St. Seraphim of Sarov

ter reality. The impetuous Motovilov was so stirred by the Elder's talk that he cried from the depths of his soul:

"Father, how I should like to have a bout with the devils!"

Father Seraphim, in alarm, cut him short:

"What on earth are you talking about, your Godliness! You don't know what you are saying. If you knew that the least of them can turn the world upside down with its claw, you would never challenge them to a fight."

"But, Father, have the devils really got claws?"

"Ah, your Godliness, whatever do they teach you at the university? Don't you know that the devils have no claws? They have been represented with hoofs, horns and tails because it is impossible for the human imagination to conceive anything more hideous. And they really are hideous, for their conscious desertion of God and their voluntary resistance to divine grace made them, who before the fall, were Angels of light, angels of such darkness and abomination that they cannot be portrayed in any human likeness. Still some likeness is necessary; that is why they are represented as black and ugly. But having been created with the power and properties of Angels, they possess such indomitable might against man and everything earthly that, as I have told you already, the least of them can turn the world upside down with its nail. Only the di-

Are the Torments of Hell a Reality?

vine grace of the Holy Spirit which has been given to us Orthodox Christians as a free gift through the divine merits of the God-Man, our Lord Jesus Christ--only this frustrates all the wiles and artifices of the enemy."

An uncanny feeling crept over Motovilov. While he was still under the Saint's protection he could defy Satan's malice. But, by the permissive will of God, his reckless challenge did not remain unanswered. It was accepted.

When Motovilov went to Kursk after Father Seraphim's death, he did not get much information about the childhood and youth of the Saint. Of the near relatives who had known Father Seraphim as a child, some were dead, while others had forgotten the facts. Even the house where the Saint was born and brought up had been destroyed, and new buildings had sprung up in its place. However, one old man was found who was a contemporary of Father Seraphim, and who supplied Motovilov with facts which have been included in all the editions of the Saint's life. The actual journey to Kursk and his stay there were without mishap. The storm broke out on his way back to Voronezh.

Motovilov was obliged to spend a night at one of the post-stations on the road from Kursk. As he was quite alone in the room for travelers, he took his manuscripts out of his suitcase and began to sort them out by the dim light of a single candle which scarcely lit up the spacious room. One of the first records he

St. Seraphim of Sarov

discovered contained a description of the cure of a possessed lady of noble parentage called Eropkin at the Shrine of St. Metrophan of Voronezh.

"I wondered," writes Motovilov, "how it could happen that an Orthodox Christian who partook of the most pure and life-giving Mysteries of the Lord could suddenly be possessed by a devil, and moreover, for such a long period as over thirty years. And I thought: Nonsense! It is impossible! I should like to see how the devil would dare to make his abode in me, especially when I frequently have recourse to the Sacrament of Holy Communion."

At that very moment he was surrounded by a horrible, cold, evil-smelling cloud which began to make its way into his mouth, while he made convulsive efforts to keep it tightly shut.

The unhappy Motovilov struggled desperately, trying to protect himself from the stench and icy cold of the cloud which was gradually creeping into him. In spite of all his efforts it got into him completely.

His hands became exactly as if they were paralyzed, and he could not make the Sign of the Cross; his mind became frozen with terror and he could not remember the saving name of Jesus. Something terrible and repulsive had happened, and Nikolas Alexandrovitch experienced a time of dreadful torture. A manuscript in his own handwriting gives us the following description of the torments he experienced:

Are the Torments of Hell a Reality?

"The Lord granted me to experience in my own body, and not in a dream or apparition, the three torments of hell. The first was that of the fire which gives no light and which can be extinguished only by the grace of the Most Holy Spirit. This agony lasted for three days. I felt myself burning, yet I was not consumed. Ten or eleven times a day they had to scrape off the hellish soot which covered my whole body and was visible to all. This torture ceased only after Confession and Holy Communion, through the prayers of Archbishop Antony of Voronezh who ordered litanies to be said for the suffering servant of God Nikolas in the forty-seven Churches and Monasteries of his diocese.

"Then I was tormented for two days by the unbearable cold of Tartarus, so that fire could neither burn nor warm me. According to the wish of His Grace, Archbishop Antony of Voronezh, I held my hand over a candle for about half an hour, and though it was thickly coated with soot, it did not get warm in the least. I described this experiment on a whole sheet of paper and signed it by stamping it with my sooty hand. Both these torments were visible to all; yet with the help of Holy Communion I could partake of food, drink and sleep to some extent.

But the third torment of Gehenna, though it was still shorter by half a day, for it lasted only a day and a half (possibly a little more), caused me the greatest terror and suffering as it was something indescribable and incomprehensible. It is a wonder that I remained alive! This torment also disappeared after Confession

213

St. Seraphim of Sarov

and Holy Communion. This time Archbishop Antony himself administered the Holy Sacrament to me with his own hands. This torment was the undying worm of Gehenna. The worm in this case was visible only to Archbishop Antony and myself. But my whole body was riddled with this pernicious worm which crawled through the whole of me and in an indescribably frightful manner gnawed at my vitals. Though it crawled out through my nose, mouth and ears, yet it went back in again. However, God gave me some power over it, and I could take it into my hands and stretch it like rubber.

I feel myself compelled to make this declaration, for God did not grant me this vision for nothing. Let no one think that I dare take the Lord's name in vain. No! On the day of the Lord's awful judgement, He Himself--my God, my Helper and my Protector--will testify that I did not lie against Him, my Lord, and against the operation of His Divine Providence which was accomplished in me."

Soon after this terrible test which is beyond the experience of ordinary men, Motovilov had a vision of his patron St. Seraphim who comforted the sufferer with the promise that he would be cured at the exposition of the relics of St. Tikhon of Zadonsk and that until that time the devil residing in him would not torment him so cruelly.

The exposition of the relics of St. Tikhon actually took place thirty years later, and Motovilov lived to see it and was in fact cured according to his great faith.

On the day of the exposition of the relics of St. Tikhon of Zadonsk (1865), Motovilov was standing in the sanctuary praying and weeping bitterly because the Lord had not granted him the cure for which his tortured soul was waiting according to the promise of St. Seraphim of Sarov. During the Song of the Cherubim, he glanced at the Bishop's throne in the apse and saw St. Tikhon there. The holy prelate blessed the weeping Motovilov and vanished from sight. Motovilov was healed instantly.

St. Tikhon of Zadonsk
At the exposition of St. Tikhon's Relics Motovilov was healed after 30 years of demonic assault, in accordance with the prediction of St. Seraphim of Sarov.

Icon of St. Seraphim of Sarov
by Master Iconographer Iouri Sidorenko.

Chapter X

Spiritual Father and Elder

Father Seraphim was a wonderful director. What a pity that the records of his instructions mostly refer to the last years of his life. But even so they are so numerous that they cannot all be included in a short biography. We shall select only the most important.

Many were amazed by Father Seraphim's spiritual insight and wisdom. Once the Abbot of Vysokogorsk, Archimandrite Antony, and a merchant of Vladimir, entered his cell together. Father asked the Abbot to take a seat and wait, and he began to talk to the merchant.

"All your difficulties and troubles are the consequences of your passionate life. Give it up; mend your ways."

And then he meekly and tenderly began to convict him of his sins, but with such warmth of heart that both his hearers wept copiously. Finally, Father Seraphim told the merchant to prepare for Holy Communion at Sarov, and assured him that if he sincerely repented, the Lord would not deprive him of His grace and mercy. The contrite merchant fell down at his feet promising to carry out all his directions, and departed in tears but with an unburdened soul.

Father Antony was astonished at the spiritual insight of the Elder and said to him later: "Father! The human soul is open to you like a face in a mirror. Before my very eyes you told the pilgrim everything

217

without waiting to hear his spiritual needs and troubles."

Father Seraphim did not say a word.

The Abbot continued: "Now I see! Your mind is so pure that nothing in the heart of your neighbour is hidden from it."

Father Seraphim put his right hand on the Archimandrite's mouth and said: "You are not quite right, my joy. The human heart is open only to the Lord, and God alone knows our hearts; but *a man will come, and the heart is deep* (Ps. 63:7)." Then he told of how St. Gregory the Theologian had been rebuked by certain people for having shown favour to Maximus the Cynic.[53] But the Saint said: "God alone knows the secrets of the human heart. I saw in him a man who had turned from paganism to Christianity, which to me is a great thing."

The Abbot asked again: "But how is it, Father, that you did not ask the merchant a single word, and told him all he needed?"

Father Seraphim then explained at some length: "He came to me just as others do, just as you came too, as to a servant of God. I, sinful Seraphim, regard myself as a sinful servant of God. What the Lord tells

---

[53] Maximus at first lived with him at his episcopal house in Constantinople, but afterwards he tried to seize his see by fraudulent means. Then St.Gregory sent him away, and to justify himself said: "He who is himself trustworthy, is most trustful."

Spiritual Father and Elder

me, I pass on to whoever seeks help. The first thought which comes to my mind[54] I accept as God's guidance and speak without knowing what is in the other person's mind; I merely believe that God's will is made known to me in this way for his benefit. Sometimes people tell me something, and without referring to the will of God, I trust to my own knowledge, thinking that it is possible to decide it with my own mind, without having recourse to God. In such cases mistakes are always made."

The Elder concluded this edifying and instructive talk with the words: "Like iron to the smith, I have surrendered myself and my own will to the Lord God. As He wills, so I act. I have no will of my own; but what God wills, I pass on."

That is Father Seraphim's own explanation of his counsels and instructions. The all-knowing Lord spoke through him. That is why he did not take time to think, but usually answered immediately and undoubtingly, or even said things which had not occurred to his collocutors, but which were revealed to him by the Holy Spirit.

The layman Bogdanov, who had come to him with a whole batch of questions, said afterwards: "I had previously written all my questions on a sheet of paper for memory's sake, and I had scarcely finished reading them to the Elder, when I at once received the answers. He spoke extremely hurriedly." At the same

---

[54] "Comes to my mind." Lit. appears in my soul.

St. Seraphim of Sarov

time "during the whole of our talk Father Seraphim was extraordinarily cheerful. He stood leaning on an oaken coffin which he had prepared for himself, and held a lighted wax-candle in his hands. In replying he often addressed me with the words: 'Your Godliness.' When he bid me farewell, he thanked me for visiting such a poor creature as he was, to use his own expression. On blessing me he even wanted to kiss my hands, and repeatedly bowed down to the ground to me."

It is also well-known that he used to give answers to letters without opening them, and would say: "This is what to say from poor Seraphim..." and so on. After his death many unopened letters were found in his cell, the answers to which had been received mostly by word of mouth through a messenger.

This was a miraculous and extraordinary gift of the Holy Spirit. But all his life had been leading up to the gift of insight and discernment. Constant reading of Holy Scripture and profound meditation on its contents, the study of the works of the Holy Fathers and the lives of the Saints, the wide experience derived from his own spiritual life, and even his natural intellectual gifts--all this had prepared the Saint for the extraordinary graces. But above all, his asceticism had paved the way--beginning with obedience, and ending with prayer and contemplation.

"Why are there no true Elders now?" they once asked an ascetic.

Spiritual Father and Elder

"Because there is no true obedience," was the answer.

St. Seraphim said the same thing: "One must obey one's Superior, for he who is obedient makes much progress to the edification of his soul; besides he acquires thereby an understanding of things and comes to compunction."

St. Seraphim had also trodden this way to perfection. His instructions to Superiors may also be fully applied to himself as a director and Elder.

"The Superior," he says, "as a shepherd of rational sheep, must have the gift of discernment, so as to be always ready to give advice to everyone who needs his direction."

But the gift of discernment is given in various ways.

"The Superior must be versed in Holy Scripture; he must meditate on the Law of the Lord day and night. Through such exercises he will be able to gain the gift of discerning good and evil."

He must be "perfect in every virtue (Heb. 13:21) and must have his senses trained by long study and experience to discern good and evil" (Heb. 5:14).

But at the same time, discernment is a gift of God. "Not everyone"--he is quoting the words of St. Peter of Damascus--"can be trusted to give advice to those

St. Seraphim of Sarov

who seek it; but only he who has received from God the gift of discernment and has acquired spiritual insight--through long training in asceticism."

Without this, that is "before he can discern good and evil, a man is not capable of feeding rational sheep, but only irrational ones; because we cannot understand the actions of the evil one without the knowledge of good and evil."

Father Seraphim was speaking out of his own experience. Having reached dispassion, he received revelations with his pure mind directly from the Lord to Whom he had surrendered his whole mind and will.

Let us take a few more examples of his spiritual insight and wise direction.

A. Of God and our Attitude to Him

"The Fathers wrote, when asked: Seek the Lord, but do not try to find out where He lives."

"Where God is, there is no evil. All that comes from God is peaceful and beneficial and leads man to humility and self-condemnation."

"When a man receives something divine, he rejoices in heart; but when it comes from the devil, he is troubled."

"Having received a divine gift, the Christian heart does not need an assurance from outside as to whether

Spiritual Father and Elder

it is truly from the Lord, but by its very action he is convinced that it is heavenly; for he feels in himself the spiritual fruits: love, joy, peace, and so on (Gal. 5:22). On the other hand, even if the devil transforms himself into an angel of light (II Cor. 11:14) or suggests plausible thoughts, yet the heart feels a certain diffidence and the thoughts are troubled."

"He who loves himself cannot love God."

"Faith is the beginning of our union with God."

"True hope seeks only the Kingdom of God and is sure that everything earthly that is necessary for this temporal life will undoubtedly be given."

"A man who has made it his aim to follow the way of inward attention, must first of all have the fear of God."

"All our enemy's endeavour is to avert our thought from the remembrance and fear and love of God" (St. Macarius the Great).

"In order to contemplate the Holy Trinity we should pray for it to Basil the Great, Gregory the Theologian and John Chrysostom who taught about the Trinity and whose intercession may attract to a person the blessing of the Most Holy Trinity. But we must beware of contemplating directly of our own accord."

St. Seraphim of Sarov

"Reverent care is needed here because *this sea*, that is, the heart with its thoughts and desires, *is great and wide; there are reptiles without number* (Ps. 103:25), that is many vain, wrong and impure thoughts, the progeny of evil spirits."

We shall also consider here the question of blasphemous thoughts. First of all Father Seraphim points out the ordinary general rule which requires us not to be disturbed when they assail us in spite of ourselves and even against our will; and "if we do not consent to the evil thoughts which are suggested to us by the devil, we do well."

St. Seraphim was able to inspire with the spirit of faith people who were most indifferent to religion.

Once the Kreditzkys, husband and wife, came to see him. Father told them much about the future life, the Saints, and of how our Lady takes care of us sinners.

"This talk did not take more than an hour. But such an hour!" writes the husband. "I never had anything like it in all my life. Throughout the talk I felt in my heart an inexplicable heavenly sweetness which came from God knows where, and which could not be compared with anything on earth. Even till now I cannot recall it without tears of compunction and a most vivid sense of joy in all my being."

"Up to that time, though I had not denied anything sacred, yet neither had I affirmed anything; everything in the spiritual world was the same to me, and I was equally indifferent to everything. Father Seraphim made me now feel for the first time the almightiness of the Lord God and His inexhaustible mercy and perfection."

"Previously, on account of my coldness of soul towards everything holy and because I liked to make godless jokes, the righteous Lord had allowed the foul spirit of blasphemy to take possession of my thoughts, and these blasphemous thoughts which until now I cannot remember without the greatest horror, continually afflicted me for three whole years, especially at prayer, in Church and, most of all, when I prayed to the Queen of Heaven. I already thought in despair that no torments would be a sufficient punishment, according to earthly judgement, and that only the eternal torments of hell would be a just retribution for my blasphemies.

"But Father Seraphim set my mind completely at rest in his talk by saying with the inexpressibly joyful smile which was peculiar to him that I ought not to fear this 'turmoil of thought,' that this was the result of enemy action caused by envy and that I should always continue fearlessly in prayer, whatever foul and blasphemous thoughts the enemy might suggest.

"From that time this turmoil of thoughts really began to disappear little by little, and completely ceased in less than a month."

St. Seraphim of Sarov

But sometimes this temptation of blasphemous thoughts is sent for experience.

Archimandrite Nikon writes that while still in the seminary, he went to the holy Elder with a question about monasticism. Father blessed him and gave him instructions. After the second visit Father Seraphim said to him:

"Good-bye. Come to me in six days' time."

"This period," writes Father Nikon, "was very troubled, for blasphemous thoughts assailed me to such an extent that I could not go to Church. I would have left the Monastery, but was restrained by Father Hilarion (the Confessor) who said: 'The Elder knows what he is doing.' At the end of nine days I was completely exhausted by the enemy's assaults, and could hardly drag myself to his cell. I came to the door and before I had time to say the prayer, Father Seraphim opened the door, and fell at my feet saying; 'Forgive me for the temptation from which you have suffered. It was to let you know that you will have such afflictions on embracing monasticism; but do not get despondent.'

"Then he put on his stole, confessed me and ordered me to have Holy Communion at the late Liturgy. As soon as I had done so, all that was dark withdrew from me into the darkness."

"Without God's help," said Father Seraphim, "it is impossible to be saved. When the Lord leaves a man to himself, then the devil is ready to grind him as a millstone grinds a grain of wheat."

B. Of Prayer

Father Seraphim lived himself in unceasing prayer and instructed others to do the same.

"Through it," he said, "if you keep peace of conscience, it is possible to approach God and to unite with Him." Therefore he advised people to train themselves in the constant remembrance of God's Name and to say the Prayer of Jesus. Many among the simple people told him that on account of their illiteracy or lack of time they could not read the appointed rules of prayer. To such people Father Seraphim gave a rule which could be carried out quite easily.

"Let every Christian on rising from sleep, stand before the Icons and read the Lord's prayer 'Our Father' three times in honour of the Most Holy Trinity, then the song to the Mother of God 'Hail Virgin Mother of God' also three times, and finally the Creed 'I believe in one God...' once.

"The above prayers," explained Father Seraphim, "are the foundation of Christianity. The first, as the prayer given by the Lord Himself, is the model of every prayer; the second was brought down from Heaven by an Archangel as a salutation to the Virgin Mary, the Mother of the Lord. And the Creed contains in brief all the saving dogmas of the Christian faith.

St. Seraphim of Sarov

"Having performed this rule let every Christian go to the work to which he has been appointed or called. But during his work, at home, or on his way to some place let him say softly: 'Lord Jesus Christ, Son of God, have mercy on me a sinner.' But if he is surrounded by people, while doing whatever he has to do let him say mentally only, 'Lord, have mercy!' and continue till lunch-time.

"Before lunch let him again perform the above-mentioned morning rule. (Three times).

"After lunch let every Christian while going about his business say softly: 'Most Holy Mother of God, save me a sinner,' and let him continue that until bed-time.

"If he happens to spend his time alone, let him say: 'Lord Jesus Christ, through the Mother of God, have mercy on me a sinner.'

"At bed-time let every Christian read again the above-mentioned morning rule. Then let him go to sleep, having protected himself with the Sign of the Cross.

"By keeping this simple rule," said Father, "it is possible to reach a measure of Christian perfection and divine love."

But if anyone cannot keep even this rule for good and valid reasons--for instance a servant--St. Seraphim recommended that it should be said in any

Spiritual Father and Elder

position at work, on the move, or even in bed--remembering the words of the Lord: *Whoever shall call upon the name of the Lord shall be saved* (Joel 2:32; Rom. 10:13).

"'Do you pray, my joy?' Father, once asked me," writes Xenia Vasilievna.

"'Oh, after a fashion, Father, but what kind of prayer is it! I am a sinner! Often there is really no time,' I replied."

"'Never mind!' said Father. 'I just wanted to tell you not to worry about that. When you have time, don't be idle, but keep the whole rule and pray. But if you haven't time, my joy, say just the small rule in the morning, at midday and at night even while at work. If possible, keep the other rule too[55]. But if not--well, do as the Lord helps you. Only don't fail somehow or other to make the prostrations to the Saviour and the Mother of God. Make them at all costs, Mother.'"

To the Sisters of the Diveyev Mill Convent Father even gave a new rule of daily Services adapted to our feeble times and to womanly weakness.

"Foreseeing a period of slackness, feeble strength and feeble people," writes Father Vasily Sadovsky, "Father Seraphim advised (the Diveyev Nuns) to give up the rule of the Sarov Monastery which was beyond the strength of womanly frailty.

---

[55] That is, the rule of the Convent, as explained below.

St. Seraphim of Sarov

"'It is difficult even for a man to keep it,' Father Seraphim said to me. 'Therefore,' he explained to me, 'I have given a new and easier rule to this Convent according to the command of the Queen of Heaven herself to me, poor Seraphim. The following should be said three times a day: *It is truly meet* once, *Our Father* thrice, *Virgin Mother of God* thrice, *the Creed*, then *Lord Jesus Christ, have mercy on me a sinner* twice, and *Lord Jesus Christ, have mercy on us sinners* once, all with bows to the waist; then *Lord Jesus Christ, through our Lady, Virgin Mary, Mother of God, have mercy on me a sinner* twice, and *Lord Jesus Christ, through our Lady, Virgin Mary, Mother of God, have mercy on us sinners* once, also with bows to the waist; then twelve times *Lord Jesus Christ, our God, have mercy on us*, and twelve times *My Lady, most holy Mother of God, save us sinners*, all with bows to the waist.

"'Also the morning and evening prayers, and the intercession[56] with the twelve select Psalms of the holy Fathers. Then one hundred prostrations to Jesus and one hundred prostrations to our Lady.

"'This is sufficient for them,' said Father Seraphim. 'If only they keep it, they will be saved.'

"Such was his simple rule of prayer which was within everyone's power.

---

[56] Russian: Pomyannik.

Spiritual Father and Elder

"'All extra Services, such as an Akathist, must on no account be obligatory for all under my direction, Father, but quite voluntary.'"

At the same time St. Seraphim valued quite rightly the spirit of prayer rather than the mere formal observance of the rule of prayer. He had an important talk on this subject with the Novice, John Petrov who was at that time reader[57] and later, master of ceremonies[58] in Sarov. Petrov writes:

"Father Seraphim wanted exterior worship to be combined with interior, spiritual prayer; because merely outward worship alone is not pleasing to the Lord. He said Himself that *cursed is he who does the work of the Lord negligently* (Jer. 45:10). Then he began to rebuke me gently, saying: 'Some people apparently read well, but they don't understand the meaning of what they are reading. Many say that they have been at the Liturgy, or at Matins, or at Vespers, and deceive themselves with the false hope that they really were there; but in actual fact, where was their mind wandering at the time? They were only bodily in the Temple of God. But you have just been at the early Liturgy. What Apostle[59] and Gospel were read? Sometimes through inattention I could give no answer. Then he usually told me himself exactly what had been read."

---

[57] Russian; Kanonarch.
[58] Russian; Ustavshtshik.
[59] The reading from the Acts of the Apostles and the Epistles is called the "Apostle." The Apocalypse is never read in Church.

St. Seraphim of Sarov

On the other hand, taught St. Seraphim, "When the mind and heart are united in prayer and the thoughts of the soul are not distracted, the heart is kindled with a spiritual warmth out of which shines the light of Christ which fills all the inner man with peace and joy.

"But if during prayer your mind is captured and your thoughts despoiled, then you must humble yourself before the Lord God and ask forgiveness, saying: 'I have sinned, O Lord, in word, deed, thought and with all my senses.'"

To the future Monk, Father Nikon, he even gave advice concerning outward methods of the Prayer of Jesus.

"Learn to say the prayer while breathing through the nose with closed lips. This art is a whip against the flesh and fleshly desires."

But the attention should chiefly be in the spirit.

"Mere exterior prayer is not sufficient," Father also said to him. "God attends to the mind, and therefore Monks who do not unite exterior prayer with interior, are not Monks, but charred logs."

"Practice mental prayer of the heart as it is taught by the holy Fathers in the Philokalia, for the Prayer of Jesus is a lamp for our paths and a guiding star to Heaven."

Spiritual Father and Elder

"This is the valuable advice which was given me by the inspired Elder," concluded Father Nikon. "It is my dearest treasure on earth."

To the layman Bogdanov Father Seraphim gave advice in the words of the Gospel: "*In praying do not speak much,*[60] *for your Father knows what you need before you ask Him. Pray then like this: 'Our Father,'* and so on (Mat. 6:7-13). In the Lord's prayer is the Lord's grace. All that the Church has embraced and handed down to us ought to be dear to the heart of a Christian. Do not forget feast days, be temperate, and go to Church unless you are unwell."

"Pray for all. You will do much good in this way. Give candles, wine and oil to the Church."

C. Of Orthodoxy

The experience of his own life and still more his knowledge of the Word of God, of the works of the holy Fathers and the lives of the Saints, gave him an undoubting confidence in the truth of Orthodoxy. This was expressed very forcibly in his wonderful conversation with N. A. Motovilov. But he spoke of it also on other occasions.

---

[60] This is how the Slavonic renders βαπολογησητε. St.Seraphim omits the next three clauses. The Greek of Mat.6:7 may be translated: "And in praying, do not jabber like the heathen; for they think that they will be heard for their volubility."

St. Seraphim of Sarov

Four Old Ritualists[61] once came to him in order to ask him about the Sign of the Cross made with two fingers, and wanting a miracle as evidence of the truth. They had hardly crossed the threshold of his cell, when Father Seraphim read their thoughts, took the first man by the hand, folded his fingers in the Orthodox way and, crossing him, said: "This is the Christian Sign of the Cross! Pray in this way and tell others to do so. This way of making the Sign of the Cross has been handed down to us by the holy Apostles; but the two-finger way is against holy tradition."

And he added with power: "I beg and implore you to go to the Greek-Russian Church. It is in all the power and glory of God! Like a ship with many masts, sails and a great helm, it is steered by the Holy Spirit. Its good helmsmen are the Doctors of the Church. The Archpastors are the successors of the Apostles. But your chapel is like a small rowing-boat without rudder and oars; it is secured to the ship of our Church, and floats behind it. The waves wash over it, and it would have certainly gone down if it had not been secured to the ship."

---

[61] Members of a group who seperated from the Russian Orthodox Church over liturgical reforms initiated by Patriarch Nikon in the seventeenth century. Known also as Old Believers, they developed into several groups, some of which preserved the Episcopate and Priesthood, and others were without Ordained clergy or Sacraments.-ed.

Spiritual Father and Elder

Another time an Old Ritualist asked him: "Tell me, old man of God, which faith is the best--the present faith of the Church or the old one?"

"Stop your nonsense," replied Father Seraphim sharply, contrary to his wont. "Our life is a sea, the Holy Orthodox Church is our ship, and the Helmsman is the Saviour Himself. If with such a Helmsman, on account of their sinful weakness people cross the sea of life with difficulty and are not all saved from drowning, where do you expect to get with your little dinghy? And how can you hope to be saved without the Helmsman?"

Once they brought him a woman whose limbs were so distorted that her knees were bent up to her breast. She had previously been Orthodox, but having married an Old Ritualist, she stopped going to Church. St. Seraphim cured her in front of all the people by anointing her breast and hands with oil from his Icon-lamp, and then ordered her and her relations to pray in the Orthodox way.

"Did some of your now deceased relatives pray with the two-finger Sign of the Cross?"

"To my great grief, everyone prayed like that in our family."

Father Seraphim reflected a little, and then re-remarked: "Even though they were virtuous people, they will be bound; the Holy Orthodox Church does not accept this Sign of the Cross."

St. Seraphim of Sarov

Then he asked: "Do you know their graves? Go, mother, to their graves, make three prostrations and pray to the Lord that He may release them in eternity.

Her living relatives afterwards obeyed Father Seraphim's instructions.

Another edifying case was that of a woman who had been adopted as a three-year-old orphan by Old Ritualists.

After their death she first joined their community, but then she started a life of pilgrimage and went from one Elder to another.

"My whole object was to find someone who could teach me, a sinner, how to save my soul. I also had a misgiving. I was in doubt whether I could have my benefactors prayed for in the Orthodox Church."

At last she reached Sarov. Reports about Father Seraphim had already spread throughout Russia.

"I saw a crowd of people preparing to go somewhere. I inquired and was told that they were going to Father Seraphim's hermitage. Though I was very tired from the journey, yet I forgot about rest and went with them. I wanted to see the Elder as soon as possible. Having passed the Monastery, we went along a forest path. We had walked about two versts; those who were stronger were ahead, but I was lagging behind and following slowly in the rear. Suddenly I looked to one side and saw an old wizened man, with

236

Spiritual Father and Elder

whitish-looking hair and a bent back, in a white cassock, gathering sticks. I went up to him and asked him whether it was far to Father Seraphim's hermitage.

"The Elder put down his faggot, gave me a serene[62] look and asked softly:

"'What do you want with poor Seraphim, my joy?'

"Only then did I realize that I was talking to the Elder himself, and threw myself at his feet, and began to ask him to pray for me, unworthy as I was.

"'Rise, daughter Irene!' said the ascetic, and he bent down to help me up himself. 'I was just waiting for you. I did not want you to have come here for nothing, when you are so tired.'

"I was astonished to be called by my name when he had never seen me before, and I trembled all over with fear; neither could I say a word, but just gazed at his angelic face."

Father Seraphim folded her fingers in the Orthodox way and crossed her himself with her hand.

"Cross yourself like that," he repeated twice; "that is how God commands us."

And after a short silence he went on: "As for your benefactors, if you happen to have a copeck, give it

---

[62] Clear, cloudless, bright, cheerful, glad.

without misgiving for them to be commemorated at the proskomidia.[63] It is not a sin!"

"Having blessed me, he held the copper cross which was hanging on his chest for me to kiss, and gave me some biscuits from his bag.

"'Now,' he said, 'go in God's name!'

"Then he hurried away into the forest. I dragged my feet slowly back to the Monastery. As for my fellow-travelers, they walked for a long time, but did not see the Elder. They did not even believe me, when I told them that I had seen him."

But if Father Seraphim spoke of the superiority of Orthodoxy to Old Ritualism, still more did he consider it superior to Roman Catholicism.

"He urged us," we read in the Diveyev Chronicle, "to stand firmly for the truth of the dogmas of the Orthodox Church, giving as an example St. Mark of Ephesus who showed unshakable zeal in defense of the Eastern Catholic[64] faith at the Council of Florence.[65] He himself gave various instructions on Orthodoxy, explaining its essence and stressing that it

---

[63] The preparatory part of the Liturgy.

[64] Here the term "Eastern Catholic" refers to Orthodoxy, not the "Eastern Rite" of the Roman Catholic Church--ed.

[65] The object of this Council was to conclude a "union" between the Orthodox and Roman Catholic Churches or rather to bring about the subordination of the former to the latter. But this dead work was accepted neither by the Greek nor the Russian Orthodox peoples.

alone contained the truth of Christ's faith in its integrity and purity. He also gave instructions as to how to defend it."

"Father Seraphim," writes the author of the Chronicle, "had a special love and reverence for those Saints who zealously defended the Orthodox faith, such as St. Clement, Pope of Rome, St. John Chrysostom, St. Basil the Great, St. Gregory the Theologian, St. Athanasius of Alexandria, St. Cyril of Jerusalem, St. Epiphanius of Cyprus, St. Ambrose of Milan, and those like them, and he called them the pillars of the Church. He often referred to their lives and labours as examples of firm and resolute faith. He also loved to speak of the Saints of our own Church-- Peter, Alexis, Jonah, Philip, St. Dimitry of Rostov, St. Stephen of Perm, St. Sergius of Radonezh and other Russian Saints, and held up their lives as models on the way to salvation. He knew the lives of the Saints as related in the *Menology* and in the works of many of the Fathers of the Church so well that he could quote whole passages by heart."

We shall insert here the account of an extraordinary vision granted to a Protestant, in which the superiority of the Orthodox Church is testified to even by an ascetic of the Western Catholic Church.

St. Seraphim and Francis of Assisi

The event which we relate below was communicated to us verbally in August 1931 by Mr. K. who

St. Seraphim of Sarov

afterwards wrote it to us in a letter. It is this letter which we shall make use of here.

It is common knowledge that St. Seraphim knew experimentally and said more than once that Christianity was preserved in all its plenitude and purity in the Orthodox Church. And what is most striking and convincing is his own sublime virtue and the fulness of grace which dwelt in him with such "power" (Mk. 9:1) as it seldom did even in the ancient Saints. It is sufficient to mention merely the talk of N. A. Motovilov with the Saint (during which he was miraculously transfigured like the Lord on Mount Tabor) in order to establish without the slightest doubt that Orthodoxy still retains in actual fact its original purity, vitality, fulness and perfection. But let us quote his own words:

"We have the Orthodox faith which has not the slightest blemish."

"I pray and beseech you," he said on another occasion to some Old Ritualists, "go to the Greek-Russian Church. It is in all the glory and power of God. It is directed by the Holy Spirit."

This has also been testified to by a follower of another confession. Here are the facts.

"A friend of mine," writes Mr. K., "forwarded to me a letter written in French in which an Alsatian lady asks him to send her something about the Russian Orthodox Church--a prayer book or something of the kind. If I am not mistaken, it was in the year 1925.

"Something was sent to her in answer to her letter; and there the matter rested for some time.

"In 1927 I was in that place and tried to make her acquaintance; but she was away for the summer holidays, and I only made the acquaintance of her mother-in-law, an old lady of great Christian charity and purity of heart.

"She told me that their family belonged to an ancient and noble line in Alsace, the N.N.s, and that they were Protestants. It must be said that in this district of Alsace the villagers are of mixed faith, one half being Roman Catholic and the other half Protestants. They share a common church, in which they perform their services in turns. At the end of the church there is a Roman altar with statues and all appurtenances. When the Protestants hold a service, they pull a curtain in front of the Catholic altar, roll their table out into the middle and pray. Recently there has been a movement in Alsace among the Protestants in favour of the veneration of the Saints. This occurred after the appearance of Sabatier's book on Francis of Assisi. Though a Protestant he was captivated by this Saint's way of life after a visit to Assisi. The family of my friends also fell under the spell of this book. Though they remained in Protestantism, they nevertheless felt dissatisfied with it and in particular they strove for a restoration of the Sacraments and the veneration of the Saints. Moreover, it was typical of them that when

241

St. Seraphim of Sarov

the pastor performed the marriage ceremony, they asked him not to pull the curtain over the Catholic altar so that they might see at least the statues of the Saints. Their heart was seeking the true Church.

"Once the young wife was ill and was sitting in the garden, reading a life of Francis of Assisi. The garden was in full bloom. The quiet of the countryside enfolded her. While reading the book, she fell into a light sleep.

"'I don't know myself how it was,' she told me afterwards. 'Suddenly I saw Francis himself coming towards me, and with him a little old man like a patriarch, bent but radiant,' she said indicating thereby his old age and venerable appearance. He was all in white. She felt frightened, but they came quite near her and Francis said; 'My daughter, you seek the true Church. It is there, where he is. It supports everyone, and does not require support from anyone.'

"The white Elder remained silent and only smiled approvingly at the words of Francis. The vision ended. She came to herself, as it were. And somehow the thought came to her: 'This is connected with the Russian Church.' And peace descended on her soul."

"After this vision the letter was written which I mentioned at the beginning.

"Two months later I was again at their house, and this time I learned from the visionary herself one more detail. They had hired a Russian workman.

Spiritual Father and Elder

When she visited his room to see whether he was comfortably settled, she saw there a small Icon and recognized in it the Elder whom she had seen, in her light sleep, with Francis. Astonished and alarmed she asked: 'Who is he, that little old man?'

"'St. Seraphim, our Orthodox Saint,' answered the workman. Then she understood the meaning of the words of St. Francis about the truth being in the Orthodox Church."

Certainly Orthodoxy has displayed itself in all its power in the Saints, but we Orthodox have borne this great name unworthily. Our life has not corresponded with the loftiness and fullness of our faith. And this, by the way, tormented N. A. Motovilov, the confidant of St. Seraphim.

"Once," he writes in his remarkable memoirs, "I was in great sorrow, wondering what would become of our Orthodox Church if the evil of our times were to spread more and more. For I was convinced that our Church was in extreme peril from both the increasing corruption of the flesh, and equally, if not even more so, from the spiritual impiety on account of the godless sects which were being spread everywhere by modern sophists. I wanted very much to know what Father Seraphim would tell me about it.

"During his long and detailed talk about the holy Prophet Elijah (as I mentioned above) he said to me among other things: 'When Elijah the Tishbite complained to the Lord about Israel, as if they had all

243

bowed their knees to Baal, and said in his prayer that he alone, Elijah, had remained faithful to the Lord, but that they were already seeking to take his life, what did the Lord answer him? *I have left seven thousand men in Israel who have not bowed the knee to Baal* (III Kings 19:18). And so, if in the kingdom of Israel which had fallen away from the kingdom of Judah (that had remained faithful to God), and had reached utter corruption, there were still left seven thousand men who were faithful to the Lord, what shall we say of Russia? I think that in the kingdom of Israel there were then not more than three million people. And how many are there in Russia now?'

"'About sixty million,' I replied.

"And he continued: 'Twenty times more! So judge for yourself now how many we still have who are faithful to God. Those whom He has foreknown, these He has also predestined; those whom He has predestined, these He has also called; those whom He has called, these He will also keep, these He will also glorify. So why should we be despondent? God is with us. He who trusts in the Lord is like Mount Zion. He who lives in Jerusalem will never be moved. The mountains are round Jerusalem, and the Lord is round His people. The Lord will keep thee. The Lord is thy shield upon thy right hand. The Lord will preserve thy going out and thy coming in, henceforth and for ever. The sun shall not burn thee by day, nor the moon by night.'

Spiritual Father and Elder

"And when I asked him what he meant, and why he said this to me, Father Seraphim answered: 'I wanted to show you that in this way, as the apple of His eye, the Lord keeps His people, that is Orthodox Christians who love Him with all their heart and all their mind, and who serve Him day and night by word and deed. Such are those who keep all the rules, dogmas and traditions of our Eastern Universal Church, and with their mouth confess the pious doctrine which is handed down by Her, and who in all the circumstances of their life act according to the holy commandments of our Lord Jesus Christ.'

"In confirmation of the fact that there still remain in Russia many Orthodox people who are faithful to our Lord Jesus Christ and live a pious life, Father Seraphim once said to a friend of mine (either to Father Gury, the former manager of the Sarov hostel, or to Father Simon who was in charge of the Maslischensk farm) that being once in the spirit, he saw the whole land of Russia, and it was filled and, as it were, covered with the smoke of the prayers of the faithful praying to the Lord."

St. Seraphim of Sarov Praying On a Rock
The Saint spent a thousand days and nights kneeling in prayer before God.

St. Seraphim Feeding the Bear

Having regained the original likeness of God that Adam possessed, St. Seraphim like certain other great Saints was able to commune with nature in paradisical innocence.

St. Seraphim Being Attacked by Robbers
In imitation of the long-suffering Saviour, the Saint did not defend himself, but abandoned himself into the hands of God.

Portrait of N. A. Motovilov
Spiritual son of St. Seraphim of Sarov and chronicler of his
teaching on the Acquisition of the Holy Spirit.

St. Seraphim Walking with an Axe
After being attacked by thieves, the Saint was left hunched over, often walking with the aid of an axe.

The Monastic Cell of St. Seraphim
with some of his personal belongings, as preserved after his death.

The Tomb of St. Seraphim at Sarov
as it appeared before its destruction in the wake of the Bolshevik
Revolution.

The Finding of the Relics of St. Seraphim, 1991
Rediscovered in the museum archives of the Kazan Cathedral,
where they had been placed by the unbelievers, the Relics of St.
Seraphim were once again returned to the Orthodox.
Above: The Relics carried in a solemn procession, to the singing
of Paschal hymns, from Moscow to Diveyevo Convent.
Below: The Faithful venerate the Relics of St. Seraphim.

Pillars of Monasticism

Mural in the Monastic Refectory at Holy Trinity Monastery, Jordanville, New York. *Left to right:* St. Athanasius of Mt. Athos, St. Symeon the Myrrh-gusher, St. Theodore the Studite, St. Onouphrius the Great, St. Macarius the Great, St. John of Rila, St. Cassian the Roman.

Chapter XI

Monasticism and the World

Scattered among Father Seraphim's instructions there is a lot of advice as to how to live in a Christian way in the world.

True, the flaming Seraphim himself loved and esteemed incomparably more (as is only right) angelic virginity, and consequently monasticism, for the sake of which he had left the world. And more than once in his talks with Monks he praised with enthusiasm the monastic life.

Once some Kursk merchants visited him in his hermitage on their way from the fair of Nizhni-Novgorod. Before taking leave they asked Father Seraphim: "What do you wish us to say to your brother (Alexis)?"

The Saint replied: "Tell him that I am praying for him to the Lord and to His immaculate Mother day and night."

And when they had gone, the Saint raised his hands to heaven and with rapture repeated several times in the presence of the Diveyev Sister Paraskeva Ivanovna who was there at the time this doxology to monasticism:

"There is nothing better than the monastic life! Nothing better!"

On another occasion when an admirer of the Saint, I. Y. Karataiev, was going to his native place of Kursk

St. Seraphim of Sarov

and also asked him whether he had any message to give to hgive to his relatives, St. Seraphim said, pointing to the Icons of the Saviour and of the Mother of God: "Here are my relatives. But for my living relatives, I am a living corpse."

And he loved the Monastery and the monastic life so much that he never, even in thought, regretted leaving the world or wanted to go back to it. And when Sister Paraskeva was thinking of leaving the Diveyev Convent in a fit of faint-heartedness, Father Seraphim foresaw it in spirit and called her to his hermitage. He started to comfort her and began to tell her about himself and his life in the Monastery. And in the end he added: "I have gone through all the monastic life, Mother; and never, not even in thought, have I left the Monastery."

"During his talk," the Sister related afterwards, "all my thoughts were gradually calmed; and when Father Seraphim had finished, I felt such a relief, as if a diseased limb had been cut away with a knife."

We shall see further on what love the Saint showed for his Diveyev "orphans," and with what tenderness he spoke of them even to strangers. He had much to suffer on their account.

"They come to me, Mother," he said to Sister Xenia Vasilievna (as she writes in her memoirs), "and they grumble at poor Seraphim for carrying out the commands of the Mother of God. Then, Mother, I opened the Prologue and showed them in the life of

Monasticism and the World

St. Basil the Great how people were suspicious of his brother Peter; but St. Basil showed them the untruth of their suspicions and the power of God. And I said: 'And my girls are surrounded in Church by a whole host of Angels and by all the heavenly powers.' And so, Mother, they went from me in shame. You see, my joy, they are displeased with poor Seraphim; they complain because he carries out the orders of the Queen of Heaven."

A most touching conversation about his love for the Nuns has been reported by the old Nun Maria Vasilievna Nikashina.

"When I was married and still a laywoman, I used to go with my husband to Father Seraphim. Once he asked me: 'Have you seen Diveyev and my girls there, Mother?'

"'Yes, I have, Father,' I replied.

"'And have you seen the bees, Mother?' he asked me again.

"'Why, of course, I have seen them, Father,' I replied.

"'Well, Mother,' he said, 'the bees always flutter round their queen, and the queen never leaves them. And my Diveyev girls are exactly like bees; they will always be with the Mother of God.'

St. Seraphim of Sarov

"'Ah,' I exclaimed. 'How good it is to be always like that, Father.' And I thought to myself: Why did I ever get married?

"'No, Mother, do not think what you are thinking,' he at once replied to my thoughts. 'Do not envy my girls! It is not good. Why should you envy them? It is good for widows there too, Mother! It is good for widows too! They will also be there! You know the Prophetess Anna; you have read about her, haven't you? Well, she was a widow; but what a widow, Mother!'"

This servant of God later became a widow and fulfilled her desire by entering the Diveyev Convent.

But while loving monasticism, the Saint regarded as true Monks and Nuns only those who had embraced the monastic life for no other reason than love for God and for the sake of the salvation of their soul. Moreover, it was not enough to go through the monastic life merely outwardly, but there must be good spiritual results. To illustrate this we must mention the case of a certain seminarist.

"In my youth," he recorded later, "before the end of my seminary course in 1827, I lived at the command of Father Seraphim about three weeks of the month of August in the Sarov Monastery. I was thinking of monasticism."

Monasticism and the World

Once Father Seraphim asked him: "Why do you want to become a Monk? Probably you hate the idea of marriage."

The seminarist replied: "I have never had bad thoughts about the holy Sacrament of Marriage. But I should like to be a Monk so as to serve the Lord better."

Then the Elder said: "Blessed be your way! But mind, write the following words of mine not on paper, but on your heart: learn mental prayer of the heart. Outward prayer alone is not sufficient. God attends to the mind. And therefore those Monks who do not combine exterior prayer with interior are not Monks but charred logs. Remember that the true monastic mantle (mantia) is to bear joyfully calumnies and false accusations. No afflictions--no salvation."

Later on this young man was professed with the name of Nikon and ended his life as the Archimandrite of the Balaklavsy Monastery in the Crimea.

Many asked Father Seraphim for his blessing to retire to Mount Athos for the salvation of their souls; but he advised them to work out their salvation in Orthodox Russia.

"It is very difficult there," he used to say. "If we (Monks) weep here, to go there means to weep a hundred times more; and if we don't weep here, it is useless to think of the holy community."

St. Seraphim of Sarov

He who embraces monasticism as he ought and according to the will of God discovers great grace everywhere. Listen how joyfully the Saint talked to Elena Vasilievna Manturova about taking the veil, comparing this in the earthly order to marriage--the happiest and most festive moment in human life.

"Now, my joy," Father Seraphim said to her after he had made her come from Diveyev to his hermitage, "it is time for you to get betrothed to your Bridegroom."

Elena Vasilievna began to sob and cried out in alarm: "I don't want to marry, Father!"

"You still don't understand me at all, Mother," Father Seraphim replied soothingly. "Only tell the Superior Xenia Mikhailovna that Father Seraphim commands you to get betrothed to your Bridegroom, to put on a black habit. This is what I mean by marriage, Mother! What a Bridegroom you have, my joy! Your Bridegroom is absent. Do not be downcast, but cheer up and have courage. And so prepare everything by prayer, by never ceasing prayer. For three years prepare yourself, my joy, in order that in three years you may be quite ready. Oh, what unutterable joy there will be then, Mother! I speak of your profession, Mother. And once you are professed, gráce will flood your heart more and more. How wonderful it will be then! When the Archangel Gabriel appeared to the Mother of God and announced the good tidings to her she felt a little disturbed, but said at once: *Behold the handmaid of the Lord! Be it unto me according to thy*

Monasticism and the World

word (Lk. 1:38). That is the marriage and the Bridegroom I am talking about, Mother."

Here Father Seraphim compared the monastic profession with the greatest and happiest event--the Incarnation of God Himself in the womb of the Virgin. It is awful even to tell it. But Father Seraphim was speaking from experience.

Lay people must also honour monasticism in heart and in deed, so as to be able at least in some measure to partake of the grace of monasticism through others. To this end Father Seraphim advised people to give alms to Monasteries or to work for them. And on the other hand, he taught that people who offended Monks and Nuns would be severely punished by the Lord.

Ivan Semionovitch Meliukov, the brother of Maria, the wonderful Saint of whom we shall speak later, became towards the end of his life a Monk in Sarov. By obedience he was the door-keeper and he used to relate:

"When I was still a peasant and a layman I often worked for Father Seraphim. And he foretold to me many wonderful things about Diveyev. And he always said: 'If anyone offends my orphans (the Nuns), he will receive a great punishment from the Lord; but the great mercy of God will be poured out from on high on whoever takes their part and defends and helps them when in need. Whoever even sighs and pities them in his heart will be rewarded by the Lord.

St. Seraphim of Sarov

And I will tell you what, remember this: happy is everyone who will stay for twenty-four hours in poor Seraphim's Diveyev, from morning till morning; for the Mother of God, the heavenly Queen, visits Diveyev every twenty-four hours.'"

But Religious[66] themselves should return all good that is done them only with prayers; and (what is still more surprising) Father Seraphim even told them not to thank people who gave them gifts.

"Pray, pray above all for anyone who does good to you," he instructed his orphans, "but never, never thank him (your benefactor) in words; because without thanks he will get all his full reward for the good he has done. But by thanking him for his kindness to you, you rob him and deprive him of the greater part of the reward which he merits for his good deed. Whoever offers you a gift, does not offer it to you but to God. It is not for you to thank him; but let him thank the Lord himself for accepting his gift."

But to take anything from a Monastery, even for one's own relatives, the Saint considered a great and dangerous sin.

"This is like carrying fire into a house. Whoever you give it to, it will burn everything; his house will be ruined and lost, and all his family will perish as a result of it. If you have something of your own, give.

---

[66] "Religious," i.e. Monks and Nuns.

Monasticism and the World

But if not, increase your prayer and pray with a contrite heart."

But on the other hand, monasticism itself, if it is worthily practiced, is a great mercy of God not only for the Religious themselves but also for all their family.

"Whether you have come to the Monastery on the advice or the authority of other people, or in any other way, do not be despondent. It is God's visitation (that is, God's mercy). If you do what I tell you, you will be saved yourself as well as your relations for whom you care. "I have not seen, says the Prophet, the righteous forsaken, nor his seed (his descendants) begging bread (Ps. 36:25)." That is how Father Seraphim taught a new Novice.

But this same thought was expressed with special force in a talk with the relatives of the wonderful nineteen year old Nun of the great habit[67] Martha, formerly the Novice Maria, after her death. When her eldest sister, Praskovia Semyonovna Meliukova, a Nun of Diveyev, came to Saint Seraphim for the coffin which he had made for the deceased, he said to her consolingly:

"Don't be downcast, Mother. Her soul is in the Heavenly Kingdom and near the Holy Trinity at the

---

[67] "Nun of the great habit." Russian: skhimnitsa. (The highest degree of Orthodox ascetics-ed.)

St. Seraphim of Sarov

throne of God. And all your family will be saved through her."

And after Maria's funeral he said to her brother John, the door-keeper mentioned above, who was then still a peasant:

"See, my joy, what mercy the Lord has granted her! In the Heavenly Kingdom she is standing with the holy virgins at the throne of God near the Queen of Heaven. She is an intercessor for all your family. She is the Nun of the great habit Martha. I professed her. Whenever you are in Diveyev, never pass by her grave without kneeling down and saying: 'Our lady and Mother Martha, remember us at the throne of God in the Heavenly Kingdom!'"

But alas, not even all Religious will be saved. Even among his Diveyev orphans some will not be granted forgiveness. This was revealed to him in a wonderful vision by the Mother of God herself in the year 1830 on the Feast of the Dormition.

"The Queen of Heaven, Father"--this was recorded by the Protopresbyter Sadovsky, the Diveyev confessor, afterwards--"the Queen of Heaven herself visited poor Seraphim. And what a joy it was for us, Father! The Mother of God covered poor Seraphim with her ineffable kindness. 'My beloved!' said our most blessed Lady, the immaculate Virgin. 'Ask of me whatever you wish.' Do you hear, Father? What mercy the Queen of Heaven showed us!"

Monasticism and the World

And the Saint became all lighted up, simply radiant with ecstasy.

"And poor Seraphim," continued the Saint, "well, poor Seraphim implored the Mother of God for his orphans, Father. And he asked that all, all the little orphans in Seraphim's Convent might be saved, Father. And the Mother of God promised to grant this unutterable joy to poor Seraphim, Father. Only for three it was not granted. 'Three will be lost,' said the Mother of God." At this the bright face of the Elder became clouded. "One will be burnt, another will be ground by the mill, and the third...However hard I have tried to remember," writes Father Sadovsky, "I am quite unable to do so. Evidently I am not meant to remember it."

Seven months later the Saint had another vision of the Mother of God, the most wonderful vision of all. Sister Evdokia Ephremovna was also present. After this vision Father Seraphim remembered the previous visitation of the Mother of God and told Sister Evdokia the following details about it:

"Listen, Mother! About a thousand people will gather in my Convent. And they will all be saved, Mother. I asked the Mother of God for it. And the Queen of Heaven condescended to fulfill the humble request of poor Seraphim. And our merciful Lady promised to save all, all of them except three, my joy! Only there, Mother," continued Father Seraphim after a short silence, "there all in the future life--will be divided into three groups: 'The United' who by their purity, their unceasing prayers and their deeds have been united to the Lord; their whole life and breath is in God, and they will be with Him eternally; 'the Elect' who will do my works, Mother, and will also be with me in my mansion[68]; and 'the Called' who will only eat our bread for a time, and for whom there is a dark place. They will be given only a hard and narrow bunk, and they will have nothing but a shirt, and they will always yearn. These are the slack and slothful, Mother, who are not concerned with the common work and do not observe obedience and are only busy with their own affairs. O, how dark and heavy it will be for them! They will sit in one place all the time rocking from side to side."

And taking me by the hand, Father Seraphim began to weep bitterly.

"Obedience, Mother, obedience is higher than fasting and prayer," continued Father Seraphim. "I tell you, there is nothing higher than obedience, Mother. And you tell all of them that."

Then he blessed me and sent me away.

Here the Saint opens mysterious pages from the future life, but it is not for our carnal and limited mind to discuss them. Only we, Religious, must remember both the three lost souls and those many "called" who alas! have not been "chosen." Further on we shall learn the awful fate of the two condemned Abbesses.

---

[68] John 14:2.

Monasticism and the World

It was not without cause that the Saint wept for us who are slack. Raise us from this mire, O Lord, by the prayers of Thy Mother and Saint Seraphim!

But Saint Seraphim ended his talk about the "called" in a strange way, as if they somehow did not belong to us.

"Their affairs are nothing to do with us, Mother. Let them eat our bread for the time being!"

Just as if they were estranged, banished, forgotten by God! And one calls to mind the robber's prayer: "*Lord, remember me when Thou comest into Thy Kingdom*" (Lk. 23:42). The judgements of God are mysteries. It is better to remember the condemnation and the "judgement-seat of Christ" as we are taught by the Church.

"At the Holy Monastery Gates"
An etching by V. P. Pavlov from *Russian Pilgrim*, 1897.

Chapter XII

The Laity and Marriage

And now let us pass on to St. Seraphim's instructions for those living in the world.

As one reads of Father Seraphim's dealings with laymen and his advice to them, one feels awe, compunction and sometimes even amazement when one sees with what love and tenderness he treated them. Sometimes it even seems as if he preferred them to Religious. Of course, it was not so in actual fact. We have already heard his own words about the excellence of virginity. But still Father Seraphim's unchanging kindness and deep compassion for laymen is worthy of profound attention.

One thinks of the laity as living married lives, bearing children, and engaged in their own affairs, some as landowners, some in military service, some in business, but the greater part labouring as peasants and workers. It would seem as if they do not deserve any special honour. And yet St. Seraphim welcomed all joyfully almost without exception and called them by endearing names, such as "father," "mother," "my treasure," but most frequently of all "my joy," and on more solemn occasions "your godliness." And in all this he acted without distinction of rank. Not infrequently he bowed down to the ground before his visitors; more than once he kissed the hands not only of persons in holy orders but also of simple laymen. And he received in this way not only pious people, but also sinners. And only on very rare occasions did he show righteous anger. That was when he saw hypocrisy, or pride, or evil and underhand deception.

One cannot help noticing that the chief persons who enjoyed Father Seraphim's intimacy and confidence were not Religious but laymen. One of them was Michael Vasilievitch Manturov, formerly the manager of an estate and himself a small landowner of the province of Nizhni-Novgorod. Father Seraphim used to call him "Micky"[69]. His wife, Anne Mikhailovna, a Latvian and a Protestant, continually grumbled at her husband for having surrendered himself in unconditional obedience to the Elder; but later, after the miraculous incident of the self-kindled lamp in her house, she was humbled and spent the last part of her life as a secret Nun.

Nikolas Alexandrovitch Motovilov, landowner, was a justice of the peace and an inspector of the district schools of the province of Simbirsk. He called himself "Seraphim's servant." With Father Seraphim's blessing he married a simple peasant girl, the daughter of Ivan Meliukov whom we already know, Elena Ivanovna who lived until the Canonization of St. Seraphim in 1903. Father Seraphim called him the "provider" (purveyor) of the Diveyev Convent and appointed him its guardian. And he proved worthy of this obedience, especially when a persecution arose against the Convent.

---

[69] Lit. "Mishenka" (accent on first syllable, and i pronounced as in machine).

The Laity and Marriage

The third confidant and collaborator of Father Seraphim in the affairs of the Convent was also a married man, Father Vasily Nikititch Sadovsky who finished the seminary of Nizhni-Novgorod in 1825 and was afterwards the Diveyev Confessor. St. Seraphim directed him himself and put complete trust in him.

These three persons, laymen and not Religious, Father Seraphim entrusted with the care of Diveyev before his death and said: "No one is to be obeyed except them." A Novice of Sarov, a certain Ivan Tikhonov who gave himself out to be "Seraphim's disciple" tried to interfere, but he was a self-willed man who afterwards did great harm to Diveyev. But even to him Father Seraphim revealed much during his life for his salvation.

"You will have no Father but me," Father used to say to his orphans. "I commit you to the Mother of God herself; she herself will be an Abbess to you. And through her all will rule."

Let us remember that the doors of his reclusion were thrown open for the first time not to Monks, not even to the strict diocesan Bishop Jonah, but to the governor Bezobrazov and his wife.

And if we remember Father Seraphim's stupendous, most wonderful revelation--his heavenly conversation about the aim of the Christian life, when he was transfigured with the light of Mount Tabor, it makes us involuntarily wonder why this was granted

St. Seraphim of Sarov

to a layman, to Motovilov, "Seraphim's servant," and not to some recluse or at least to Father Sadovsky, a Priest.

Besides these outstanding personalities, we see in the background many more laymen: peasants like Meliukoff and Euphim Vasiliev, a noble lady--the widow Eropkina, Aksakova and others. In fact, everyone who visited the holy Elder considered himself a close friend.

How can we explain this relationship of a hermit, a recluse, a Monk who was dead to the world, with those who lived in the world?

Father Seraphim himself more than once gave an answer to this question in his teaching (or rather, it is the common Christian doctrine) about the essence of Christianity--the acquisition of the grace of the Holy Spirit. And this acquisition is not only possible, but even obligatory for all without distinction. In his wonderful talk on this subject the Saint said to Motovilov: "The fact that I am a Monk and you are a layman is utterly beside the point. What God requires is true faith in Himself and in His only-begotten Son. In return for this the grace of the Holy Spirit is granted abundantly from on high. The Lord seeks a heart filled to overflowing with love for God and our neighbour; this is the throne on which His loves to sit and on which He appears in the fullness of His heavenly glory. 'Son, give Me thy heart' (Prov. 23:26), He says, 'and all the rest I Myself will add to thee,' for in the human heart the Kingdom of God can be con-

The Laity and Marriage

tained...The Lord listens equally to a Monk and to a simple Christian layman provided they are both Orthodox, and both love God from the depth of their souls, and both have faith in Him, if only as a grain of mustard seed (Lk. 17:6); and both will move mountains" (Mk. 11:23).

The Saint had a similar talk with another layman, Bogdanov, shortly before his death. "*The Kingdom of God is not food and drink, but righteousness and peace and joy in the Holy Spirit* (Rom. 14:17). Only we must not desire anything vain; but all that is of God is good. Virginity is glorious. Even marriage is blessed by God: *And God blessed them saying, Increase and multiply* (Gen. 1:22). Only the enemy disturbs everything."

And so, our whole business consists in the acquisition of the grace of the Holy Spirit, or, what amounts to the same thing, the Kingdom of God. And this is given by God irrespective of our state of life, but according to the efforts we make to attain the aim of the Christian life. And therefore there is really no essential difference between Monks and laymen. The difference can be only in degree; but even then it depends on the will and labour of each.

Yet besides all this there were other reasons why St. Seraphim entertained such cordial relations with laymen. The Monks were already being saved by living in the Monastery, but the laymen were in need of great care, all the more so because they mostly came to Father Seraphim with their sorrows, afflictions,

273

St. Seraphim of Sarov

perplexities and sicknesses. Once there came to the Saint his constant admirer and spiritual friend, the Abbot and founder of the Nadyaiyevsky hermitage, the blessed Hieromonk Timon. On foot in spring when all the roads are flooded he slowly made his way from the province of Kostroma to that of Nizhni-Novgorod, to see his beloved Father whom he had not seen for more than twenty years. On reaching his cell, he waited with impatience for a happy meeting with the holy Elder. But Father Seraphim went on receiving other people, both men and women, and only towards evening did he admit Father Timon. The Abbot fell down at the Saint's feet and asked him with sorrow: "Why have you been angry with me, a sinner, and have not admitted me all day?"

Father Seraphim gave his friend a seat and with great love said to him: "No, it was not so, Father Timon! I love you, but I have done this because you are a Monk, and even a solitary. So you should have patience. I was also testing you to see what you had learned by living so many years in solitude. You have not come out of it empty, have you? As for the other people, they are worldly and even sick. They must be treated and dismissed first, for *they that be whole need not a physician, but they that are sick* (Mat. 9:12), as the Lord said. But with you it is necessary to talk more at leisure." "And so," Father Timon ends his reminiscence, "we spent the whole night with him in conversation."

Here I shall mention the direction which was given by the Saint to Father Timon: "Sow, Father Timon,

The Laity and Marriage

sow! Sow everywhere the wheat which has been given to you. Sow on the good ground, sow on the sand, sow even on the rock, sow by the wayside, sow among the thorns. Somewhere or other it will sprout, and grow, and produce fruit, even though not soon. And do not hide in the earth the talent which has been given to you, lest you be called to account by your Lord, but give it to the exchangers and let them trade with it.[70] One thing more I have to tell you, Father Timon. Have no friendship and no union firstly, with enemies of Christ's Church, i.e. heretics and schismatics; secondly, with those who do not keep the holy fasts; thirdly, with women, for they do a lot of harm to us Monks."

Though, strictly speaking, all but Saints are sick, those who came to the Saint from a distance of hundreds and even thousands of versts were special sufferers. How was he not to comfort them before the Monks? I shall mention a case which has not been printed in any of the other lives, but which is comforting to every sufferer. In the book *The Sacred Ministry of a Priest* (Father Tikhon), we read the following: "There lived a husband and wife. They were both educated people and lived together in love. But the husband had a vice--he was addicted to wine. As time went on, his passion overcame him more and more. Neither the entreaties of his wife nor his own efforts were of any avail. The tortured wife went to Sarov to Father Seraphim and told him her grief with bitter tears. The Saint felt compassion for her, com-

---

[70] Cp. Mat. 25:27.

275

St. Seraphim of Sarov

forted her and gave her the following instruction, namely, to read daily for forty days an Akathist to the Mother of God and to keep it a secret from her husband. She returned home and began to do what the Elder had told her, but her husband's passion did not abate in the least. Towards the end of the forty days, to her horror and distress, his drunkenness increased to madness. However, she continued to read daily an Akathist to the Mother of God. On the fortieth day something extraordinary and unexpected happened to her husband. He humbly went to his wife, asked her forgiveness for all his sins and for all the pain he had caused her, and promised never to drink again. The poor woman could hardly believe it for joy; but she thanked the Mother of God and Saint Seraphim. And from that day her husband was completely cured."

Now let us return to other laymen, especially to those who were intimate and trusted friends of the Saint. There was one other special reason for his confidence in them: they were devotedly obedient to him. This was not the case with most of the Sarov Monks; among many of them there was even some antagonism towards the Saint. But for the creation of a community, and especially a women's community, he needed collaborators whose obedience was absolute. Life shows us that it is sometimes easier to find a trustful simplicity of soul in a humble layman than in some opinionated Monk. Besides, it would have been a cause of scandal and criticism to entrust a community of Nuns to Monks. Even a Monk of such perfect chastity as St. Seraphim never visited his own com-

The Laity and Marriage

munity except on a single occasion, after a funeral, when he was a Hierodeacon. And even then he did not stay for lunch, but, in spite of the rain, walked back to Sarov. And on another occasion, when the Church of the Nativity had been built in Diveyev by M. V. Manturov, and Father Paul, who occupied the next cell in Sarov, invited Father Seraphim to its consecration, the Saint replied: "No! Why disturb them? I shall not go. And don't you go either. It is better to give them what they need. They will do everything themselves and make all the necessary arrangements. There is no need for us to go there."

In spite of all that we have said, it is not perfectly clear why the Saint appeared to prefer good laymen to Monks. But perhaps we can discover a further reason for it. That spiritual deadness among Monks as well as among Hierarchs and Priests which the Saint had so sharply rebuked when he called those whose life was external and formal "charred logs," had it not already begun in his life-time? Was not the time at hand when true Christians would be determined not by their badge of office, rank or profession, not by their name or label, but by their actual life? Are we not witnessing in our days how those who ought to defend the truth remain indifferent to it, while people who hold no official position in the Church, simple laymen with a religious outlook, are the mainstay of the Church? And the word of God comes true: *The last shall be first* (Mat. 19:30).

It is well known that among the prophecies of St. Seraphim one still remains unpublished in order that it may not give offense. This is the prophesy about the fall of the members of the Episcopate and their lack of zeal for the glory of God. Neither can the Monasteries boast of such zeal, for they are more concerned with outward organization than with the art of contemplative prayer and holiness of life. It is not for nothing that in our time both Bishops and Priests are having to bear a purifying punishment. It is not without the will of God that the Monasteries, which were previously provided with everything, have been closed, even the best of them.

And finally, in our days of the decline of true Christianity throughout the world, was it not high time to make it perfectly clear that Christianity is not only for Monks and clergy, but for the whole world, and consequently first of all for the laity themselves? Is it not striking that our Saviour Himself worked His first miracle at a marriage in Cana of Galilee by changing water into wine? Thereby He called humanity to a spiritual transformation and transfiguration of its life in the world. This is possible everywhere and for everyone. And the essence of it consists in sanctifying one's soul and thereby all the surrounding life. Is Christianity only for Monks? No, it is for everyone. And all are called to that "acquisition of the grace of the Holy Spirit" or the Kingdom of God of which St. Seraphim reminded the whole world which had forgotten the very essence of Christianity. That great servant of God Saint Simeon the New Theologian[71] had also reminded the Greeks

---

[71] St. Simeon lived in the 10th century.

The Laity and Marriage

who had grown cold towards religion (both Monks and laymen) of their forgotten conception of Christianity as a life in which the power of the Holy Spirit was consciously realized. The importance of Saint Seraphim's conversation will soon be appreciated.

And so both ways, the monastic and the married life, can lead to salvation. The question as to which of them to choose is solved differently by each individual. Both have essentially one and the same aim--the acquisition of the grace of the Holy Spirit. But according to the degree of self-denial and asceticism a good monastic life is higher than the married life. *The unmarried man,* says the Apostle, *cares for the things of the Lord* (I Cor. 7:32). But the monastic way is harder. "The monastic life is not suitable for everyone," said the Saint to an elderly lady. Therefore it is clear that people must generally choose the way of married life which is blessed by God. But in this case too God does not force anyone against his will. "The Lord does not compel anyone to accept virginity"[72] said Father Seraphim, but at once added: *"All things are possible to him who believes"* (Mk. 9:23). And only in flagrant cases of unfitness for virginity and lack of decision, is it better and safer to contract marriage without any misgivings and to obtain salvation in this "middle way", according to the words of St. Gregory the Theologian. And after all, both ways are "gifts of God," for both are given as ways of salvation, as is clearly said by the Apostle Paul: *I wish that*

---

[72] Cp. Mat. 19:12: "He who is able to accept it, let him accept it."

279

St. Seraphim of Sarov

all were as I am myself (i.e. in the state of virginity).
*But everyone has his own gift from God--one in one
way, and one in another* (I Cor. 7:7)."

> Stone walls do not a prison make,
> Nor iron bars a cage;
> Minds innocent and quiet make
> That for an hermitage.

> If I have freedom in my love
> And in my soul am free,
> Angels alone, that soar above,
> Enjoy such liberty.

Neither do walls or rich furniture make a home.
Millionaires in magnificent mansions may never
know a home. But where there are good relationships,
where love binds the family together and to God,
there happiness is always to be found. For good relationships are heaven anywhere. Monotony and misery
cannot exist where there is love. But the fire of love
must be kept burning warmly and brightly with the
sweet wood of sacrifice. In teaching us to cross the I
out of life our Lord tells us the secret of happiness,
what the Saints call the ecstasy of self-forgetfulness.
For divine love is always self-effacing, seeks to give
rather than to receive, to serve rather than to be
served, to love rather than to be loved, and will sacrifice anything for the Beloved. Only then does love
become a clean and holy fire in the heart, and not an
ugly flare of lust.

The Laity and Marriage

Christian marriage is a life-work. It is easy only in ideal circumstances. Fidelity to the end, St. Seraphim taught, is essential to happiness. If Christians find they cannot live together, they go on living together for their homes, their children, for the Church and for God. It may mean much suffering, but this married life is the way to heaven. For only those who take up the cross can follow Christ.

Prayer, discernment, and especially the experience of wise directors gifted with spiritual insight will lead to knowledge of God's will and the acceptance of one's own "gift of God." But if you are still uncertain or doubtful, you ought to choose the way of marriage which, as a gift of God, is also good and blessed, and not blamable. (God preserve us from such blasphemy!), and labour in that. However when the Lord sends us Spirit-filled directors, we should consider it a mercy of God and apply to them in doubtful cases. That is why many people asked for St. Seraphim's blessing to choose the monastic life.

The following is related in the Chronicle: "In the year 1830, a Novice of the Glinsky Monastery who had not yet finally decided as to his way of life, came with this intention to the Sarov Monastery and asked Father Seraphim whether there was God's blessing for him to become a Monk. The young man did not quite know his own mind and was not sure of his vocation; he was hesitating between the world and the Monastery. He had no one to whom he could disclose his thoughts. There was no one at hand who could solve the problem of his life. And so the Novice came

St. Seraphim of Sarov

to Father Seraphim, fell at his feet and begged him to release his soul from the turmoil of doubts, asking: 'Is it the will of God that I and my brother Nikolas should choose the monastic life?' Had not Father Seraphim, some years previously, asked the Recluse Dositheus the same question in Kiev? And so he answered the Novice thus: 'Save yourself and save your brother!' Then he reflected a moment and said: 'Do you remember the life of Johannikius the Great? When he was wandering among the mountains and rapids, his staff happened to slip from his hand and fell down a precipice. It was impossible to get the staff, and without it the Saint could go no further. In deep anguish he cried to the Lord God, and an Angel of the Lord invisibly handed him a new staff.'

"So saying, Father Seraphim put his own stick into the right hand of the Novice and said: 'It is difficult to direct human souls! But among all your trials and sorrows in directing the souls of the brethren, the Angel of the Lord will be constantly with you till the end of your life.'

After this the Novice decided to enter a Monastery. At his profession he received the name of Paissy, and in 1856 he was appointed Abbot of the Tchurkinsky Nikolas cenobitic Monastery in Astrakhan. Six years later he was raised to the rank of Archimandrite in the same Monastery. In this way he became, as St. Seraphim had foreseen, a pastor of human souls. And his brother, of whom Father Seraphim had said, 'Save your brother,' entered a Monastery under the name of Nazarius and ended his life in St. George's Monastery

The Laity and Marriage

in Kozeletsk as a Hieromonk." How decisively did the Spirit-bearing Seraphim determine the fate of those who asked his advice!

Recently, at the Theological Academy in St. Petersburg there was a student called Nikolas V. S. For his geniality his fellow students gave him the nickname of Koletchka. In his second or third school-year he thought of becoming a Monk. He thought and prayed, and he asked the advice of a number of spiritual persons. But no one gave him a definite and final answer. "You may become a Monk; but you might also be a good parish Priest," said those whom he asked.

"Koletchka" was not satisfied, and his longing for monasticism grew. The Canonization of St. Seraphim and the exposition of his relics had taken place a short time before this. Two years later a friend had a desire to venerate the Saint, and went to Sarov. From there, laden with small souvenirs of the Monastery, he returned to the Academy at the beginning of the school year. Incidentally, he brought Kolya a small Icon of the Saint. He had had for a long time a special veneration for the Wonder-worker of Sarov, even before his Canonization. His friend had had no special intention in bestowing his gift. But this is what happened.

Having received the welcome present, as he afterwards told his friend, he decided to ask the Saint in prayer to solve finally his torturing problem regarding monasticism. He only wanted to know one thing: Was it the will of God for him to become a Monk?

St. Seraphim of Sarov

"And so," he told his friend, "I put your Icon before me in my room and I said aloud to my Saint: 'Little Father, Saint Seraphim, great Wonder-worker of God! You said yourself during your life-time that we were to come to your grave and tell you everything as if you were alive. Dear little Father! I am quite tortured by my problem regarding monasticism. Tell me, is it the will of God for me to become a Monk or not? Look, I shall make three prostrations to you, as to a living person; and then I shall open your "Life" (I think it was Levitsky's book on St. Seraphim), and where my glance falls, let it be the answer to me.'"

And he did as he said. He made three prostrations, opened the "Life" on the left side, and his eyes lighted upon the paragraph which begins with the words; "In the year 1830 a Novice of the Glinsky Monastery"...which we have just quoted.

Nikolas V. S. was overjoyed and began with tears to thank his Wonder-worker who had now blessed his vocation in a similar manner. His doubts were at an end. And soon, instead of the servant of God Nikolas, he became after his profession "our Brother Seraphim," being so called on account of the wonderful revelation made to him by the Saint. Other details from the same account of the Glinsky Novice were also fulfilled. Brother Seraphim subsequently also became a pastor--a Bishop.

There was also another extraordinary coincidence with regard to his own brother, whom Nikolas V. S.

had not thought of during his prayer, as his thoughts were busy about himself. He also had a brother who, from time to time, suffered from headaches and from an inexplicable anguish. In those moments, his elder brother Nikolas was a great help to him, comforting and cheering him. And suddenly there was now an answer for him too: "Save your brother." This he did. After he had graduated from the Academy Father Seraphim took his mother (a widow) and his brother to live with him. Then he professed him and gave him the name of Sergius. Now he is an Archimandrite and he is working out his salvation with his brother the Bishop. As to their mother, she passed peacefully away.

Of course, we should not make a rule of this way of finding out the will of God, for it will be similar to fortune-telling. And it is not approved by the Church. In the history of the Diveyev Community great confusion arose in this way. Nectarius, Bishop of Nizhni-Novgorod, in whose diocese this Convent stood, wanted to appoint as Abbess a certain Sister, Glykeria Zanyatova, against the wish of the majority of the Sisters who wanted to remain with their former Abbess, Elizabeth Ushakova. To this end, contrary to law, he used the method of casting lots, inscribing the names of Mother Elizabeth, Sister Glykeria and another of her party, Paraskeva Yerofeyeva. The lot fell on Glykeria who had only forty adherents, while the other four hundred were for Mother Elizabeth. This gave rise to a notorious lawsuit. And this is what the deceased Metropolitan Philaret of Moscow wrote in his resolution: "I have learned that His Grace looks upon the lot cast by him as upon the will of God, and therefore considers his case above the decision of the Holy Synod."

Metropolitan Philaret considers this opinion erroneous. Afterwards the same view was expressed by the Holy Synod; the settling of the matter by lot was cancelled, and Mother Elizabeth was reinstated in her lawful office. As for Sister Glykeria and her adherents, she was removed from the Convent. Peace was restored.

Another heirarch, one of the leaders of the Church, wrote with regard to another case: "We should pray that the Lord may show us the way and crown our work with success; but a decision ought to be taken only with a clear conviction of its soundness and adequateness, and we should take upon ourselves all responsibility for this decision."

If we have mentioned the case of the Novice, it was not as a rule, but merely as an exceptional instance of the manifestation of the will of God, which was afterwards justified in deed.

The holy Fathers, Barsanufius the Great and others, including the author of the "Invisible War," recommend the following way of solving doubts. Having interiorly renounced your own will and your pre-conceived opinions, turn to God three times in prayer, as the Lord did in the Garden of Gethsemane, and then consider the matter again in your soul, taking all responsibility upon yourself. After this, accept the decision to which your heart inclines, be it ever so slightly.

But besides all this the gift of discernment is a special gift of God which is granted by the Holy Spirit. *For to one is given by the Spirit the word of wisdom...to another discerning of spirits* (I Cor. 12:8-10), says the Apostle Paul.

And St. Seraphim teaches: "The Superior, as a shepherd of rational sheep, must have the gift of discernment, in order that he may be able to give at any time useful advice to all who require his guidance." And according to St. Peter Damascene: "Not everyone can be trusted to give advice to those who seek it, but only he who has received from God the gift of discernment, and through long exercise in asceticism has acquired spiritual insight."

But besides its being a gift of God, discernment is acquired, according to the words of St. Seraphim, through a continuous, "daily and nightly study of Holy Scripture, the law of the Lord": finally, he indicates a further way to it: "He who is obedient makes great progress in building up his soul; and besides, he acquires through it an understanding of things and comes to compunction."

When there is the direct order of a competent authority, Father Seraphim orders it to be carried out unquestioningly for the sake of holy obedience.

St. Seraphim of Sarov

One must not discuss the affairs of the Superiors and judge them. In that way we offend the Majesty of God by whom the authorities have been appointed. *For there is no authority except from God, and the existing authorities have been appointed by God* (Rom. 13:1)."

"He who obeys, obeys in everything. But he who has renounced his will in one thing and has not renounced it in another has had his own will even in what he renounced."

"What is done in one's own way is not pleasing to God, even though it may seem good."

That is why the Saint insisted on obedience for all "Religious," and especially for his "orphans." "Obedience is higher than prayer and fasting," he constantly repeated.

The lay-people have their own way. But here too, as we shall see, there are special ways of obedience and of discovering the will of God. Here too, in the world, it is not only possible but imperative that people should live a holy life in order to work out their salvation. For the business of the Church is to make Saints in every walk of life.

It is impossible for us to collect all the counsels of St. Seraphim; in fact, not everything has been published. So we shall choose what is most important and practically useful for those living in the world.

Chapter XIII

Piety in the World

When talking with laymen, St. Seraphim displayed a supernatural perception of the spiritual state of each individual. It seemed as if he saw the other person's soul within him. And that is why his counsels were not general directions, but answered the hidden feelings and thoughts of his visitors. And he also advised people to adapt themselves to others.

With the natural man one must talk of natural things; but with a person of spiritual understanding, one must talk of heavenly things. Sometimes there is no need to talk of spiritual things at all, "especially when you do not observe any desire to listen."

But as the people who came to him came with open souls, St. Seraphim not only showed them his love, but poured out his very soul to them. "Often," writes the author of the Chronicle, "he revealed the innermost thoughts of his visitors, and then torrents of tears burst forth even from people who had hard, stony hearts." And all left him edified, sometimes for the whole of their lives.

According to St. Seraphim, or rather according to Christian teaching in general, one can and must work out one's salvation in every calling and state of life. The great Apostle Paul also says the same: *Let everyone lead the life which God has assigned to him, and in which the Lord has called him. This is my rule in all the Churches. Everything is in keeping the commandments of God. Let everyone remain in the voca-*

tion in which he was called. Were you a slave when called? Never mind. (And yet if you can get your freedom, you had better take it.) For a slave who is called by the Lord is the Lord's freedman. Likewise he who was free when called is a slave of Christ (I Cor. 7:17-22).

Therefore in the life and instructions of Saint Seraphim we see neither a depreciation of marriage nor an unconditional recommendation of monasticism, neither a disparagement of the rich if they are humble and pious, nor a preference for the poor if they do not live a spiritual life. *Truly everything is in keeping the commandments of God.*[73]

The clergy, officials, armymen, merchants and most of all peasants came to him, and Father Seraphim received them all in an equally friendly and earnest manner; to all he gave the instructions, comfort and answers which they needed.

First of all, how many people came to him with questions about marriage, and sometimes about monasticism! And he solved their doubts and difficulties with such faith that it seemed as if the all-seeing eye of God were looking through him. Often he did not give the decision that was expected. Here are a few striking examples.

---

[73] This is the Russian version of I Cor. 7:19 as quoted by St. Seraphim.

Piety in the World

Once two ladies visited him. One was young and belonged to a merchant family; the other was middle-aged and of noble birth. The latter had a great desire for the monastic life, but her parents would not give her their blessing; the former did not even think of monasticism. But the Saint's spiritual insight led him to give them advice which was just the opposite of their intentions. He firmly urged the noble lady to marry.

"Married life," he said to her, "is blessed by God Himself. It is only necessary for both parties to keep marital fidelity, love and peace. You will be happy in marriage. Monasticism is not the way for you. The monastic life is difficult; not everyone can endure it."

But the Saint told the younger woman to enter monasticism, and even told her the name of the Monastery where she would be saved. Both visitors were dissatisfied with the talk, and left the Elder disappointed. But subsequently everything turned out exactly as Father Seraphim foretold.

The thought of the blessedness of marriage the Saint often repeated to his visitors. Once a young man came to him and asked him to bless him to enter a Monastery. But the Saint, wishing to test his firmness and strengthen him in his good intention, spoke to him of marriage: *"Not all can receive this counsel* (Mat. 19:11), and the Lord does not compel them to do so. But," he added, "*all things are possible to him who believes* (Mk. 9:23). Remain in the world, get married. Don't forget conjugal intercourse and hospi-

291

St. Seraphim of Sarov

tality. Practice the virtues which will be remembered at the awful judgement of God, according to the Holy Gospel: *I was hungry, and you gave Me food; I was thirsty, and you gave Me drink; I was naked, and you clothed Me* (Mat. 25:35-36). Herein is your salvation! And also observe chastity. Remain continent on Wednesdays and Fridays, as well as on Sundays and all holidays. For not practicing chastity on Wednesdays and Fridays children are born dead, and for not observing holidays and Sundays wives die in childbirth."

The young man returned home, but Father Seraphim's advice kindled still more his desire for monasticism and a year and a half later he entered the Sarov Monastery.

Sometimes Father Seraphim unexpectedly linked the lives of people who had never met before. An officer came to ask for his blessing to marry. Father Seraphim told him that his bride was already there, at the hostel. This young lady also soon came for his blessing to marry some other man.

"No, your bridegroom is here, in Sarov," the Elder told her.

The young people became acquainted, and later both came to the Saint who gave them his blessing to marry. The marriage was an extremely happy one.

St. Seraphim often saw what would happen to families in the future. A father brought him his baby

Piety in the World

daughter to be blessed. The Saint looked at her and said: "She will have a difficult way. She will marry a husband who will not even know God."

E. P. Gooseva, a young woman, wife of a merchant of Elatma, came to the Saint. He took her by the hand, led her into his cell and kissing her on the head, said to her: "This head will see much sorrow! You will conceive in sorrow and reap them all in joy." And so it turned out.

"I had many children," she said afterwards, "and he foretold the truth to me in a parable. I brought them up, married them all and buried them all. And now I am left alone in the world."

Those who were married Father Seraphim would not allow to separate, however hard it might be, even under the pretext of a subsequent life of virginity. There was such a case.

A married couple separated and divided their children. The husband went to Sarov and came to Father Seraphim. As soon as the Saint saw him, he began to rebuke him sternly and, contrary to his wont, said to him in a menacing tone: "Why don't you live with your wife? Go to her, go!"

The rebuked husband obeyed the Saint, and returned to his wife; and they spent the rest of their life in harmony and unity.

St. Seraphim of Sarov

However, two instances are known when St. Seraphim blessed married people to enter a Monastery, but it was under special conditions.

A pious visitor to the Monastery made a vow that he would embrace monasticism. But on returning home he got married and had two children. However, his conscience gave him no peace, and on the advice of the Sarov Monks, he applied to the holy Elder. He saw him coming out of his cell with a hoe in his hands and threw himself at his feet, begging him for advice and again asking for his blessing for the longed for monastic way. The Saint listened to everything, and then said:

"If you will keep all the monastic rules strictly according to your vow, go your way in peace."

Then the Elder blessed the supplicant who went home, committing everything to the will of God. Soon his wife died; then both his children. Having buried them, the penitent sinner went to Sarov, where he was professed as a Monk and ended his life as an exemplary ascetic.

Another time Father Seraphim of his own accord said to a merchant: "Leave the world." After long reflection the husband began to urge his wife to go to a Convent with her daughter, so that he might become a Monk. But the wife did not want to, and gave as an excuse the precarious situation of her parents. Then she openly declared that she had not the slightest wish to go to a Convent. But soon both the old parents and

Piety in the World

the wife died; and then father and daughter went to different Monasteries. Subsequently he was professed and given the name of Melchisedek.

But cases of this kind were extremely rare. For the most part Father Seraphim gave instructions as to how to live in a family. We have already heard some of his advice. Let us cite some further examples. He told people to care more for the education of their children's souls than for the grafting into them of various branches of knowledge, though he did not deny the need for that either. A certain Bogdanov asked him whether he should teach his children foreign languages and other subjects. Father Seraphim said:

"What harm is there in knowing something?"

"I, a sinner," writes Bogdanov, "thought, judging by worldly standards, that he ought to have been educated himself in order to answer this. But I was at once rebuked by the clairvoyant Elder: 'It is not for a child like me to answer a learned person like you. Ask someone cleverer!'"

Here is an edifying narrative for parents who care for the religious upbringing of their children.

"In 1829," says the cavalry officer, African Vasilievitch Teplov, one of the Saint's devoted admirers and friends, "in the summer, I went to Sarov with my wife and children. On the way, noticing that our eldest son, who was about ten, was entirely engrossed with the reading of spiritual books and did not pay the

St. Seraphim of Sarov

least attention to his surroundings, my wife began to complain that our children were too fond of spiritual books, and that they did not care at all for their lessons, for science and for other things which were necessary in the world. On our arrival in Sarov, we went at once to Father Seraphim and received a friendly welcome from him. Blessing me, he told us to remain there three days. When he blessed my wife, he said:

'Mother, mother! Do not be in a hurry to teach the children French and German, but first prepare their souls; *and all these things shall be added* to them afterwards (Mat. 6:33).'

"When he blessed both our children, he deigned to call our eldest 'his treasure.' In this way the just Elder rebuked my wife for her unjust murmuring."

The Saint loved children, those flowers of paradise. Some touching incidents from his life have been recorded.

The wife of a landowner of Simbirsk, E. N. Pasuchina, came in 1830 to visit the Father. But when she approached his cell, she became aware that it was locked from inside; the Elder was not receiving anyone. Some people tried to say the monastic prayer (By the prayers of our holy Fathers, Lord Jesus Christ, our God, have mercy on us), but the door did not open.

"At last," says the visitor, "I turned to a lady with a little girl who was standing beside me close to the

Piety in the World

door, and I asked her to make her baby say the prayer, since she was the most worthy of us all.[74] And as soon as the baby had said the prayer, the door opened."

A similar incident happened on another occasion at the hermitage. A crowd of people had gathered there to see the Saint and at least get his blessing. But this time the holy Elder had decided for some reason to receive no one; unnoticed, he slipped out of his cell into the forest and hid in the tall grass. Among the visitors was a lady called Aksakova with her children. As the pilgrims did not dare to disturb the Elder or even to look for him, they told the innocent children to walk in the grass and to call the Father, hoping that he would answer their shouts. They soon found the Saint's hiding place, but he made signs to them not to betray him. But the children were so delighted at their discovery that they began to call all the louder to the waiting pilgrims. Then Father Seraphim rose from the grass with a joyous smile, and approached with love his guileless traitors who, being pure in heart, surrounded him without the least fear and began to caress him as another child of God. Then the grown-ups also drew near.

Sometimes the Saint would take children in his arms. "I came to Father Seraphim for the first time with my parents when I was still quite young," says Anastasia Protasova, a Diveyev Sister. "For the second time I came to him with my mother and a Diveyev Sister, Irene Prokopievna. He blessed us and

---

[74] Cp. Judith 4:8; Luke 18:16.

St. Seraphim of Sarov

told us to kiss the Icon of the Mother of God. And as I could not reach the Icon which stood on the table, he lifted me up and let me kiss the heavenly Queen."

During this visit the Saint predicted that she would be a Nun in Diveyev. When she was in her sixteenth year, Father Seraphim said openly to her: "The Mother of God chose you as a Nun when you were seven." When they brought her three-year-old brother Ivan to him, Father Seraphim took him from the arms of the nurse and, "giving him to me," says Protasova, "asked: 'Have you a garden?' I replied: 'Yes, we have.' Then he said: 'Well, mother, carry him in the garden and say all the time: Lord, have mercy! Lord, have mercy! Lord, have mercy! He will grow strong and will be our dearest treasure. And feed him yourself, out of your own hands.'"

Afterwards Anastasia became a Sister in the Diveyev Convent.

A certain Natalia Evgraphova related of herself: "When I was five, I was accidentally scalded with boiling water. Medical aid brought me no relief. My aunt, through whose carelessness I was suffering, turned in prayer to Father Seraphim. She brought me his Icon and taught me to call upon the good Elder for help myself. His Icon was hung at the head of my bed."

Then she fell asleep and saw herself in Sarov, and Father Seraphim said to her: "You will be well, baby." The pain stopped. The baby was then taken to the

Piety in the World

Monastery, and she saw there everything just as she had seen it in her vision. She was specially struck, even to tears, by the fact that Father Seraphim was exactly like the face she had seen in her dream.

"The Elder kindly turned to me," she relates further on, "and said: 'Oh, the baby has come to me too!' At the same time he took me in his arms, kissed my head and for a long time caressed me."

Later we shall see once again with what unusual tenderness the holy Elder met a twelve-year-old girl, a child ascetic, the future Nun of the great habit[75] Martha.

In conclusion I shall relate an incident which has been recorded by its little hero, J. M. Neverov. While still a boy, he came with his mother from he grandfather's estate, Veryakush, in the Ardatov district, to Sarov. They went to see Father Seraphim. They found him with a crowd of people. According to his custom, he was offering his visitors prosphora crumbs with red wine from a spoon. One young lady would not accept it and kept turning away. Then Father Seraphim said to her: "With your little finger, mother, with your little finger," meaning, take it from the spoon with your finger and put it in your mouth. The young lady began to laugh at these words. Then the boy also burst into an uncontrollable fit of laughter. The lady went out. Then the mother also took out her son and as a punishment left him without food. After some time

---

[75] Skhimnitsa Nun of the great habit.

St. Seraphim of Sarov

she took him to Father Seraphim's cell to ask for forgiveness. She herself remained behind the door. Having said the prayer,[76] the boy entered Father Seraphim's cell and saw him sitting in a coffin with a book in his hands.

"How are you, my friend, how are you? What do you want?" The Elder greeted him in an extremely friendly manner.

"Mother sent me to ask your forgiveness for having laughed at you a short time ago."

"Your mother sent you?" said Father Seraphim in the kindest tone but with a stress on the word "mother." "Well, thank your mother from me, my friend! Thank her from me for having taken the side of an old man. I shall pray for her. Thank her!"

"Realizing my inner guilt before the Elder, I allowed myself to say: 'No, it is not mother who sent me. I came myself.'

"'You came yourself, my friend? Well, thank you, thank you. God's blessing be with you!'

"At the same time he called me to his side, gave me his blessing and said: 'Repentance takes sin away; but here there was no sin. Christ be with you, my friend!'"

---

[76] By the prayers of our Holy Fathers, Lord Jesus Christ, our God, have mercy on us.

Piety in the World

Thereupon Father Seraphim told the forgiven sinner to sit on the single bench which stood near his coffin, and opening the Gospel which was in his hands, he began to read: *Judge not, that ye be not judged*, and so on from the seventh chapter of St. Matthew. The words of the Lord made a tremendous impression on the child for the whole of his life. Father Seraphim dismissed with love the involuntary culprit who went away chastened. And afterwards he always welcomed him affectionately whenever he visited him. Subsequently he was granted to be a witness of an extraordinarily touching scene, when the Elder partook of the Holy Mysteries in his cell. But this we have already mentioned.

"Even to this day," concludes the now grown-up Neverov, "when I approach the chalice and repeat after the Priest the words of the Communion prayer, I mentally see before me the majestic features of Father Seraphim with the chalice in his hands."

Father Seraphim told children to respect their parents, even if they had some infirmities. For instance, a boy came to him with his mother who suffered from the vice of intemperance. But as soon as he wanted to complain of her weakness, the Saint covered his mouth with his hand. Then he turned to the poor woman and said: "Open your mouth!"

When she opened it, Father Seraphim breathed three times on her. And dismissing her, he added:

St. Seraphim of Sarov

"This is my bequest to you. Never have in your house not only wine, but even wine bottles, for," he said turning to the mother, "you will not be able to bear wine any more."

On another occasion the following conversation took place.

"Once," says M. V. Nikashina who afterwards became a Diveyev Sister, "I came to Father Seraphim with my sister who had been married to a Priest, but had become a widow. The Elder blessed my sister and said to her : 'Your life, Mother, will be blessed until your very death.' My sister thereupon answered: 'I sin all the time quarrelling with my father because he has given up his job to my brother and lives with me all the time.'

"Father Seraphim replied: 'But with whom ought you to live, Mother, if not with your father?'

"'I have a son, Father, who is now finishing his studies, and I hope that he will support me.'

"'There is no hope for you whatever, mother, none whatever,' the Elder retorted.

"Actually, her son soon died, and she had to live with her father."

Father Seraphim gave instructions not only on the married life which concerns all lay people, but also on various kinds of service and activity.

Piety in the World

Let us give a few examples from different levels of society.

At Christmas 1830, Bogdanov, a high official, came to the Sarov Monastery and asked Father Seraphim: "Shall I go on working or shall I live in the country (on his estate)?"

"You are still young; work," replied the Elder.

"But my work is no good," replied the visitor.

"That depends on your will," explained Father Seraphim, "because it is possible to be saved in every kind of work, in every occupation."

In the life of the Saint there are many cases when army men applied to him for advice. And he never gave the slightest hint that it was a questionable calling. On the contrary, it was noticeable that he was particularly attentive and kind to them.

In October 1830, Ivan Yakovlevitch Karatayev drove past Sarov on his way from Kursk on business in connection with his regiment. Having heard many reports of St. Seraphim's holiness, he had an ardent desire to see him; but he was scared by a thought common to sinners. "It seemed to me," he said, "that the Elder would solemnly convict me of all my sins, especially of my error concerning the veneration of the holy Icons. I thought that an Icon painted by the hand of a man, perhaps even a sinful man, could not be pleasing to God."

St. Seraphim of Sarov

And so the timid officer drove past. But the following year in March he was again returning with his men through Sarov on his way to a war with Poland. This time he went to the Elder's cell with a joy that even he himself had not expected. He found the Saint with a crowd of people. Blessing the pilgrims, Father Seraphim glanced at the officer and called him into his cell.

"I obeyed his command with fear and love, prostrated at his feet and asked for his blessing on my journey and for the coming war, and that he should pray that my life should be spared. Father Seraphim blessed me with his copper cross which was hanging on his chest, and having kissed me, he began to confess me, telling me my sins himself, as if they had been committed in his presence. At the end of this comforting confession he said to me: 'You should not surrender to the fear which is sent to young men by the devil, but you should at that time be specially watchful in spirit and, rejecting cowardice, remember that though we are sinful, we are all in the grace of our Redeemer without Whose will not a single hair will fall from our head.'"

"After this he began to speak about my error with regard to the veneration of the holy Icons.

"'How bad and harmful for us is the wish to probe the mysteries of God, which are inaccessible to the human mind--for instance, how the grace of God works through the holy Icons, how it heals sinners like you and me,' he added, 'and not only their body, but their soul too, so that even sinners, according to their faith in the grace of Christ present in the Icons, were saved and attained the Kingdom of Heaven.'

"Then Father mentioned instances of the veneration of Icons: 'Even in the Old Covenant, by the Ark of the Covenant, there were golden Cherubim; and in the Church of the New Covenant the Evangelist Luke painted the face of the Mother of God; and the Saviour himself has left us His Icon not-made-with-hands.'

"At the end of the talk Father said: 'One must not pay attention to blasphemous thoughts of that kind for which eternal punishment awaits the spirit of the evil one and his accomplices on the day of the awful judgement.'"

On his departure the officer left three roubles on the table; but as he went out, he was disturbed by the diabolic thought: "Why should the holy Father want money?" The earthly soldier was still inexperienced in the spiritual warfare. But still he hurried back to the great Elder, and the latter met him with the words:

"During a war with the Gauls a chief was to be deprived of his right hand; but this hand had given a hermit three coins for a holy Temple. And by the prayers of Holy Church the Lord saved it. Think it over well, and in future do not regret your good deeds. Your money will go towards the establishment of the Diveyev community, and they will pray for your health."

St. Seraphim of Sarov

Then Father confessed him again and poured into his mouth some holy water, saying:

"May the evil spirit which is besetting the servant of God John, be driven away by the grace of God!"

On dismissing him, the Elder said: "Put your trust in God and ask for His help. And learn how to forgive your neighbour; and everything you ask for will be given you."

"During the Polish campaign," concludes Karatayev, "I took part in many battles, and the Lord always saved me through the prayers of His righteous servant. The soldiers who were returning with me to the regiment also received his blessing. He gave them some advice on this occasion and foretold that none of them would perish in battle. This actually came to pass; not a single one was even wounded."

Another army man, O. A. Lodyzhinsky, had four sisters, who wrote of him as follows:

"In 1832 our brother O. A. L. was sent to China. As his road lay through Nizhni Novgorod where we had a grandmother, who was Abbess of the Convent of the Holy Cross, he decided to stop at Nizhni in order to visit our grandmother and to meet us.

"During the last Turkish campaign he had been wounded in his left hand, and now the pain had returned and forced him to undergo treatment.

Piety in the World

"We urged him to come with us to the Sarov Monastery in order to see Father Seraphim and to receive his blessing on such a long and dangerous journey. Only after much persuasion did he finally accede to our request, for he did not fully believe in Father Seraphim's sanctity. Although he respected him, he was far from sharing our feelings for him, and he consented to go with us only to pacify us.

"On the eve of our departure we had a long talk with our brother about the holy Icons. He said that it was sheer superstition to call some Icons wonder-working, and that they were all alike.

"On our arrival[77] we all went to the early Liturgy at which Father Seraphim generally made his communion. When it was over, our brother went into the sanctuary to get Father Seraphim's blessing and at the same time convey messages from our grandmother (the Abbess) and Bishop Athanasius who was then in charge of the diocese of Nizhni Novgorod.

"When our brother came back to the hostel, we noticed a great change in him. His first word was an admission that Father Seraphim had worked a miracle on him.

"'While I was giving Father Seraphim the messages from grandmother and the Bishop,' he told us, 'he took my bad hand and pressed it so hard that only shame

---

[77] It was Sunday morning.

prevented me from shouting. But now I feel no pain in the hand whatever.'

"After refectory we all went to the forest, to Father Seraphim's hermitage. Seeing him from afar sitting opposite his spring, we suggested to our brother that he should go to him alone, while we waited at a distance and watched them.

"Our brother went and was received by Father Seraphim evidently very kindly, because he blessed him and seated him beside him, and they talked together for about half an hour. At last Father Seraphim raised his head and made a sign to us that we should go to him. While we were making our way to him, he rose from his place, and we found him with a spade in his hands, digging his garden.

"We received his blessing, and when our brother also went up to him, he said to him: 'Wait a moment, I shall come out to you immediately.'

"He went into his cell and at once came out with half a prosphora. Offering it to our brother, he said lovingly: 'For you, from my soul.' Then he added, as if with sorrow: 'We shall not meet again.'

"Our brother was touched and replied: 'No, Father, I shall come to you tomorrow.'

"But Father Seraphim repeated: 'We shall not meet again.'

Piety in the World

"Our brother retorted: 'Father! On my return journey I shall visit you.'

"But the Elder repeated for the third time: 'No, we shall not meet again.'

Having said good-bye to Father Seraphim we all went to the Monastery. My sisters were walking ahead, while I was a little behind them. Noticing a great change in my brother, I asked him the reason and he replied:

"'Now I am completely convinced of the holiness and spiritual insight of that amazing man. All that you said of him is true, and you did not exaggerate at all.' I asked my brother to tell me more in detail and he continued:

"'When I went up to him for his blessing and explained that I was on my way to China and therefore had come to Sarov specially to get his blessing and ask for his holy prayers for such a long journey, the Elder blessed me, and seating me beside him said:

"'What is my sinful blessing! Ask the Heavenly Queen for help. Here in our Cathedral there is an Icon of the Life-Giving Font. Have a Moleben.[78] It is a miraculous Icon. She will help you.'

"And he continued with a smile:

---

[78] A short service (a miniature matins) performed by a priest. (A service of Intercession to Our Lord, the Mother of God, or one of the Saints - ed.)

St. Seraphim of Sarov

"'Have you read the life of Joannikius the Great? I advise you to read it. He was an army man, a very kind and good man. He was a Christian too, for he believed in the Lord. But he erred in the matter of Icons just as you do.'

"At these words he pointed at me with his hand.

"'After this, Father Seraphim went on talking with me and giving me instructions. He said that I must be merciful myself if I wanted the Lord to be merciful to me. In conclusion he foretold that I should fulfill the mission entrusted to me and return safely.'

"My brother was now aflame with faith and love for Father Seraphim, so that we went at once to the Cathedral to serve a Moleben to the Heavenly Queen.

"After this he threw away all his medicines, for he no longer needed them. He felt healed in body and soul, and wrote us on the way that he had never felt so well in his life."

When he returned from China he wanted to visit Father Seraphim again, but the Saint was no longer in this world.

One of his most touching and edifying conversations was with General L. who had called at the Monastery out of curiosity. Having inspected the premises, he wanted to go, but he met A. N. Prokudin, a landowner, and had a talk with him. The latter advised him to visit the hermit without fail. The proud

Piety in the World

general consented with difficulty and went with his friend to the cell of the Elder. Father gave them an eager welcome and bowed to the ground before the general, to his great astonishment! Prokudin went out of the cell, and the general talked to the Elder for half and hour. When he came out later, Father was supporting him by the arm, and he was crying like a child. In his grief he had even forgotten in the cell his decorations and his cap. Father carried them out afterwards and gave them to the general.

Later he said that he had traveled all through Europe, but had never seen such humility in his life; he had never even suspected that there was such a thing as spiritual insight, and meanwhile the Elder had disclosed his whole life to him, and even intimate details. And when his decorations dropped from his chest, Father said to him: "That is because you received them undeservedly."

Once the manager of the estate of a landowner, who was at the same time his serf, came to him with his wife. They began to ask for Father's blessing to undertake a journey to Moscow for the purpose of seeing their master and asking him to free them or at least to release the manager from his difficult post. But Father Seraphim took him by the hand, led him towards the Icon of Our Lady of Compunction[79] and said: "I beg you for the sake of the Mother of God, do not give up your post. Your management is to the glory of God; you do not wrong the peasants. There is

---

[79] Or, Our Lady of Tenderness.

311

no opening for you in Moscow. Look, this is your way: I blessed a manager to ask for his freedom after his master's death. When that master died, his mistress gave him his freedom and put him in charge of everything on the estate except herself!"

The visitor carried out Father Seraphim's orders, and later on, everything that the Elder had apparently said about someone else, happened to himself.

Father Seraphim always ordered his visitors to show pity and consideration to their subordinates, especially to serfs.

"Are not some apparently lawful punishments repugnant to God?" he was asked by a certain Superior. "And how am I to preserve the morals of my subordinates?"

"By charity,[80] by making their work easier, and not by wounds," replied the gentle Elder. "Give them food and drink, be just! The Lord is tolerant (with you). You too forgive. Isaac, Abraham's son, did not get angry when his wells were stopped up, but went away." (Gen. 26:15).

These were hard times for the peasants, and it was necessary to insist repeatedly on the mercy of masters to slaves. But if some of the serfs left their masters of their own accord, the Saint did not connive with such. A young girl who wanted to run away from her mas-

---

[80] Or, almsgiving.

ters, put on the cassock of a Monk, cut off her hair, and in that get-up went roaming about the world. When she was discovered by the authorities, she put the blame on St. Seraphim in the hope that she would be pardoned out of respect for the holy Elder. He was subjected to cross-examination; it all proved to be untrue. Even the Elder was grieved at all this and did not leave his cell for a whole day, passing his time in prayer.

No calling is sufficient in itself to save a man. Once a peasant made a special effort to get to Father through the crowd, but it seemed as if some power was driving him back. At last, turning his attention to him, Father Seraphim suddenly asked him with a sternness quite unusual for him: "Where are you climbing to ?"

"Beads of perspiration stood out on the peasant's face," writes an eye-witness, "and in the presence of all who were there, he began to repent of his sins, especially of stealing, with a feeling of deep humility, confessing that he was not worthy to appear before the face of such a light."

Father always showed great severity with regard to stealing. When he gave directions to his Diveyev Sisters, he was generally very moderate and lenient in his regulations about prayer, eating, etc. But on the other hand, he required obedience and work and, moreover, he ordered that those who had succumbed to stealing should never be kept but should be sent out of the Convent immediately.

St. Seraphim of Sarov

"There is no one worse than a thief," he said to Xenia Vasilievna. "He is the cause of a multitude of sins. It is even better to keep a prodigal, Mother, for he ruins his own soul and answers for it himself. But a thief ruins everything, both himself and his neighbour, Mother."

Father rebuked not only the simple people, but the nobles too, if he saw that they could not be saved by gentleness.

Once a certain landowner stopped at Sarov on his way from the Crimea. During the Liturgy he prayed on his knees and with tears before an Icon of the Mother of God. Father was in the hermitage that day. The traveler was given a Novice of the Monastery to guide him to the Elder, but Father refused to receive him and said to the Novice:

"I beg you in the name of the Lord to avoid such people in future. This man is a hypocrite. He is a most miserable, lost soul."

There was nothing to be done. The guide told the man that the Elder had refused to see him, and on the way to the Monastery he gently explained the reason to the landowner. Then the man began to sob with utter sincerity and confessed to the Novice his wrong thoughts and intentions.

Archimandrite Nikon (Konobeyevsky) who was asked by Father during their talk on monasticism "whether he did not loathe marriage," recorded later a

Piety in the World

case in which Father Seraphim rebuked a high official.

On his arrival from Nizhni-Novgorod with his family, he went several times to the Saint's cell in order to receive his blessing. All the members of his family had already been granted a blessing; he alone was not admitted by the Elder. When this man knocked, Father Seraphim answered from inside:

"I am not at home, I have no time."

This was repeated five times. Then he asked Konobeyevsky, who was then a young seminarist, to take him to the Elder. They said the prayer, and at once Father opened the door and welcomed the official as if nothing had happened. Then he said to him:

"I said to you through the door what your servants say to those who come to you with their needs: 'The master is not at home!' 'He has no time!' By making your neighbour angry through your refusal, you anger God Himself."

The worldly general humbly accepted the rebuke, bowed down in the presence of the seminarist at Father's feet and promised never again in future to allow this lying practice which is so common among the rich but is such a temptation to poor callers.

Father Seraphim even sometimes refused money which was brought for the building of the Convent and of the Church, as "unclean and not pleasing to the

St. Seraphim of Sarov

Heavenly Queen." Once Sister Xenia Vasilievna came to him and without naming the giver, joyfully told him that they had received the promise that a Church would be built in Diveyev. But Father answered:

"Don't rejoice too much, and don't put much hope in benefactors. And who has promised you this, my joy?"

"Prokudin," answered Xenia.

"That man!" exclaimed Father Seraphim. "You can't take that money on any account, Mother, and you must refuse. He has already spoken to me and to Mishenka[81] about it, but I have not given my consent, Mother. Remember once for all, not every kind of money is pleasing to the Lord and to His most pure Mother. And not every kind of money will find its way into my Convent. And what if some people would be only too glad to give if we would only take it! But the Heavenly Queen will not accept every sort of money. See what kind of money it is! There is the money of injustice, tears and blood. We don't need that kind of money. We must not accept it, Mother!"

And so he refused the unjust landowner's offering.

Father Seraphim ordered all to work. A famous ascetic, Daniel of Atchinsk, had forbidden a certain pilgrim, Maria Ikonnikova, who lived in Tomsk, to wan-

---

[81] Michael Manturov.

Piety in the World

der idly about the world. He even angrily threatened her with his stick and said:

"Go and live in Tomsk. Live on your earnings from your handwork. Knit stockings. And when you get old, then collect alms. But mind, don't wander about Russia any more!"

At first she obeyed, but half-a-year later her relatives and friends prevailed on her to guide them to Kiev. She consented. On the way they visited Father Seraphim. Father looked at her severely and shouted loudly at her, as the ascetic of Atchinsk had done:

"Why are you wandering about Russia? Did not Brother Daniel forbid you to wander about Russia? Go back home at once!"

Maria began to ask for a blessing on her last pilgrimage, saying that she had not even the money for her way back. But Father Seraphim again shouted loudly:

"I have told you: go back! There is no blessing for you to go on. Go back, go back! Even without money you will drive all the way to Tomsk."

The pilgrim obeyed against her will. She left her companions, and went on foot to Nizhni. By the Providence of God and as a reward for her obedience, she found some Tomsk merchants and safely reached her town.

St. Seraphim of Sarov

Many other edifying incidents about laymen could be told here, but we have already devoted much space to them. However, this is easy to understand. Father had to deal mostly with laymen.

Father did not recommend people to invent special ascetic feats or even unusual things. A visitor asked Father Seraphim to interpret his dream for him.

"I saw someone who ordered me to build a Church," he said.

Father answered: "That is your own desire. But if God has chosen you for this purpose and there is need for it, then go ahead and God bless you."

We have already seen that Father did not approve of people who of their own accord became fools for Christ's sake. He once sent back to his family and to his trade such a would-be ascetic who had abandoned his trade without a blessing and had taken to wandering barefooted and laden with chains. "I think," Father Seraphim said to him, "that it is very good to trade in grain."

Another time he said: "There was hardly one among the fools for Christ's sake who was not in delusion. And so they were lost or went back. Our Fathers did not allow anyone to become a fool. In my time only one showed such a tendency and began to mew in Church like a cat. The Elder Pachomius ordered the fool to be taken instantly out of Church and be put out of the Monastery gates. There are three ways which

Piety in the World

require a special vocation: the way of a recluse, the way of a fool for Christ's sake and the way of a Superior."

We know of only two or three instances in the life of the Saint when he blessed people to undertake this kind of asceticism. These people were Pelagia Ivanovna Cerebrennikova (who will be mentioned later), Paraskeva Semionovna Melinkova, and one other Nun. Later on there lived in Diveyev a fool for Christ's sake who went by the name of "Pasha of Sarov." Her name in the world had been Irene and she was a serf of the landowner Bulygin of the Spask district. These were the only ones for a whole century, and even they lived in Convents. But, generally speaking, we must try to avoid singularity and live like everyone else, and must seek salvation in whatever walk of life we happen to be placed. And we have seen how many extraordinary laymen shone round Father Seraphim, like tiny stars round a big star. And everywhere the Elder preached humility, obedience and meekness, and especially love and compassion.

To those in Monasteries Father Seraphim advised, in accordance with the general teaching of the Fathers, obedience as a way to humility. And humility is the death of the passions. "Renounce your will and preserve humility throughout your life. Then you will be saved. Humility and obedience are the eradicators of all the passions and the planters of all the virtues" (Barsanufius the Great, Ans. 309 etc.). "As cloth which the dyer beats, tramples on, combs and washes, becomes white as snow, so a Novice who suffers humiliations, offenses, reproaches, is purified and becomes like pure, shining silver, refined in the fire" (Ant. hom. 113).

And though these words were addressed primarily to Novices, yet in a certain sense the Lord has made the world so that everyone has to submit to someone else, subordinates to their superiors, children to their parents, wives to their husbands, and so on. And everywhere one has to humble and break one's own will and subject it to the will of others. A mother has to humble herself even with her own children, so as not to be irritated, and not spare a punishment when it is necessary. And what patience, what sufferings are required throughout the education of her children, in their illnesses and the correction of their faults! Sometimes the outward circumstances of life are difficult and painful. Humility and patience are needed everywhere. At other times, the Lord sends us, even in the world, someone to break and crush our pride. Certainly no one in the world is abandoned by the Lord Who cares for the salvation of all; but there is no salvation without humility. And therefore we must watch attentively and ask ourselves: What is the Lord doing this very moment to humble me? And this lesson of God must be at once accepted, without waiting for another, without rejecting it, and without devising one's own seemingly better ways of salvation. The Lord surely knows best what is best for us, sinners, at a given moment. And what we plan ourselves is usually only the enemy's red herring to draw us away from the work of God.

But even if there are no directors and experienced Elders, a layman always has a helper at hand. Bogdanov, whom we have already mentioned, prepared a whole batch of questions for Father and asked him about spiritual direction:

"Can we trust ourselves to the direction of others?"

"Our Angel Guardian, given us at Holy Baptism is enough," replied Father Seraphim.

But at the same time he added a few words about counselors.

"If there is anger in a man, do not listen to him. If a man preserves virginity, he is acceptable to the Spirit of God (consequently, he is worthy of attention). However, use your own judgement, and read the Gospel."

And at the same time he gave him a whole series of simple instructions such as everyone knows:

"Do not forget the holidays. Be temperate. Go to Church, unless prevented by illness. Pray for all. You will do much good in that way. Give candles, wine and oil for the Church. Almsgiving will do you a lot of good.

St. Seraphim of Sarov

And so let not laymen despond! It was not in vain that the Saint gave them consoling names as "my joy," "my treasure," "father," "mother." And it was from the ranks of the secular clergy that he singled out a parish Priest, Father Alexis Gnyevashev, who lived in the village of Busurman, province of Simbirsk. Of him he said:

"This man, on account of his prayers for Christian souls, is like a candle burning before the throne of God. He is a toiler who, without making the monastic vows, stands higher than many ascetics."

Father Vasily Sadovsky, who was so closely associated with Father Seraphim, was also a married man. And yet how the Saint loved him! He always called his wife by the respectful Slavonic word *podruzhye* ("companion"), and he sent her some of the dry bread which was left over after his vision of the Mother of God (1830, after the Dormition). He foretold to both of them their death. His words were recorded by Father Vasily.

"Your 'companion' will depart to the Lord before you," Father Seraphim told me. "Two years after her you will go too, Father. Remember, twelve! And you will be the thirteenth, Father. And this is what I command you, when you die. You must lie on the right side of the altar in the Church of the Nativity, and Mishenka (Michael Manturov) will lie on the left. Give them orders to bury you there. How nice it will be, Father! You will be on the right, and Mishenka on the left, and I shall be between you in the middle. And so we shall all be together."

Chapel Built Over the Grave of St. Seraphim
Here the Saint's Relics remained until his Canonization in 1903.

323

St. Seraphim With Children
Aquarelle by Archimandrite Kyprian of Holy Trinity Monastery, Jordanville, New York.

Chapter XIV

The Joyful Director of Souls

Father Seraphim made such a fascinating and striking impression on everyone, that people left him delighted. Some went away sobbing, but almost all were comforted, cheered, gladdened, touched, uplifted, as if he had injected into each of them some vital force, new joy, fillip of spiritual effort, strength in virtue, desire for a new life. In brief, the flaming Seraphim kindled men with celestial fire and with the grace-given spirit of regeneration.[82] This is hard to realize. Only from the records of his dealings with men and from his remarkable influence can we have an inkling of the extraordinary power that was latent and at work in the poor "twisted" Elder. He especially knew how to cheer his visitors and give them joy. A meeting with Father was a true feast. People went away from him as on wings, or, on the contrary, unusually grave, subdued, but firmly resolved to fight evil.

What was the secret of St. Seraphim's spiritual power? It lay in his constant sense of the Resurrection and of the all-conquering paschal joy.

The Church sees Easter in Christ the Redeemer. Easter is in fact Christ Himself risen, glorified, ever abiding with the Church. *Christ our Passover has been sacrificed; therefore let us keep festival* (I Cor. 5:7). It is Easter that is the new factor in the New Testament. The new power *is the power of His Resurrection* (Phil. 3:10). By the power of the

---

[82] Cp. Luke 3:16; John 3: 3-8.

St. Seraphim of Sarov

Resurrection He was sanctified, and He departed glorifying it.

Usually St. Seraphim saluted his visitors with the Easter greeting. Kissing the people who came to him, he would say: "Christ is risen!" The joyful face of the ascetic who was exhausting himself with superhuman labours was a ray of heavenly sunshine. The light of his soul shone in his face, and men were led to glorify the Father in heaven (Mat. 5:14-16).

"For of the soul the body form doth take.
"For soul is form and doth the body make."

The Saint's perpetual Easter joy was the joy of *the victory that overcomes the world* (I Jn. 5:4), the eternal joy *which no man can take away* (Jn. 16:22).

Father Seraphim inspired men with the desire to be and do good. Therein lies the power of spiritual people. The Pharisees also spoke, but their words were dead, lifeless. Our Lord's teaching was *with authority* (Lk. 4:32). The Apostle Paul also says of himself: *My speech and my preaching were not in the plausible phraseology of human wisdom, but in the demonstration of the Spirit and power* of God (I Cor. 2:4).

We shall now try to convey a little more of the gladdening and joyous spirit which manifested itself in the instructions of Father Seraphim and in his dealings with laymen.

The Joyful Director of Souls

"Once," relates Father Paul, St. Seraphim's cell-neighbour, "I brought to Father Seraphim a young peasant with a bridle in his hand who was crying over the loss of his horses, and I left them alone. After some time I met that peasant again and asked him: 'Well, have you found your horses?' 'Of course, I have, Father,' answered the peasant. 'Where and when?' I asked him again. And he replied: 'Father Seraphim told me to go to the market-place, and there I would see them. So I went, and I saw them at once, and took home my little horses.'"

This seems a trifling incident, but for the peasant his horses were his whole fortune and their loss would have meant ruin and bitter poverty. And all of a sudden such joy! As St. Seraphim had foretold, the "little horses" (as their master affectionately called them) were found. It is easy to understand that the young peasant will be drawn more than once to Father Seraphim and Sarov, and in his old age may end his life in the Monastery. And what joy for all his family! The "little horses" were found! What bitter tears must have been shed by his wife and children, if the peasant himself was crying in the Monastery with the bridle in his hands.

Here is another incident. Prince N. N. Golitsyn came to Sarov on his way from Moscow to Penza. The Elder was in his hermitage. The prince hastened there. On the way he met Father and asked his blessing.

"Who are you?" Father Seraphim asked affably.

St. Seraphim of Sarov

The prince modestly called himself a traveler.

The Elder embraced him with brotherly love, kissed him and said: "Christ is risen!" Then he asked him: "Do you read the Holy Gospel?" The prince replied: "Yes, I do." "Read more often," said the Elder, "the following words in that Divine Book: *Come to Me all you who labour and are heavy laden, and I will give you rest. Take My yoke upon you, and learn from Me, for I am meek and humble in heart, and you shall find rest for your souls. For My yoke is easy, and My burden is light*" (Mat. 11: 28-30).

So saying, the Elder again embraced the prince with tears. On the way he continued talking to him of the future life and of various trials which were going to befall him, all of which actually happened. On reaching the Monastery the Elder invited the prince to his cell, gave him some holy water to drink and offered him a handful of dry bread. On bidding him farewell, he asked the traveler whether he intended to remain long in the Monastery. The latter replied that he proposed to go in the morning after the early Liturgy.

Then Father Seraphim said "with inexpressible love" (to use the prince's own words), that he had become fond of him and wanted to see him again on the following day after the early Liturgy, and that for this reason and for his sake he would not go to the hermitage next day, but would remain in the Monastery. On the following day the Elder came out to meet him on the balcony leading to his cell. He blessed him and,

The Joyful Director of Souls

embracing him, led him into his cell. There he again gave him some holy water to drink, presented him with some dry bread and blessed him on his journey. He again advised him to read frequently the above-mentioned words of the Gospel and also the Creed, in which he asked him to direct his attention especially towards the twelfth article.[83] Unfortunately the other conversations of the Elder and the prince have remained unknown, but they were of great comfort to the prince and brought much benefit to his soul.

Peace, comfort, consolation, affability, love, attention, a tearful kiss and the greeting "Christ is risen!"--the whole visit had been a sheer joy. Moreover, a rule had been given him for his whole life--to seek consolation in sorrows (which the Saint already foresaw) in Christ and Christlike humility. *I will give you rest* (Mat. 11:28).

We have already mentioned Anna Petrovna Eropkina. As she had lost both her parents in childhood, she lived with her uncle who was a true father to her. He had just decided to marry her for her own good when she met a young man whom she fell in love with, as she found in him a kindred soul. She was then seventeen. In her uncle's house she occupied a room with his two daughters and a young lady who was their guest. One evening they had a lively talk about her happy future.

---

[83] "The life of the age to come."

St. Seraphim of Sarov

"When we all went to bed," she says, "I do not know about the others, but I could not sleep for a long time and remained half awake. All of a sudden in a light doze I saw my uncle entering our bedroom with an unknown old man. Vividly conscious of decency, I at once tried to pull the blanket over me. But from under it I heard them come up to my bed, and then uncle said: 'See, she's asleep,' But the elder replied: 'It is useless for her to get married. Her husband will not live more than two or three months at the most. How hard it will be for her to change from an orphan into a widow! It is like jumping out of the frying-pan into the fire.' After these words all grew still in the room, no one and nothing could be heard. But I was afraid to uncover myself. Having received the fatal news of my brief married life, I wept bitterly under the blanket and fervently prayed to God to have mercy on me. But I did not remain long in this state. The violent agitation of my soul soon woke me up, and when I regained full consciousness, I made the Sign of the Cross while the tears poured down my face in streams. It was hard for me after that to wait for the morning. The hours seemed ages, and my soul was suffering cruelly. God alone knows what I then experienced. When dawn came, the dear friends of my childhood, not knowing my sorrow, greeted me with happy jokes, but my face was pale and the words died on my lips. I was at a loss to know how to answer them, but their kindliness and curiosity forced me to tell them the secret of my heart. Through them it became known at once to everybody in the house. Whether they considered my words to be true,

The Joyful Director of Souls

whether they thought in their hearts that the words of the old man might come true I do not know. I only remember that everyone tried to undeceive me and to interpret my dream as a mere fancy, a trick of the imagination.

"At first I used to argue with them a lot, but they in turn tried in every way to refute my words, and they soon won me over completely. I was even ready to laugh at my own credulity, though I had to repent bitterly afterwards; but then it was too late.

"Everyone was looking forward to my marriage with impatience, for it was to take place exactly three weeks after this incident, namely on the 8th of February 1829. And I, unhappy creature, did not know then that the words of the old man whom I had seen in my dream were holy and prophetic, and would be realized without fail--that in three months I would lose my husband and would bury with him in the grave all my earthly happiness.

"The marriage ceremony was magnificent. Crowds of people gathered for the occasion, and no one thought, as they saw my husband and me looking the picture of youth and health, that our joy would shortly vanish for ever. After the ceremony there was no end to the kindliest greetings, and we passed from one family gathering to another unceasingly. But after a few weeks my husband began to feel a change in his health and, gradually losing his strength, he finally took to his bed. We called in the most experienced doctors, we tended him ourselves with the greatest

St. Seraphim of Sarov

care, but he got no better. On the contrary, he seemed to waste away from day to day. Though I was very young, it became clear to me that he had but a few days to live. But I tried to hide from him my gloomy thoughts and to soothe him in every way. He did the same with me, especially when he saw me looking particularly sad. He even assured me that he was getting better and said that his youth and strong constitution would carry him through this illness and that he would get well. We allowed ourselves to be carried away by our tender feelings towards one another, and lacking the direction of experienced people, we were ourselves the cause of a misfortune which I consider worse than bodily death itself. I did not suggest that he should receive the Holy Sacraments for fear of frightening him by the sad news of his approaching end. And although he was also very religious, he was probably afraid to scare me by asking me to send for a Priest to administer the last Sacraments. On the day after the Feast of St. Nikolas, i.e. the 10th of May, when all nature revives and all rejoice, I was suddenly struck with a terrible sorrow--I was separated from my husband. At first I could not even believe my eyes and was quite out of my mind. But when I realized what had happened, I either lost consciousness, or was immersed in an abyss of most dreadful thoughts. Deploring my premature widowhood and the loss of my husband's soul, I was almost ready in my folly to curse the hour when I had met him for the first time in my life and when I had become attached to him.

The Joyful Director of Souls

"To die without the last Sacraments seemed to me a special punishment of God for my sins and those of my husband. I thought that my husband would be for ever alienated from the life of God. I hardly remember how my husband's body was committed to the earth. After the burial my relatives and friends did not know what to do with me, how to comfort and soothe me, for I was in despair and would have perhaps committed suicide if I had not been strictly watched.

"I do not know how and from whom my uncle heard of the ascetic life and spiritual gifts of Father Seraphim, an elder of Sarov. My uncle was so firmly convinced of the holiness of the wonderful ascetic that he considered my going to Sarov to ask for the prayers and advice of the holy Elder Seraphim as the only means of obtaining deliverance from my sorrow. He did not even take into consideration that the Sarov Monastery was at a distance of five hundred versts[84] from our place. Moreover, owing to the Spring season, I might have great difficulties on my way back owing to the flooded roads. When he told me his conviction about Father Seraphim and advised me to go to him, I accepted his offer gladly.

"On our arrival in Sarov we put up at the hostel and I was burning with impatience to learn where Father Seraphim was, whether in the Monastery or in retirement at his hermitage. Fortunately I was told that he was then in the Monastery and that I might go

---

[84] 1 verst = 3,500 ft. or almost 2/3 of and English mile.

St. Seraphim of Sarov

to him. Hurriedly entering the Monastery I was struck
by an extraordinary sight.

"Between the Cathedral of the Dormition and the
one-storied building opposite, compact masses of
people were moving like waves. From my inquiries I
learned that Father Seraphim lived in this very building. I mixed with the crowd of people of all sexes,
ages and positions and made my way through it towards the porch where everyone else was pressing. I
squeezed myself with great difficulty into the ante-
room, and through the open door got into Father
Seraphim's cell. The room was simply packed with
people. I tried to approach him like the others, and
reached out my hand for his blessing though I had not
yet been able to see his face properly. Giving me his
blessing and some biscuits, he said: 'The servant of
God Anna partakes of the grace of God.'

"What was my surprise when I heard my name in a
unknown place! And looking straight into Father
Seraphim's face, I recognized in him the very Elder
who had warned me as a father from an unhappy marriage. This meeting showed me instantly how close he
was to God. But one could not stop for a minute near
him, because the people who were following me
pushed me aside to receive his blessing too and hear a
few words from him.

"I was crowded out into the anteroom and, feeling
with my feet a few logs near the wall, I clambered on
to them and began to look fixedly at Father Seraphim
through the door. His angelic face, the meekness he

The Joyful Director of Souls

showed in his dealings with all, singled him out as an extraordinary man. I did not take my eyes off him for a single minute. Following all his movements, I soon noticed that he apparently wanted to end the reception, because he began to send away everyone out of the room, saying meekly: 'Go in peace.'

"At the same time he moved nearer to the open door near which I stood. Seizing the door-handle with one hand, with the other he quite unexpectedly led me into his cell, and without asking me anything, he at once began to speak to me. 'Well, my treasure, why have you come to me, poor Seraphim? I know, your sorrow is very great. The Lord will help you to bear it.' After these and other comforting words he told me to prepare myself to confess with Father Hilaron and to receive Holy Communion.

"All this I did. As regards my deceased husband, when I was thinking whether he would be deprived of the heavenly Kingdom because he had neither confessed nor partaken of the Holy Mysteries, Father Seraphim said: 'Do not be distressed about it, my joy. Do not think that just for that his soul will be lost. Only God can judge who and how to reward or punish. It sometimes happens that here on earth people receive Communion while with the Lord they remain uncommunicated; and another person wants to receive Communion, but for some reason his wish remains unfulfilled quite independently of himself. Such a person is granted Communion in an invisible manner through an Angel of God.'

St. Seraphim of Sarov

"In order to drive away from me all gloomy thoughts connected with the memory of my husband and save me from despondency and despair, Father Seraphim commanded me on my return home for forty days to go without fail to my husband's tomb and say: 'Bless me, my lord and father! Forgive me in so far as I have sinned against you, and the Lord God will also forgive and release you.' He also told me to take for forty days the ashes from the censer which would be left over from the Services performed in the Temple of God, and then, having dug a hole about one foot deep in the grave, to pour the ashes into it and say three times 'Our Father,' the Prayer of Jesus, 'Virgin Mother of God,' and once the Creed.

"After Holy Communion, however pleasant it was for me to undergo spiritual treatment and to enjoy the Elder's favour I had to hasten home. The roads would soon be impracticable and my uncle's estate, as I have already said, was five hundred versts from Sarov. I told the Elder of my intention to go home and of my fear that the roads would be flooded. But he said to me: 'Fear nothing, my joy, and God will prepare the way for you. The snow will be a foot deep, and you will go back better than you came here. But be here again for the Fast of Sts. Peter and Paul.'

"After this it was as if I had been completely reborn. Such quiet settled in my soul as I had never felt since my husband's death. It was just as if I had been relieved of a heavy burden. I began to feel pleasure again in the circle of my family and in society. At home I found a suitable occupation and did not get

The Joyful Director of Souls

tired of it. Whenever it was possible, I went to Church or to my husband's grave which no longer made the dreadful impression it did before. I did not torture myself over it and I was no longer a cause of alarm to others.

"In this way I spent two months in the country after my arrival from Sarov. The Fast of Peter and Paul came round, and I went to Father Seraphim again according to his appointment. My journey was a joyful one this time. It seemed as if I was going to my own father.

"On my arrival at the Monastery, without losing a minute, I dashed like a deer into the forest to him, having learned that he was in his hermitage. I ran and found a crowd of people there and asked someone: 'Where is Father Seraphim?' They pointed towards the river and said: 'There he is.' Only by straining my sight could I make out that he was moving about in the water, taking out a big stone and carrying it to the shore. In a minute I had threaded my way through the crowd to him, and as soon as he saw me he greeted me with a joyful countenance: 'Well, my treasure, have you come? The Lord bless you! Be our guest for a time.' Soon he began to send me and all the people to the Monastery, telling us to make haste; but no one wanted to leave him. All wished to feast their eyes on him and to hear something for the good of their soul. Moreover, the day was fine, the weather clear, there was plenty of time till evening; so our common sense supplied us with many reasons for staying a little

St. Seraphim of Sarov

longer with him. But the consequences soon showed us that we ought to have obeyed the Elder at once.

"Having delayed rather long in the forest, when we started in a long, unbroken line towards our night quarters in the hostels of the Monastery, we were overtaken by a dreadful cloud. Loud peals of thunder and flashes of lightning frightened us out of our wits, and we were all soaked to the skin by the heavy rain.

"On the following day, when I went to Father Seraphim, he received me very kindly and said to me with an angelic smile: 'Well, my treasure, what a downpour it was! What a storm! You would not have been caught in it if you had obeyed me. You can't say that I did not send you away in good time.'

"On this occasion as well as afterwards Father Seraphim talked to me on various subjects, for with his blessing I stayed eight days at Sarov, and he received me every day, except on Friday. On that day he remained in silence, and one must suppose that he was completely immersed in meditation on the passion of our Redeemer.

"Having spent just over a week in Sarov, I went home with Father Seraphim's blessing. It was sad to leave that sanctuary where I had received so many useful lessons for my life, where I had been face to face with the blessed Elder Seraphim who was truly a model of Christian asceticism. My separation from him was all the sadder because I had a kind of foreboding that I would never see him again; and to my

The Joyful Director of Souls

sorrow, this proved true. How much he helped me from beyond the grave, of this I dare not speak, but I believe that by his holy prayers I have been granted a longer time for repentance."

Here is another comforting case. A mother lost her only son who had disappeared, no one knew how or where. One can imagine her inconsolable grief. She went to Sarov with a broken heart, fell down at Father Seraphim's feet and asked his prayers for her lost son. The Elder comforted her, cheered her, revived her hope and, to her surprise, told her to wait for her son at the Monastery hostel. Incredible as the consolation seemed to be, yet the unhappy mother obeyed him, clinging to the Saint's word as a drowning man clutches a straw. A day passed, then another, then a third, and still there was no son. Sadly she went to Father Seraphim to get his blessing and return home with the same stone on her soul. Imagine her surprise when, just as she was going from the hostel to Father, her son also came to him for his blessing. Father Seraphim took him by the hand, led him towards his mother and congratulated them on their happy reunion.

There is no end to the stories of how he consoled his orphans. Let us take two or three examples.

"When I came to Father Seraphim," says the old Nun Agathia Gregorievna, "I was thinking in my troubled state of mind that after death there would be no reward for anybody. Father was in his cell, in the anteroom. He put his head on my sinful shoulder and

St. Seraphim of Sarov

said: 'Don't be despondent, don't be despondent, Mother! In the Heavenly Kingdom we shall rejoice together.'

"And he added: 'Mind, Mother, always have mental prayer with you.'

"And sinner that I am, I had succumbed to despondency.

"'Do not listen, Mother,' he said, 'to where your thoughts send you, but pray like this, Mother: *Lord, remember me when Thou comest in Thy Kingdom*, and repeat it from beginning to end with the Beatitudes. Then say, *O all-hymned Mother*. Then: Remember, Lord, our Father Hieromonk Seraphim (and mention your own name too). In this way, Mother, the Lord will forgive my sins and yours as well. And so we shall be saved!'"

He also told lay people to invoke him in their prayers in moments of despondency, affliction and melancholy, or during an attack of the invisible foes. Once a young peasant woman, Alexandra Lebedeva of the village of Elizarievo (Ardatov district), succumbed to a mysterious illness. Here is an account of her case as stated by her husband.

"On the 6th April 1826 which was a holiday, my wife Alexandra returned from the Liturgy, had dinner and then went out with me for a short stroll beyond the gates of our house. All of a sudden, God knows why, she became faint and dizzy, so that I could

The Joyful Director of Souls

hardly lead her back to the hall. There she fell on the floor; she began to vomit and had frightful convulsions in all her limbs. Finally, she fell into a deathly stupor. She remained in this awful state for about half-an-hour. Then she partly regained consciousness, but began to gnash her teeth and gnaw at everything that she could lay her hands on. Then she fell asleep.

"On the following day she felt better and in reply to her mother's question as to what had happened to her the day before, she said that their house had collapsed over her, as it seemed to her, and even now everything had assumed a terrifying appearance. Two days later she had another fit of the same kind. Then it came on again a month later. Then for a whole year these fits were a daily occurrence, so that everyone regarded her as possessed.

"At first, at the request of the land-steward, she was treated by the district practitioner, but when all his efforts proved fruitless, another doctor was summoned from Ardatov; but this one too, after three weeks of careful treatment, refused to proceed with the case, said that he had never seen such an illness and that there was something strange about it.

"Finally, owing to the efforts of the land-steward who took a genuine interest in the patient, another doctor was summoned from the Vyksoonsky factory; but this one too, after examining the patient, said decisively that her illness was incomprehensible and that the evil spirit was certainly at his tricks in this case, but that he could not take it upon himself to drive him out. In his opinion, it was useless to torture the patient by trying to cure her with human means, but that it was better to have recourse to the help of God. In spite of this advice, we still tried to help her with simple remedies; but they were all useless. The patient was at the point of death.

"At the beginning of the second year from the day when her sufferings had increased, on the 20th May 1827, the sufferer suddenly saw at night a stranger enter her room. It was an old woman of middle stature, dry, with fair, short hair and a round face, with closed eyes, bare feet and all powdered with dust. She said to her: 'Why are you lying in bed and not looking for a doctor?' Frightened by this strange apparition, the sick woman protected herself with the Sign of the Cross and began to say the prayer: *Let God arise, and let His enemies be scattered.*

"Then the unknown woman said to her: 'Don't be afraid of me. I desire your well-being and health. I love this prayer and rejoice when anyone says it.' The sick woman asked her: 'But who are you? Aren't you from the other world? And haven't you seen my boy there?' The unknown woman replied: 'I have. He is angry with you. But there is no need to talk of him; we must think of you. Why don't you try to get healed?' The sick woman replied: 'I have had many doctors, but not one of them could help me.' The stranger said: 'I shall find you a true physician who has wanted to heal you for a long time. He specially asked me to go to you. Go as quickly as you can to

The Joyful Director of Souls

Sarov to Father Seraphim. He can help you.' After this the vision vanished.

"The sick woman decided to wake up her mother, but the latter was not asleep and had heard all her daughter's conversation with the unknown woman. When all was still again, and the daughter turned to her mother, the mother asked her who she had been talking to. The daughter replied: 'Oh, Mother, I had such a fright! Didn't you see the woman who told me to go to Father Seraphim and said that he would help me?' The mother coldly replied: 'Yes, when you are better, then you may go.' And soon after she fell asleep.

"Meanwhile my wife saw again, on the night of the 11th June 1827, the same unknown woman who reminded her reproachfully that she should not delay, but should make haste, as Father Seraphim was waiting for her and was expecting her to come soon. Then the sick woman took courage and asked her who she was and where she came from. The woman replied: 'I am from the Diveyev Convent, their first Abbess, Agathia. But go quickly, don't dawdle.' So saying, she disappeared again.

"The sick woman at once woke up her mother and earnestly begged her to ask the land-steward for a cart for a journey to Sarov. The mother consented, and though it was early dawn, she went at once to the land-steward, told him the reason of her early visit and asked him for a cart to convey her sick daughter to Father Seraphim. The land-steward immediately

complied with her request and told her that he had
seen Father Seraphim himself that very night in a
dream, and that he was attending to a sick woman and
was holding the cross which he wore on his chest over
her, and that after that the sick woman had gone away
completely healed.

"And so the mother went to Sarov with her sick
daughter, and when they entered the Sarov forest, the
sick woman, who had lost her hearing through her illness, heard for the first time the ringing of the bells of
Sarov and to her mother's surprise and joy said:
'Listen, they are ringing for the Liturgy!'

"They arrived in the Monastery at dinner time and
found the Brothers in the refectory. They were told
that Father Seraphim had shut himself in his cell and
was receiving no one. Meanwhile there was such a
crowd of people near his cell that it was impossible to
reach it. The mother with her sick daughter applied to
a Monk of Sarov and earnestly begged him to get
them through to Father Seraphim. The good Monk led
them through the crowd and, leaving them in the ante-
room, went to the Elder to tell him about them. But
Father Seraphim forestalled him.

"The Monk had hardly said the customary prayer at
the entrance, when the Elder came out to him and
said: 'Bring the suffering Alexandra in quickly.'
Astonished at such spiritual insight the Monk returned
to the two clients, told them to go and at the mother's
request helped to lead the patient himself.

The Joyful Director of Souls

"As soon as they had entered Father Seraphim's cell, the sick woman tore herself from their hands with extraordinary force and instantly threw herself at Father Seraphim's feet. Then the Elder covered her with his epitrachelion[85] and said a prayer over her. After that, he took her by the head with both his hands and lifted her up a little. At that moment the sick woman was aware of a kind of noise as if someone had stripped her fur coat off her, and she felt as if she had been poisoned by charcoal fumes.

"Then Father Serpahim gave her some holy water and antidoron, told her to kiss the cross which was hanging on his chest and the Icon of the Mother of God which stood on his table, and said: 'There is your Mediatress! She interceded for you before God!'

"Having obtained in this way a complete cure, and fully realizing the greatness of the favour shown her by Father Seraphim, the patient was extremely sorry that she had nothing at the time with which to reward her benefactor. But he read her thoughts and said: 'I need nothing from you. Only pray to God. But if you have a desire to give me something, spin some threads for me on three Wednesdays and twist them on three Fridays, abstaining during these six days from food, drink and conversation. And at the beginning of every action say three times the Lord's Prayer and pray to the Mother of God unceasingly during those six days.' And he added: 'Go to Diveyev to the grave of the servant of God Agathia. Take some earth for yourself

---

[85] Or, stole.

345

and make as many prostrations as you can on that spot. She is sorry for you and wants you to be healed. And when you are sad, pray to God and say: Father Seraphim! Remember me in your prayers and pray for me a sinner, so that I may not fall again into that disease from the adversary and enemy of God.' Then he blessed them and sent them home in peace. This cure took place on the 11th June 1827."

The woman was completely healed and subsequently bore four sons and five daughters besides the two children she already had. They always remembered Father in their prayers.

He also used to say to Captain Teplov: "When you are in trouble, come to poor Seraphim's cell. He will pray for you." This was efficacious even during his life-time, and is still more so now after his death owing to his intercession before the throne of God.

During his talks with his orphans he gave them among other things just the advice against despondency which we find in the writings of other holy Fathers, namely, to offer to a person in sorrow some nice dish to eat. But what nice dishes could there be in poor Diveyev? Instead of that, Father told the Sisters to eat their fill of such food as there was, and even to take some bread with them when they went to their work.

"Put a little bit into your pocket," he said to Xenia Vasilievna. "When you are tired or exhausted, do not

The Joyful Director of Souls

despond, but eat your bread; and then get to work again!"

He even told them to put some bread for the night under their pillow. "When you feel worried or despondent, Mother, take out your bread and eat it. And the despondency will pass, the bread will drive it away, and it will give you a good sleep after your labours, Mother."

And when later the strict cook began to refuse to give bread to the Sisters, referring to an order of the Superior, Father called her, gave her a sharp rebuke and even added: "Let the Abbess talk (of economy), but you should give on the quiet and not lock it up. And thereby you would be saved!"

Here is a still more touching incident which even perhaps seems unbecoming in a Monk. But Father Seraphim foresaw the future and at the same time he wanted to cheer his despondent Sisters.

"Once I came to Father with Aquilina Vasilievna," says Barbara Ilinitchna, an old Nun. "He spoke to her alone for a long time and was doing all he could to persuade her, but evidently she did not want to obey him. He came out and said: 'Take out of my ark (so he called his coffin) some dry bread.' He gave a big bundle to Aquilina, and another one to me. Then he filled a whole sack with dry bread and began to beat it with a stick. This made us roar with laughter. Father glanced at us, and then beat it all the harder. We could make nothing of it. Then he tied the sack, hung it round Aquilina's neck and told us to go to the Convent. We understood it afterwards, when Sister Aquilina Vasilievna left the Convent and had to suffer terrible beatings in the world. She came back to us later and died in Diveyev."

Later Barbara Ilinitchna was slandered and the Superior of Mother Alexandra's community, Xenia Mikhailovna, put her out of her Convent.

"I cried and cried, and then I went to Father Seraphim and told him everything. I even cried while I knelt before him. But he just laughed and clapped his hands. Then he began to pray and told me to go to his Sisters in the mill, to their Superior Paraskeva Stepanovna. And she let me stay in her Convent according to his blessing."

It was this Sister who once saw flies sitting on Father's face and the blood running in streams down his face. She wanted to drive them off, but Father forbade her: "Don't touch them, my joy," he said. "*Let every breath praise the Lord* (Ps. 150:6)."

In the face of such patience our troubles are bound to appear trifling. And how many similar incidents there were! But is it not comforting for laymen to know that their earthly calling, whatever it may be, leads them to salvation, if only they bear it with faith, humility and patience, in the name of Christ, and carry it out as a commandment of God? Every work, every labour is spiritualised in this way. Then, the whole of a man's life is changed into an unceasing

The Joyful Director of Souls

labour of salvation. And we have seen how Father loved his worldly collaborators and confidants.

And so, however simple Father Seraphim's advice and instructions to laymen may seem to us, yet those who fulfill them as the "commandments of God" according to the words of the Apostle Paul, may be granted the gifts of the Lord which follow them, from the heavenly joy of the Holy Spirit, to the actual manifestation of Christ the Saviour to them. These are wonderful words, but they were uttered by the Son of God Himself: *I will not leave you orphans; I will come to you. Yet a little while, and the world will see Me no more; but you will see Me , because I live, and you will live. In that day you will know that I am in My Father, and you in Me, and I in you. He who has My commandments and keeps them, he it is who loves Me; and he who loves Me will be loved by My Father, and I will love him, and will manifest Myself to him* (Jn. 14:18-21).

This thought is developed in the Saint's wonderful conversation with the layman Motovilov. And we are at once reminded of our Lord's further words: *These things I have spoken to you, that My joy may be in you, and that your joy may be full* (Jn. 15:11). Saint Seraphim simply radiated joy. Often it even streamed from him quite visibly like some extraordinary light which sent into ecstasy those who were granted this vision. And there were many witnesses--his closest confidants, Eropkina, Aksakova, Meliukov, Tikhonov as well as many of his Nuns.

St. Seraphim of Sarov

What else shall we mention of his instructions to laymen? Of course, it is easy to write all this and it is still easier to speak of another's salvation. But in reality everyone knows, be he Monk or layman, that it is difficult to obtain salvation, that everyone must bear his cross all his life. And the man of God often reminded people of it, and only tried to lighten their burden.

Once a professor of a seminary, accompanied by a Priest, came to him and wanted to receive his blessing to become a Monk. But Father kept talking to the Priest and did not pay the least attention to the learned theologian. Then he asked casually: "Has he anything else to learn to complete his studies?"

The Priest explained that the professor knew well the different branches of the science of theology.

"I know that he is skilled in composing sermons. But teaching others is as easy as throwing stones from the top of our Cathedral, but to put into practice what you teach is like carrying the stones yourself to the top of the Cathedral. That is the difference between teaching others and doing things oneself."

In conclusion he advised the professor to read the life of the holy and learned John Damascene, where it is told among other things, how this great theologian had been forbidden by his director to compose sacred hymns as a mortification. And when, out of compassion for the brother of a deceased Monk, he composed funeral songs, the Elder wanted at first to expel him

The Joyful Director of Souls

from the Monastery. Then at the request of the Monks he consented to let him stay, but he ordered the theologian who had been found guilty of disobedience to clean the lavatories. And only after this humiliation and a special vision of the Mother of God to the Elder, were the lips of the Church hymn writer unsealed.

Yes, salvation is not easily given. And the Sarov ascetic knew it himself out of his own vast experience better than anyone. That is why he warned earthly pilgrims that they would certainly meet with afflictions on their way.

"According to the Saviour's word," he said to Captain Karatayev, "we must enter by the narrow way into the Kingdom of God" (Cp. Mat. 7:13-14).

"All the Saints had temptations," he said, "but like gold which, the longer it remains in the fire, the purer it becomes, so the Saints grew more skillful through temptation. By their patience they propitiated the Creator's justice and drew near to Christ in Whose name and for Whose love they suffered."

Occasionally he would refer to himself in order to convince and comfort sufferers. The husband of a woman became seriously ill. As he had a great regard for the man of God, he sent his wife to Sarov. The Saint was not receiving anyone, but seeing in spirit human sorrow, he suddenly opened the door and at once turned to the anxious woman.

St. Seraphim of Sarov

"Daughter Agrippina," he said, "come to me quickly, because you must hurry home."

Then taking her hand, he put it on his shoulder, where she felt a big cross.

"There, my daughter," said the Elder, "at first it was very heavy to carry this, but now it is very pleasant. Make haste now and remember my burden. Good-bye!"

Her husband was still alive, he took some of the wine, antidoron and holy water which Father Seraphim had sent him, blessed his children and peacefully departed to the Lord.

But at the same time the Saint always exhorted all not to despond. He reminded people of the words of the Lord Himself Who says that though the fulfillment of His commandments is a burden, yet this burden is light (Cp. Mat. 11:30). But Father Seraphim especially comforted the afflicted by the expectation of future happiness for those who were worthy of it. To a young widow, A.P. Eropkina, he spoke with extraordinary enthusiasm of the Kingdom of Heaven.

"I cannot now transmit exactly either all his words or the impression which he made on me at the time," she writes in her last reminiscences. "The appearance of his face was quite extraordinary. Through his skin shone a supernatural light. I cannot remember everything, but I know that he was speaking to me of the three holy Prelates--Basil the Great, Gregory the

The Joyful Director of Souls

Theologian and John Chrysostom--and of the glory in which they dwell there. He described vividly and in detail the beauty and glory of St. Fevronia and many other martyrs. In all my life I had never heard such vivid narratives. But it seemed as if he could not tell me everything then, and he added in conclusion: 'Oh, my joy! There is such bliss there that it is impossible to describe it.'"

Once he was asked: "Can a person who has been in a state of grace rise again through repentance after a fall?"

"Yes, he can," he replied, "according to the word: *I was thrust and fell, but the Lord helped me* (Ps. 117:13). When the holy Prophet Nathan rebuked David for his sin, he repented and at once received forgiveness (II Kings 12:13). When we sincerely repent of our sins and turn to our Lord Jesus Christ with all our heart, He rejoices over us, makes a feast, and calls together His beloved Powers (Angels), and shows them the drachma which He has found again, that is His royal image and likeness. Laying the lost sheep on His shoulders, He brings it to His Father. In the mansion of all who rejoice, God establishes the soul of the repentant sinner with those who never ran away from Him."

When he wanted to encourage desponding sinners, Father Seraphim used, among other things, to quote an ancient episode related in the "Prologue." A hermit set out to fetch water and on his way fell into sin. As he was returning to his Monastery, the enemy began to disturb him with thoughts of despair, representing to him the gravity of his sin and the impossibility of forgiveness and amendment. But the soldier of Christ withstood the attacks of the evil spirit and resolved to expiate what he had done by repentance. God revealed this to a certain holy Father and told him to praise the Brother who had fallen into sin, for his victory over the devil, and for not having given way to despondency and despair.

"And so," we read in the instructions of Father Seraphim which were recorded by his spiritual children, "let us not fail to turn quickly to our merciful Lord, and let us not yield to carelessness and despair on account of our grave and countless sins. Our despair is the most perfect joy for the devil. It is a *sin unto death* as Scripture says (I Jn. 5:16). 'If you do not give way to despondency and carelessness,' says Barsanufius the Great, 'you will have to wonder and to glorify God when you see how He changes you from non-existence to existence (that is, from a sinner into a righteous man)'" (Answer 114).

In teaching repentance the Saint quoted the words of the holy Martyr Boniface (commemorated on 19th December): "The beginning of repentance is born of the fear of God and attention to oneself. The fear of God is the father of attention, and attention is the mother of interior peace. The fear of the Lord awakens the sleeping conscience, which enables the soul to see its ugliness as in a kind of pure and clear water. In this way the germ[86] of repentance is produced and its roots grow and spread."

Another way of cultivating the spirit of penitence is unceasing prayer. "All our life we offend the Divine Majesty by our sins, and therefore we must always humbly ask the Lord for the remission of our debts."

Father Seraphim specially advised penitent sinners to pray in the words of St. Antioch's contrite and confident prayer (See following).

"Repentance from sin consists, among other things, in not doing it again."

"Despair," according to St. John of the Ladder, "is born either of the consciousness of the multitude of our sins, despair of conscience and unbearable sadness, or of pride and haughtiness, when anyone thinks that he does not deserve the sin into which he has fallen" (that is, he is surprised at his sin, for he thinks himself not so bad after all). "The first is cured by abstinence and good hope, and the second by humility and non-condemnation of our neighbour."

"The Lord cares for our salvation. But the homicidal devil tries to bring man to despair. A firm and lofty soul does not despair in misfortunes, whatever they may be. Judas the traitor was a coward and unskillful in warfare; and therefore the enemy, seeing his despair, attacked him and deluded him into

---

[86] The word translated *germ* may also mean first-fruits.

hanging himself. But Peter, that firm rock, being skillful in warfare, did not despair and become dispirited when he fell into sin, but shed bitter tears from a fervent heart. And on seeing his tears, the eyes of the enemy were scorched as by fire, and he fled far from him with a painful wail."

"Therefore, brethren," teaches St. Antioch, "when despair assails us, let us not yield to it; but being strengthened and shielded by the light of faith, let us say with great courage to the evil spirit: 'What have we to do with thee who art alienated from God, a fugitive from Heaven and a wicked slave? Thou darest not do anything to us! Christ, the Son of God, has power both over us and over all. Against Him we have sinned, and before Him we shall justify ourselves. But thou, pernicious spirit, depart from us! Strengthened by His precious Cross, we trample on thy snaky head.'"

But though we must by all means avoid despair, we need to live in penitence, as the Church constantly prays in the litanies: *That we may finish the remainder of our life in peace and penitence*, grant, O Lord. An Orthodox Christian must constantly remember this and pray for it. Holy Orthodoxy, notwithstanding all its confidence in the mercy of the Redeemer, tries above all to train and establish her children in penitence. That is why the normal, ordinary state of both ascetics and laymen seeking salvation is the spirit of contrition, and sometimes tears, and their best prayers 'Lord, have mercy,' and the prayer of Jesus. St. Seraphim's own training throughout his monastic life

The Joyful Director of Souls

consisted essentially in penitence and prayer. He advised people to say no other prayer than 'Lord, have mercy' even when nursing a baby, so that these words should be heard even by an innocent child. How wonderful and edifying this is!

Truly narrow is the gate into the Kingdom of God. And there is no other way but the way of penance, continual effort and unceasing prayer for grace. But all efforts and labours must be transfused with faith and love.

Therefore, Father Seraphim not only taught those who came to him to trust in the Lord's mercy, but he also talked to them of the Cross and taught them penitential prayers. And among others he specially recommended two prayers.

"Undoubtingly approach repentance, and it will intercede with God for you. Continually say this prayer of St. Antioch" (such was St. Seraphim's advice):

"Trusting, O Lord, in the abyss of Thy loving-kindness, I offer Thee this prayer from my foul mouth and my unclean lips. Remember me, for Thy holy Name was invoked over me and Thou hast redeemed me with the price of Thy blood, for Thou hast sealed me with the betrothal of Thy Holy Spirit and Thou hast raised me from the depth of my transgressions, that I should not be seized by the enemy.

St. Seraphim of Sarov

"O Jesus Christ, defend me and be my strong helper in my struggle, for I am a slave of lust and I am assailed by it. But Thou, O Lord, leave me not cast to the earth and condemned by my deeds. Free me, O Lord, from the evil slavery of the prince of this world and make me Thy own in Thy commandments. Thy Person is the way of my life, O my Christ, and the light of my eyes. O God, Master and Lord, give me not roving eyes, and dispel from me evil lust. Defend me with Thy holy arm. Let not longings and lusts overwhelm me, and give me not up to a shameless soul.

"May the light of Thy presence shine in me, O Lord, lest darkness overwhelm me, and I be snatched by those who walk in the night. Do not surrender to invisible beasts, O Lord, a soul which confesses to Thee. Do not allow Thy servant, O Lord, to be wounded by alien dogs.

"Grant me to be a receptacle of Thy Spirit, and make me a house of Thy Christ, Holy Father. O Guide of the lost, guide me lest I stray to the left. I long to see Thy face, O Lord. O God, guide me by the light of Thy countenance.

"Grant me, Thy servant, a fountain of tears, and give Thy creature the dew of Thy Holy Spirit, lest I wither like the fig tree which Thou didst curse; and let tears be my drink, and prayer my food.

"Turn, O Lord, my weeping into joy and receive me into Thy eternal tabernacles. Let Thy mercy over-

The Joyful Director of Souls

take me, O Lord, and Thy bounty encompass me, and pardon all my sins, for Thou art the true God Who pardonest transgressions. 'And do not allow, O Lord, the work of Thy hands to be put to shame on account of the multitude of my transgressions, but call me, O Lord, through Thy only-begotten Son, our Saviour.

"And raise me who lie prostrate like Levi the publican, and quicken me who am slain by my sins, like the son of the widow.

"For Thou alone art the Resurrection of the dead, and to Thee is due the glory for ever. Amen."

What a penitent and contrite spirit this prayer breathes! And the Saint orders us to say it "continually."

And here is another prayer which is still more contrite, which Father Seraphim advised people to say in moments of despondency and as an antidote to despair.

"Master and Lord of Heaven and earth and King of the ages! Deign to open the door of repentance to me, for in anguish of my heart I pray to Thee, our true God, the Father of our Lord Jesus Christ, the Light of the world. Look upon me in Thy great loving-kindness and accept my prayer. Incline Thy ear to my prayer and forgive me all the evil that I have done by the abuse of my free-will. Behold, I seek rest, yet I do not find it, for I have not received forgiveness from my conscience. I thirst for peace, but there is no peace

359

St. Seraphim of Sarov

in me from the dark abyss of my transgressions. Hear, O Lord, a heart which cries to Thee. Regard not my evil deeds, but consider the agony of my soul and make haste to heal me who am badly wounded. By the grace of Thy love for men give me time for repentance and deliver me from my shameful deeds. Reward me not according to Thy justice and requite me not according to my deeds, lest I finally perish.

"Hear me, O Lord, in my despair. Behold, I am bereft of my will and of every thought of amendment. Therefore, I have recourse to Thy compassion. Have mercy on me, cast down and condemned on account of my sins. O Lord, rescue me who am enslaved and held by my evil deeds, as if I were shackled with chains. Thou Alone knowest how to set prisoners free; and as Thou Alone knowest secret things, Thou healest wounds which are known to no one, but seen by Thee.

"Therefore, being tortured in every way by cruel pains, I cry only to Thee, the Physician of all who are afflicted, the Door of those who knock without, the Way of the lost, the Light of those in darkness, the Redeemer of those in bonds, Who ever restrainest Thy right-hand and witholdest Thy anger prepared for sinners, but Who givest time for repentance through Thy great love for men.

"O Thou Who art quick to show mercy and slow to punish, shine upon me, who have fallen badly, the light of Thy countenance, O Lord. And in Thy loving-

The Joyful Director of Souls

kindness stretch out Thy hand to me and raise me from the depth of my transgressions.

"For Thou Alone art our God, Who dost not rejoice at the destruction of sinners, and Who dost not turn away Thy face from those who cry to Thee with tears.

"Hear, O Lord, the voice of Thy servant who cries to Thee, and manifest Thy light to me who am deprived of light. And give me Thy grace, for I have no hope whatever, that I may always trust in Thy help and power. Turn my weeping into joy, rend my rags and gird me with gladness.

"And grant that I may rest from my dark deeds and enjoy the morning calm with Thy chosen, O Lord, whence all pain, sorrow and sighing have fled away. And may the door of Thy Kingdom be opened to me, that I may enter with those who rejoice in the light of Thy countenance, O Lord, and that even I may receive eternal life in Christ Jesus our Lord. Amen."

That is the cry of penitence which the "joyful" Seraphim advised people to offer to God! This helps us to understand one of his sayings which is rarely quoted by his biographers.

"We must," he says, "banish from us every earthly joy, following the teaching of the Lord Jesus Christ Who said: *Do not rejoice that the spirits are subject to you, but rather rejoice that your names are written in heaven* (Lk. 10:20)."

St. Seraphim of Sarov

"This he said apropos the veneration shown him by people who had derived benefit from his instructions. And if he would not allow himself this natural joy, what must we say of us sinners?

But, besides that, we find he also gave direct instructions with regard to weeping and tears.

"All the Saints and the Monks who have renounced the world, wept all their life in expectation of eternal consolation, according to the assurance of the Saviour of the world. *Blessed are they who weep,*[87] *for they shall be comforted* (Mat. 5:4). So we too must weep for the remission of our sins. Let the words of the purple-robed Prophet convince us: *Going they went and wept as they cast their seeds; but they will come with joy, bringing their sheaves* (Ps. 125:6), and the words of Isaac the Syrian: 'Moisten your cheek with the tears of your eyes, that the Holy Spirit may rest upon you and that you may wash away the foulness of your wrong-doing. Propitiate your Lord with tears that He may come to you' (Chap. 68). He who sheds tears of compunction has his heart illumined by the rays of the Sun of Righteousness, Christ God."

But then how are we to reconcile with this penitent attitude the radiant joy of Father Seraphim and his joyful greetings to his visitors: "my joy, "my treasure" and the like?

---

[87] So the Slavonic.

The Joyful Director of Souls

We must stop for a moment and give this our special attention. The reason is this. In the minds of many there has arisen an erroneous opinion as to Father Seraphim's appearance. And this one-sided interpretation has spread throughout Christendom. Father Seraphim's Christianity, they say, seems different from that of other Orthodox Saints. Theirs is more rigorous, penitential, ascetic, but Father Seraphim's is consoling, encouraging, joyful, if not to say, merry.

And then, without going the way of penitence, people try to live joyfully, and fall.

We must correct this erroneous view which is rather widely held among educated Christians. If Father Seraphim's way and appearance were really different from that of other Orthodox Saints, this alone ought to make us, who are faithful to Orthodoxy, think and put us on our guard and ask ourselves: "Is the Saint's way right?" But as no one shows any doubts on that score, we must question the judgement of our contemporaries. For the salvation of the sinful world there is no other way than repentance and a laborious struggle. This is the inevitable law for all Christians. And Father Seraphim went through it all. One need only remember his one thousand days' standing on a stone with the ceaseless penitent cry: "God, be merciful to me a sinner." But even if he followed a lighter, easier way (the inner life of the Saints is really hidden from us), those who came to him were ordinary people with all their infirmities, such as they have been *from the days of John the Baptist until now*, when, according to the words of Truth Itself, *the*

St. Seraphim of Sarov

Kingdom of Heaven suffers violence, and the violent take it by force (Mat. 11:12). And if so, they needed the way of penitence which is common to all. Father Seraphim could teach them no other way than through the narrow gate. He would not have lured them through the temptation of the *broad and wide way*, the easy and pleasant way *that leads to destruction*, and by which unfortunately many of us are already going (cp. Mat. 7:13). After an attentive perusal of the Saint's life it will be quite obvious that he went the narrow way, the way of the Cross, so that it is often painful to write, to read or to hear about his labours. And what do we know of them? A tiny drop, only a fraction of them. It is sufficient to read Motovilov's temptation about the torments of hell (see Chapter IX) to feel terrified. And St. Seraphim himself had to endure a cruel struggle with the powers of darkness. There were in fact all kinds of temptations, and people, and incredible fastings, and exhaustion.

Having gone the way of the Cross, the holy ascetic reached while still on earth that blessed state which is prepared by the Father in the Heavenly Kingdom for those who love Him. And though he never desponded, being pure in heart, and always enjoyed peace of soul, as one who had kept the grace of Baptism unstained, yet we must not forget that the fiery Seraphim reached a state of complete joy only towards the close of his ascetic life. God alone knows how much time and labour he had previously spent in the Monastery, in the hermitage, in quiet and in seclusion.

The Joyful Director of Souls

But when a Christian attains the heights of sanctity, then he sheds his joy, like the sun, on all without distinction, both on the good and on the evil, on the just and on the unjust (Cp. Mat. 5:45). This may explain, among other things, his kindness to the Novice Ivan Tikhonov who later caused much sorrow to his orphans and whose soul he had seen a long time previously.

Besides, everyone knows that true joy is the fruit and companion of the Cross. And in repentance we always feel the consolation of grace. In fact without it there is only death and delusion.

But we must take into special consideration the good aim the man of God had in view when he so joyfully received his visitors. Most of the people who came to him were in trouble, in despondency, sick in soul or in body, often living in sin. And they were all in need of encouragement, kindness, peace, joy. They all had enough sorrow of their own. What they lacked was the warmth of God. This grace had been given to the man of God by the Comforter and he diffused it all around him.

Consolation and encouragement is especially necessary at the beginning of the spiritual life, and particularly for weak and sinful people, in order to kindle fervour in them. Only after having been strengthened can they live on the solid food of contrition and tears. Besides, the festive joy which they received from St. Seraphim was usually the beginning of subsequent spiritual labours and a life of penitence, of a desire to

St. Seraphim of Sarov

amend, to change, to expiate former sins, to be reborn in the Holy Spirit. How many examples we have seen of people leaving "poor" Seraphim's cell or hermitage in tears! How many deep confessions were heard by the walls of St. Seraphim's cell! And for the most part this was brought about by the joyful and gentle love of the Christlike Father. It was not for nothing that on taking leave of Father Antony, the future Abbot of the Monastery of the Holy Trinity and St. Sergius, the collaborator of the austere Metropolitan Philaret of Moscow, St. Seraphim gave him the following commandment: "Submit in everything to the will of the Lord, be diligent in prayer, carry out your duties strictly, be merciful and indulgent with the brethren. Be a mother, and not a father, to the brethren," he said, "and in general be merciful to all and humble. Humility and discretion make the beauty of the virtues." Be a mother, not a father. And he was just such a tender mother himself, especially to his "little orphans" of Diveyev. "Have I not begotten you in the Spirit?"[88] he often used to say to them. And you should have seen how they were reborn by that joyful love! I shall mention a touching incident and then bring this chapter to an end.

"Once I began to complain about myself," says Xenia Vasilievna, one of the Diveyev Sisters who was nearest to the Saint, "of my hot temper and impetuous character, but Father only said: 'What are you talking about, Mother? What are you talking about? You have the most beautiful, gentle character, Mother, the most

---

[88] Cp. I Cor. 4:15; Philem. 10.

The Joyful Director of Souls

lovely, peaceful, meek character.' And he said it with such a serene expression and so humbly that his words 'gentle and meek' seemed worse to me than any scolding. And I felt so ashamed that I did not know which way to look. And I began to subdue my hot temper little by little. I had always been severe and strict. Father forbade me to be too strict with the young Sisters. On the contrary, he ordered me to encourage them. And though he did not permit frivolous talk or gossip, he never forbade anyone to be cheerful. He would ask for instance: 'Tell me, Mother, do you have lunch with the Sisters?'

"'No, Father,' I replied.

"'How is that, Mother? No, my joy, if you don't want to eat, don't, but always sit at the table with them. You know, they will come tired and depressed, but when they see you sitting among them, affectionate and cheerful, and in good spirits, they will also feel cheered and gladdened, and will eat all the better, with great joy. Cheerfulness is not a sin, Mother. It drives away weariness which breeds despondency. And there is nothing worse than that; it brings everything evil in its wake. To say a kind, friendly, cheerful word in order that all may be in the presence of the Lord in a cheerful and not in a despondent spirit, is not all sinful, Mother.'"

St. Seraphim Blessing a Pilgrim

Chapter XV

Amazing Wonderworker

"Rejoice Saint Seraphim, Wonderworker of Sarov!" the Church now sings in the Akathist to the holy servant of God.

No one knows or ever will know all the wonders which were worked by God through His "sinful servant," "poor Seraphim."

"I, sinful Seraphim, consider myself a sinful servant of God, and what the Lord tells me as His servant I pass on to those in need of benefit. Like iron to the smith, so I have surrendered myself and my will to the Lord God. As He wills, so I act." These were the Saint's words to Father Antony, Abbot of Vysogorsk, in explanation of his spiritual insight. But the same must be said of all his other wonders. Everything was done in and through him by the Lord God. There can be no other explanation. Besides, it is unnecessary. To a believer miracles are both simple and necessary, for God can do everything. In the case of an unbeliever the irrefutable facts remain, deeds which are too numerous to be denied and which force a man to think and to stand lost in amazement. And for us, these works of God are not only instructive and edifying, but they are, so to say, windows into the other world. Through them we become aware of the reality of "that world." And the mere fact that it really exists is both a joy and a consolation to us. The existence of the other world is proved neither by syllogisms nor by our feelings and wishes, but by its irrefutable existence, that is by spontaneous self-revelation. It has been re-

St. Seraphim of Sarov

vealed time after time through St. Seraphim. And it is particularly comforting and convincing to know that all these miracles occurred almost in our life-time.

But it is time to enjoy the wonderful spectacle of the miracles of God. One hardly knows where to begin. They are so numerous. And God alone knows how many have remained unrecorded. All Russia abounds in tales about the miracles of "Father Seraphim."

And he still continues to work miracles, even beyond the borders of his native land. Our boundaries and frontiers do not exist for the Saints. They belong to everyone and can be everywhere. Just as God is everywhere, and they are in God (Jn. 17:20-23), so they are everywhere in Him.

Miracles in Father Seraphim's life began, as we know, in his early childhood. He fell down unhurt from the belltower in Kursk; he was healed by the Icon of Our Lady of the Root while he was still in the world. In the Monastery a miraculous cure was effected through the intervention of the most holy Mother of God who appeared to him twelve times according to his own words. Then he had a striking heavenly vision of our Lord Jesus Christ Himself in company with a host of Angels, while he was assisting at the Liturgy as a Deacon. And how many extraordinary instances of spiritual insight we have seen in his life! And how many facts there are that are, humanly speaking, quite incredible in connection with the foundation of his favourite work--Diveyev. But

Amazing Wonderworker

now let us take the most important of his innumerable miracles.

The earlier biographies usually began with a case of "divination." Let us do the same. It is easy to see in it how "simple" it is for Saints to work miracles. I shall copy it straight out of the "Chronicle."

"Once a simple peasant with his cap in his hand, with his hair disheveled, came running to the Monastery and asked in despair the first Monk whom he met:

"'Father, are you by chance Father Seraphim?'

"They directed him to Father Seraphim. He rushed there, fell at his feet and said imploringly:

"'Father! I have been robbed of my horse, and now, without it, I am quite a beggar. I do not know how I shall feed my family. But they say you divine.'

"Father Seraphim took him affectionately by the head and, putting it close to his own, he said:

"'Wrap yourself in silence and hasten to the village of (he named it). When you come to it, turn off the road to the right and pass along the back-yards of four houses. There you will see a small wicket-gate. Go in, untie your horse from the log and lead it out without a word.'

St. Seraphim of Sarov

"The peasant immediately ran back with faith and joy without stopping anywhere. There was a rumour in Sarov afterwards that he had actually found his horse at the place indicated."

The peasant had come to Father Seraphim well informed. "They say you divine." It means that there had been so many miracles of this kind that reports had long since spread among the people and had taken root. In Sarov there is a Monk with the gift of spiritual insight--Father Seraphim! And so people who sought the mercy of God flocked to him.

Two Diveyev Sisters, Aquilina and Maria, were in his anteroom, when he said to them: "Stand aside, stand aside, Mothers, many ladies and gentlemen are coming to see me!"

"But there was no one there at all," said Aquilina, "and no one in sight. Of course, he could see everything at a distance, for in a very short time, a matter of minutes, there really came many visitors. We stepped aside and listened.

"'This is my daughter, Father,' said a lady. 'And this is my son,' said a gentleman. 'Bless him to take her, the daughter I mean, in marriage.'

"'No, no,' replied Father. 'He must marry the one who was left there. And she will marry the one who lives here near you.'

Amazing Wonderworker

"And Father mentioned the names of all the places, which I do not remember now. But how did he know everything in advance, and about everyone? It is really just marvellous!"

But it is still more marvellous when he foresaw the future many years in advance: life and death, poverty and prosperity, marriage or the monastic life, and so on without end. Let us mention two more cases, one from the married and one from the monastic life, which are both edifying.

"A widow who had three small children and was burdened with their upbringing, often complained of her bitter fate. Having heard of Father Seraphim's kindness, she decided to apply to him in order to ask his blessing and tell him her grief. Having blessed her, the Elder said:

"'Do not murmur at your fate. Your sorrow will soon end. One will be your support.'

"A week later two of her children died. The mother was struck by their unexpected death and went again to Father Seraphim. When the Elder saw her, he anticipated her words and said: 'Pray to our Mediatress, the most holy Mother of God and to all the Saints. You have greatly offended them by cursing your children. Confess everything to your spiritual Father, and in future, control your anger, so as not to be a great sinner. I bless you for the last time; only forgive them.'"

St. Seraphim of Sarov

On another occasion a young girl came to him to ask the holy Elder's advice as to how to save her soul. But before she had time to open her mouth, Father Seraphim began to speak to her himself:

"Do not be over-anxious. Live as you have been living. As regards higher things, God will teach you Himself."

Then, bowing to her to the ground, he said:

"Only one thing I ask you. Please, see that all your orders are carried out; and judge justly. In this way you will be saved."

The girl had never thought of the monastic life, so she could not understand what orders the Elder was referring to, when he bowed down to the ground. But, reading her secret thoughts, he added:

"When the time comes, then you will remember me."

The girl asked him whether God would grant her another interview with Father.

"No," he replied, "we are parting for ever, and that is why I ask you not to forget me in your holy prayers."

The girl in her turn asked him to pray for her.

Amazing Wonderworker

"I shall pray. And now go in peace. They are already grumbling at you."

And in fact her fellow-travelers met her in the Monastery hospice with a sharp complaint for her delay in Father's cell. Later she embraced monasticism under the name of Callista and became an Abbess in the Convent of Sviazhak of the Khazan district. That is why Father had bowed down to the ground to her and had addressed her respectfully as an Abbess.

The wonderful cures of sick people are no less numerous. His first spiritual healing, according to his own testimony, was effected on his favourite and ever-obedient Novice "Mishenka", Michael Vasilievitch Manturov.[89]

When he was serving in the army in Lithuania, he probably caught cold and therefore he returned to his estate Nutch which lay in the province of Nizhni-Novgorod, forty versts from Sarov, and applied to physicians for medical treatment. But his illness not only did not improve, but it grew to menacing proportions: bits of bone began to fall from his legs. Hearing of the ascetic of Sarov, Manturov decided to apply to him for help. He was brought with great difficulty by his serfs into the ante-room of the elder's cell. Father came out and asked him kindly:

---

[89] The word used in Russian for Novice is *poslushnik*, which means "one under obedience." The author is using the term here to refer to Manturov's obedience as a spiritual son, and not in the sense of a monastic.--ed.

St. Seraphim of Sarov

"What is it you want? To look at poor Seraphim?"

But Manturov fell at his feet in tears and begged him to heal him from an incurable disease.

Then Father asked him three times with the deepest sympathy and fatherly love:

"Do you believe in God?"

And having received a thrice-repeated vigorous affirmation of his sincere and absolute faith in God, St. Seraphim said:

"My joy, if you have such faith, believe also that to a believer everything is possible through God. And I, poor Seraphim, will pray."

After this, Father seated Manturov near the coffin which stood in his ante-room, while he himself retired to his cell. After a short interval he came out with some oil in his hands and told the patient to strip his legs.

"According to the grace given me by the Lord, you are the first whom I heal," he said, and he anointed the diseased legs with oil.

Then he pulled on his legs linen stockings which had been brought to him as a gift by some peasants, brought out of his cell a great quantity of dry bread, emptied it into the flaps of his client's coat, and then told him to walk with this load to the hostel.

376

Amazing Wonderworker

Manturov got up and walked, not without fear, but quite firmly and feeling no pain whatever. Amazed and overjoyed at the miracle, he went back to Father, and throwing himself at his feet again, began to kiss them rapturously, thanking him for his cure. But the great Elder raised him from the ground and said to him sternly:

"Is it Seraphim's work to kill and to make alive, to bring down to hell and to raise up again? (I Kings 2:6). What are you thinking of! This is the work of the Lord alone, Who does the will of those who fear Him! (Ps. 144:16). Give thanks to the Lord Almighty and to His immaculate Mother."

With these words the Elder dismissed the healed man, and Manturov returned with joy to his estate, and to his wife and sister. Their joy together was unbounded, but they soon forgot both the illness and the healing. But suddenly Michael Vasilievitch remembered Father Seraphim's injunction to thank God and the immaculate Virgin. And he had not even thought of it till then in his joy and out of forgetfulness. Abashed he went to Father again. On meeting him Father Seraphim said at once:

"My joy! Didn't we promise to thank the Lord for having restored our life to us[90]?"

"I do not really know how, Father," said Manturov amazed at his perspicacity. "What do you command?"

---

[90] Cp. I John 5:16.

St. Seraphim of Sarov

Then the holy Elder gave him a penetrating glance, as if he foresaw all his future in a flash, and said merrily:

"Well, my joy! All that you have, give to the Lord, and take upon yourself voluntary poverty."

He had not expected this, and was disconcerted. He remembered among other things the rich young man of the Gospel (Mt. 19:22). The thought of his young wife, who moreover was a Lutheran, also came to his mind, and his impecunious sister who was dreaming of a rich marriage. How were they to live? Michael Vasilievitch was at a loss to know what to reply to his benefactor, or rather, to God Himself.

The Saint read his thoughts and interrupted his troubled silence.

"Leave everything and do not worry over what you are thinking about. The Lord will not leave you either in this life or in the next. You will not be rich, but still you will have your daily bread."

Ardent in soul and strong in faith, resolute as an ex-soldier, Manturov suddenly felt a change in his soul as well as a whole-hearted love for the Saint, and he said firmly:

"I agree, Father! What do you bless me to do?"

But the wise Elder, wishing to test the impetuous Novice, replied:

Amazing Wonderworker

"Well, my joy, let us pray, and I shall direct you as God instructs me."

With that they parted for the time being. But the grace of God had already united them for life in the work of the building of the Diveyev Convent. Soon, with St. Seraphim's blessing, Manturov liberated his serfs, sold his estate at Nutch, bought a small plot of land of about forty acres at Diveyev and settled nearer to his Elder. His friends laughed at him and thought he was quite mad. His wife complained for a long time; being a Lutheran, she had no inclination to lead an ascetic or frugal life. But having once made this decision, Michael Vasilievitch abandoned himself to the will of the holy Elder with unquestioning obedience, and bore everything unmurmuringly, humbly, silently and even generously.

It was particularly difficult to deal with his wife.

"I used to say to him," Anna Michailovna (his wife) wrote afterwards, 'You may respect the Elder, you may love and trust him, but not to such an extent!' But Michael Vasilievitch would listen, sigh and remain silent. This irritated me all the more. Once, when we had reached such an extremity in winter that we had nothing to light our room with (and the evenings are long, depressing and dark), I felt very bitter, began to grumble and then gave way to uncontrollable weeping. First I felt indignant with Michael Vasilievitch, then with Father Seraphim himself, and then I began to grumble and to complain of my bitter fate. All the while Michael Vasilievitch kept silent and sighed. Suddenly I heard a crackling sound. I looked up. O Lord! Fear and horror seized me! I was afraid to look and I could not believe my own eyes. The empty lamp which stood without oil before the Icons suddenly began to burn with a bright flame and became full of oil. Then I burst into tears and repeated amidst my sobs: 'Father Seraphim! Saint of God! Forgive me, a wretched, grumbling, unworthy creature, for Christ's sake. I shall never do it again!' Even now," she concludes, "I cannot recall it without fear. From that time onwards I never allowed myself to murmur, and however hard it would be, I bore everything patiently."

Afterwards she became Orthodox and lived as a secret Nun in Diveyev. And Michael Vasilievitch completely surrendered himself to Father and became his most faithful Novice and dearest friend. This is why Father Seraphim always gave him the affectionate name of "Mishenka" (Micky). This was the first miracle of healing which afterwards proved so beneficial for Diveyev; for Manturov became the undisputed executor of Father's orders. Everyone knew it and looked upon him as upon the Elder himself in what concerned the affairs of the Convent. All this took place in 1822.

This reminds us of another still more wonderful occurrence.

Sister Xenia Vasilievna of Diveyev, who was the sacristan, came to the Church of the Nativity of Christ in order to trim the lamp which was always kept

Amazing Wonderworker

burning before the Icon of the Saviour according to Father's order. She went to pour out the remains of the oil before the Service; but then she saw that it had all burned out and that the lamp had gone out. She began to reflect bitterly that Father Seraphim's prediction about the ever-burning lamp had not been fulfilled, though the Sisters had tried to keep his order. If so, his other predictions about the Convent might also prove unreliable. And doubts as to the Saint's spiritual insight assailed the soul of one of Father's most faithful and intimate Novices. Covering her face with her hands, in bitter disappointment, Xenia went a few steps away from the Icon of the Saviour. Suddenly she heard a crackling sound.

"Raising her head," writes the author of the Diveyev Chronicle, "she saw that the lamp was burning. She went up closer to it and noticed that the glass of the lamp was full of oil and that two silver roubles were on the oil. In consternation she closed the Church and hastened to tell the wonderful vision to her spiritual Mother, Elena Vasilievna Manturov. On her way she was overtaken by a Sister accompanied by a peasant who was looking for the sacristan and wanted to give her something. When the peasant saw Xenia Vasilievna, he asked her:

"'Are you the sacristan here, Mother?'

"'I am,' replied Xenia. 'What do you want?'

"'As Father Seraphim has given you an order about an ever-burning lamp, I have brought you three

St. Seraphim of Sarov

hundred roubles in paper money for some oil for the lamp, so that it may burn for the repose of the souls of my parents.'

"At the same time he gave the names of his deceased parents and handed over the money."

Manturov's sister, Elena Vasilievna, a beautiful seventeen year old girl, was attracted by worldly pleasures. She liked evening parties and nice clothes. She was already engaged, when she suddenly felt an inexplicable repulsion for her fiancee and broke off the engagement. Once when she was returning home and was just getting into a carriage, she saw above her head a terrible serpent which was about to swallow her in its jaws. She cried out: "Save me, Queen of Heaven! I swear to you that I shall never marry, but will go to a Monastery." The serpent rose into the air and vanished.

For three years St. Seraphim prepared Elena Vasilievna for the monastic life, and when she began it, she showed extraordinary zeal. She died at the age of twenty-seven in obedience to the Saint. This is what happened. Michael Vasilievitch Manturov fell ill with a pernicious fever and wrote a letter to his sister, Elena Vasilievna, requesting her to ask Father Seraphim how to get well. Father Seraphim told him to chew the crumb of hot well-baked rye-bread, and thereby healed him. But soon he sent for Elena Vasilievna who came to him with her Novice, Xenia Vasilievna the sacristan, and he said to her:

Amazing Wonderworker

"You have always obeyed me, my joy, and now I want to give you an obedience. Will you do it, Mother?"

"I have always obeyed you," she replied, "and I am still ready to obey you!"

"That's right, my joy!" exclaimed the Elder. "Well, you see, Mother, Michael Vasilievitch, your brother, is ill and it is time for him to die. He has to die, Mother, though I still want him for our Convent, for our orphans, I mean. And so, this is your obedience: die for Michael Vasilievitch, Mother!"

"Bless me, Father!" answered Elena Vasilievna humbly and with apparent calmness.

After this Father Seraphim had a long talk with her, comforting her heart and discussing the question of death and eternal life. Elena Vasilievna listened to him in silence, but suddenly she looked troubled and said:

"Father! I am afraid of death!"

"Why should we be afraid of death, my joy?" Father Seraphim replied. "For you and me there will only be eternal joy!"

Elena Vasilievna took leave of him, but she had hardly crossed the threshold of his cell when she fell down. Xenia Vasilievna picked her up. Father Seraphim told her to put her in the coffin which stood

St. Seraphim of Sarov

in his ante-room, while he fetched some holy water. He sprinkled it over Elena Vasilievna, gave her some of it to drink and so brought her back to consciousness. On returning home, she fell ill, took to her bed and said: "Now I shan't get up any more!"

Her end was remarkable. She sent for Father Basil Sadovsky so as to be anointed and make her communion for the last time. In her confession she told Father Basil of a wonderful vision she had been granted. This is how he recorded it with his own hand.

"I was not allowed to tell this before," explained Elena Vasilievna, "but now I can. In Church I saw in the open Royal Doors a majestic Queen of unutterable beauty. Beckoning to me with her hand, she said: 'Follow me and see what I shall show you.' We entered a court; to describe its beauty is quite impossible, Father! It was all of transparent crystal, and the doors, handles and fittings were of purest gold. The brilliance made it difficult to look at; it all seemed to be burning. As soon as we reached the doors, they opened of themselves, and we entered a kind of endless corridor on both sides of which were closed doors. As we drew near to the first doors, which also opened of themselves, I saw a huge hall in which were tables and armchairs all ablaze with indescribable splendour. It was full of dignitaries and young men of extraordinary beauty who were all sitting down. When we entered, all silently rose and bowed to the Queen. 'There, look!' she said, pointing at them all with her hand, 'these are my pious merchants.' Having given me time to have a good look at them, the Queen

Amazing Wonderworker

went out and the doors closed behind us of themselves. The next hall was of even greater beauty; everything seemed to be flooded with light. It was full
of young women dressed in garments of extraordinary
brightness and with shining crowns on their heads.
The crowns varied in appearance, and some were
wearing two or three crowns at once. The women
were sitting, but when we appeared all silently rose
and bowed to the Queen. 'Look well at them to see if
they are nice and whether you like them,' she said to
me kindly. I looked at the side of the hall she was
pointing at, and all of a sudden I saw that one of the
women was terribly like me, Father." So saying, Elena
Vasilievna was confused, stopped, but then continued:
"That woman smiled and looked at me. Then at the direction of the Queen I began to look at the other side
of the hall, and I saw on one of the girls a crown of
such beauty that I even envied it!" said Elena
Vasilievna, sighing. "And they were all our Sisters,
Father, those who had been before me in the Convent,
and those who are still living now, and future ones.
But I cannot name them because I am not allowed to
speak. We came out of that hall, and the doors closed
behind us of themselves. Then we went up to the third
entrance and suddenly found ourselves again in a hall,
this time far less bright, in which were all our Sisters,
past, present and future; they were also in crowns, but
not such splendid ones, and I was not allowed to tell
their names. After that we crossed over into a fourth
hall, almost in semi-darkness, also full of Sisters, but
only present and future ones, who were either sitting
or lying; some were contorted with illness and with-

out any crowns, with terribly dejected faces, and on each and all of them there lay, as it were, the seal of pain and inexpressible sorrow. 'Those are the careless,' the Queen told me, pointing at them. 'You see,' she continued, 'how terrible is carelessness! On account of their carelessness they will never be able to rejoice.' They were all our Sisters too, Father, but I am forbidden to tell their names," explained Elena Vasilievna, and wept bitterly.

She died after a short illness on the eve of Pentecost, 28th May 1832. She was twenty-seven years of age and had spent altogether seven years at the Diveyev Convent. She was extremely beautiful and attractive, tall, with a round face, quick dark eyes and black hair.

At the very hour of her death Father Seraphim hurriedly and joyfully sent the Sisters who were working with him at Sarov to Diveyev, saying:

"Quick, quick, go to the Convent. There your great lady has departed to the Lord."

On the third day after Elena Vasilievna's death, Xenia Vasilievna went to Father Seraphim all in tears. On seeing her, the great Elder who loved the late Superior no less than all the Sisters was involuntarily troubled and at once sent Xenia home, saying:

"Why are you crying? We ought to rejoice! Come here on the fortieth day, but now go home. You must see to it that all the forty days there is a daily Liturgy.

Amazing Wonderworker

If necessary, beg Father Basil on your knees, but there must be the Liturgies."

Choking with tears Xenia Vasilievna went away. But Father Paul, who occupied the cell next to Father Seraphim, saw how the Saint for a long time walked up and down in his room and exclaimed:

"They understand nothing! They are weeping! If only they had seen how her soul flew away like a bird taking wing! Cherubim and Seraphim made way for her! She has been granted to sit not far from the Holy Trinity, as a virgin."

When Xenia Vasilievna came on the fortieth day after the death of Elena Vasilievna to Father Seraphim according to his instructions, the Elder comforted his beloved sacristan and said to her joyfully:

"What stupids you are, my joys! What is there to cry about! It is a sin, you know. We ought to rejoice. Her soul took wing like a dove, and has been borne aloft to the Holy Trinity. Cherubim, Seraphim and all the host of heaven made way for her. She is an attendant of the Mother of God, Mother! She is a lady-in-waiting of the Queen of Heaven, Mother! We can only rejoice; we must not weep."

In September 1831 Nikolas Alexandrovitch Motovilov obtained a miraculous cure through the prayers of Father Seraphim. In his notes on the Diveyev Convent this is what he writes about his healing:

St. Seraphim of Sarov

"The great Elder Seraphim healed me of extremely severe rheumatic pains and other ailments accompanied by bodily debility and paralysis of my legs which were twisted and swollen at the knees. I also suffered for more than three years from incurable bedsores on my back and sides. The cure was effected in this way. I gave orders that I was to be carried, a very sick man, from my estate in the village of Britvin in the Nizhny-Novgorod district to Father Seraphim. On the 5th September 1831 I was brought to the Sarov Monastery. On the 7th September and on the 8th, the day of the Nativity of the Mother of God, I was granted two interviews, the first that I had had with Father Seraphim, one before and one after dinner, in his cell at the Monastery, but I received no healing as yet. On the following day, 9th September, they brought me to his near hermitage, by his well. Four men were carrying me in their hands and a fifth was holding my head when they brought me to him. He was then talking to the people who came to him in great crowds. They put me down near a tall and very thick pine-tree which still stands until now on the bank of the Sarovka river, in the meadow where he made hay. To my request that he should help me and heal me he replied:

"'But I am not a doctor. One must apply to doctors when one wants to be cured of some illness.'

"I told him in detail of my sufferings, of how I had experienced all the main kinds of treatment, without having obtained healing from a single one. And now I saw no other way of salvation and I had no other hope

388

Amazing Wonderworker

of being healed of my ailments other than the grace of God. But as I was a sinner and had no boldness towards the Lord God, I asked his holy prayers that the Lord should heal me. He asked me:

"'Do you really believe in the Lord Jesus Christ, that He is the God-Man, and in the most pure Mother of God, that she is Ever-Virgin?'

"I replied: 'I do.'

"'And do you believe,' he continued, 'that as formerly the Lord healed instantly with one word or by His touch all the diseases which afflict men, so now too He can heal as easily and instantaneously as before those who ask His help, by a single word of His, and that the intercession of the Mother of God is all-powerful, so that at her intercession the Lord Jesus Christ can even now heal you completely, in an instant and by a single word?'

"I replied that I truly believed all this, I believed it with all my soul and heart, and that unless I had believed it, I would not have ordered my servants to bring me to him.

"'But if you believe,' he concluded, 'you are already well!'

"'How am I well,' I asked, 'when my servants and you are holding me in your hands?'

St. Seraphim of Sarov

"'No,' he said, 'you are completely well now in the whole of your body.'

"And he told my men who were holding me in their hands to leave me, and taking me by the shoulders, he raised me from the ground himself. Then, putting me on my feet, he said to me:

"'Stand more firmly, fix your feet squarely on the ground, there--like that. Don't be afraid, you are quite well now.' And then he added, looking at me joyfully: 'There, you see how well you are standing now!'

"I replied: 'I can't help standing well since you are holding me so firmly and well.'

"Then he took his hands off me and said: 'Well, now I am no longer holding you, and you are still standing firmly even without me. Now walk boldly. The Lord has healed you. So go and move from your place.'

"Taking me by the arm with one of his hands, and with the other pushing me a little between the shoulders, he led me on the grass and on the rough ground near the big pine-tree, saying: 'There, your Godliness, how well you walk!'

"I replied: 'Yes, because you are so kind as to lead me so well.'

"'No, ' he said taking his hand off me, 'the Lord Himself has been pleased to heal you completely, and the Mother of God herself has prayed to Him about this. Now you will walk without my help and you will always walk well. So walk!'

"And he began to push me in order to make me walk.

"'But I shall fall and hurt myself,' I said.

"'No,' he contradicted me, 'you will not hurt yourself, but you will walk firmly.'

"And when I felt in myself some power from on high overshadowing me, I took courage a little and began to walk firmly. But he suddenly stopped me saying: 'That is enough now.'

"Then he asked me: 'Well, are you sure now that the Lord has actually healed you, and healed you completely? The Lord has taken away your transgressions and He has cleansed your sins. Do you see what a miracle the Lord has worked with you? So always undoubtedly believe in Him, Christ our Saviour, and firmly hope in His lovingkindness towards you, love Him with all your heart and cling to Him with all your soul and always firmly trust in Him, and thank the heavenly Queen for her great mercies toward you. But as your three-year sufferings have seriously exhausted you, do not walk much all of a sudden now, but do so gradually. Accustom yourself to walking little by little, and take care of your health as a precious gift of God.'

St. Seraphim of Sarov

"And he went on talking with me even after this for a considerable time. Then he sent me away to the hostel completely healed. And so my men went back alone from the forest and the near hermitage to the Monastery, thanking God for His wonderful mercies to me which had been displayed before their own eyes, and I got into the carriage along with Father Gury, without human support, and drove back to the hostel of the Sarov Monastery. As there had been many pilgrims present at my healing, they had returned before me to the Monastery, telling everyone about the great miracle."

In May 1829 the wife of Alexy Gurievitch Vorotilov of the village of Pavlovo fell dangerously ill. Vorotilov had great faith in the power of St. Seraphim's prayers, and the Elder loved him as one of his own disciples. Vorotilov went to Sarov, and although it was midnight when he arrived, he hastened to Father Seraphim's cell. The Elder was sitting on the steps and, on seeing him, greeted him with the words:

"Well, my joy, why have you hurried at such a time to poor Seraphim?"

Vorotilov told him with tears what had brought him to Sarov and asked him to help his sick wife. But St. Seraphim declared to Vorotilov's extreme sorrow that his wife was to die from her illness. Then Alexy Gurievitch fell at the ascetic's feet shedding a flood of tears, and with faith and humility begged him to pray for the restoration of her life and health. Father Seraphim instantly immersed himself in mental

392

Amazing Wonderworker

prayer for about ten minutes. Then he opened his eyes and, raising Vorotilov to his feet, he said joyfully:

"Well, my joy, the Lord is granting life to your wife. Go home in peace."

Vorotilov sped home joyfully. There he learned that his wife had felt relief precisely during those minutes which Father Seraphim had spent in prayerful labour. Soon she recovered completely.

"In 1826," wrote General P. A. Galkin-Vrassky to Father Raphael, Abbot of Sarov, "I visited the Sarov Monastery while still a captain in the army, and, like the other pilgrims, I went for a blessing to Father Seraphim. In the corridor leading to his cell it was intensely cold and I was shivering in my light overcoat. His attendant[91] said that Father Seraphim had a Monk with him and that he was talking to him just then; and as I stood in the corridor I prayed to the most holy Mother of God. The door opened, the Monk came out, and a few minutes later Father Seraphim opened his door and said: 'What joy God has granted me!' He led me into his cell and, as it was crowded with various things, he sat me on the threshold of his cell, while he himself sat down on the floor in front of me, holding my hand. And he talked affectionately to me and even kissed my hand. Such was his love for his neighbor! Sitting in front of him, I was in a kind of extraordinary ecstasy. After a talk on various subjects I told

---

[91] Keleynik.

him that I felt a pain in my chest (I was a thin pale youth). To this he replied:

'That is nothing,' and he got up, took a bottle, and handed it to me saying: 'Take a good draught.' What was my horror when I gulped down some lamp oil! I expected instantly bad consequences, but on the contrary, the oil proved delicious. From that moment, thanks to God, I had no more pain in my chest and from a thin, pale youth I became a strong and healthy man. A considerable time later I was obliged to leave the army and to go on leave for an indefinite period. This absence from Petersburg brought on such a state of depression that for a whole year I did not know what to do with myself. On my way to Arzamas I visited the Sarov Monastery and went at once to Father Seraphim's grave. I asked a Priest to serve a Pannikhida[92] for his soul, and as soon as it was finished, my depression vanished instantly and I became well again."

The grace of the Holy Spirit which acted in the cures of those who had recourse to St. Seraphim's intercession, made its presence apparent both in the special signs which accompanied his prayer and in its special power which even released the dead from the torments of hell.

Princess E. S. Shahaeva reported a most astonishing prodigy, namely a case of levitation during prayer.

---

[92] Memorial service of prayer for the departed.

Amazing Wonderworker

She received a visit from Petersburg of G. Y., her sick nephew. Without delay she brought him to Sarov, to Father Seraphim. The young man was so ill and weak that he could not walk, and he had to be carried on a bed into the Monastery enclosure.

"Father Seraphim was standing at the time at the door of his cell as if he had expected to meet the paralysed man. He asked them at once to bring the patient into his cell and, turning to him, he said:

"Pray, my joy, and I shall also pray for you; only mind, lie as you do and do not turn to the other side."

The sick man remained lying in obedience to the Elder. But his patience wore out; curiosity urged him to look and see what the Elder was doing. Glancing back, he saw Father Seraphim standing in the air in an attitude of prayer. This unexpected and extraordinary spectacle made him cry out.

After finishing his prayer, Father Seraphim went up to him and said:

"Now you will tell everyone that Seraphim is a Saint, that he prays in the air. The Lord will have mercy upon you. But mind, protect yourself with silence and do not tell anyone till the day of my death, otherwise your illness will return."

G. Y. actually rose from his bed, and though he still had to lean on people for support, he walked out of the cell. At the Monastery hostel he was assailed

St. Seraphim of Sarov

with questions: "What did Father Seraphim do? What did he say?" But to everyone's surprise he never said a word. The young man was completely healed and went back to Petersburg, but after some time he returned to the estate of Princess Shahaeva. There he learnt that St. Seraphim had rested from his labours, and then he related the miracle of levitation.

One instance of this kind of prayer happened to be seen by chance, but, of course the Elder was more than once raised into the air by the grace of God in the course of his extensive spiritual labours.

On another occasion St. Seraphim himself related the following facts. "Two Nuns, who had both been Abbesses, died. The Lord revealed to me how their souls had been subjected to the aerial tests, how they had been tried and then condemned. For three days and nights I prayed, wretched as I am, entreating the Mother of God for them, and the Lord in His goodness pardoned them through the prayers of the Mother of God; they passed all the aerial tests and received forgiveness through God's mercy."

The water of St. Seraphim's well had a special miraculous power according to his prayer, even during his life-time.

Hieromonk Anastasius of Sarov related that he once happened to be with St. Seraphim who said to him during their conversation: "I have prayed, Father, that this water in the well should have the power to heal diseases."

Amazing Wonderworker

This prayer of the Saint, who even then had great boldness towards God, explains two facts: 1) that the water from Seraphim's well never becomes fetid, however long it may stand even in an open vessel; and 2) that those who visit the Sarov Monastery and bathe in the pavilions by the well at all seasons of the year experience no harmful after-effects, but on the contrary get better and recover from their illnesses, though the water in the well even in summer has a temperature of 6° to 10° R. Let us now relate instances of miraculous cures from the water of St. Seraphim's well, which occurred during the Saint's life-time.

In the course of a visit to Father Seraphim Tatiana Vasilievna Barinova complained to him of her disease. She had an incurable cancer on her arm, and the whole of her arm was bandaged. Father Seraphim told her to wash her arm with water from the well. Tatiana Vasilievna thought at first: "How can I do that when my arm gets worse at the slightest contact with anything moist?" However, she obeyed and washed her arm. At once the scaly skin appeared to slip off her arm, and ever since then both her arms have been well.

Father Seraphim told many people, even those who had wounds, to pour over themselves the water from his well and all were cured by it from their various diseases.

"In 1830," related Abbess Pulcheria of the Slobodsky Convent in the Viatka diocese, "while I

397

St. Seraphim of Sarov

was still living in the world, I undertook in accordance with a vow, a journey to Sarov by water on the Volga. On the way I fell ill near Nizhny-Novgorod and my disease (a swelling of the whole body) soon grew so much worse that I had to stay at Nizhny-Novgorod for four weeks and wait there either for recovery or death. I was given shelter and nursed by the hospitable Nuns of the Kresto-Vozdvizhensky Convent, and I even received the viaticum for my passage to the other world by the blessing of Abbess Dorothea.

"But as I had firm faith in the salutary power of Father Seraphim's prayers, I asked him more than once with tears, though absent, to pray for me a sinner, that the Lord should prolong my life, if only for a short time, so that I might go to Sarov and receive a blessing from the holy Elder. God heard my prayers; my health improved a little, and I decided to continue my journey, in spite of the swelling of my whole body. On my way I was again obliged to stop for two weeks with the Alexeyievsky Community at Arzamas owing to complete exhaustion. Besides being swollen and weak, my body became quite yellow, and it was evident I was suffering from dropsy. After two weeks I again felt some relief. I continued my journey, though with the utmost difficulty, and at last by God's help I reached Sarov.

"On the following day, after the early Liturgy, we went at the appointed time to the Elder's ante-room and I saw there among the crowd of visitors a man who was weeping bitterly. Father Seraphim was

Amazing Wonderworker

sternly rebuking him for something, and when he wanted to hand him a gift, the Elder replied: 'I won't take it now, I won't take it now.' I had also prepared a gift, but on hearing his last words, I did not dare to offer it, but hid it and backed towards the door, so that I stood behind everyone else. And what do you think? Neither my thought nor my act had escaped Father Seraphim's perspicacity. Making his way through the crowd of visitors, he came up to me with a smile and silently stretched out his hand.

"Not knowing what to do for joy and surprise, I hastily handed him my gift--a towel. He took it, wiped himself three times with it and said to me: 'Follow me, my joy.' Bringing me into his cell, he blessed me, gave me some prosphora[93] and holy water and then said to me: 'I shall see you tomorrow.' On my return to the hospice, I felt that my illness, which seemed to have left me for a time, had returned again.

"On the following day, after the early Liturgy, Father Seraphim went to his hermitage; and we had to go there to get his blessing. I could hardly follow my companions.

"We sat by Father Seraphim's cell for about an hour, and while we waited for him to come out, we all silently said the Prayer of Jesus. At last he came out to

---

[93] A prosphora is a tiny "cottage" loaf used in the Holy Liturgy. Individuals may also send to the sanctuary a prosphora from which the priest takes a few crumbs, and puts them on the paten with the Lamb, in the name of the living or the departed.

St. Seraphim of Sarov

us in a half-mantle[94] with a lighted candle in his hands, and began to bless all who came up to him in turn, saying to everyone something for the good of his soul. I went up to him last of all and he said, looking at me: 'You are not well, mother.' Then he blessed me and continued: 'Go and wash in the well, drink a little and you will be well.' I replied: 'I have already drunk and washed, Father, when I came here.' To this he again said: 'Take some water from the well with you, mother, drink and wash, and wash your body. Christ's Apostles will heal you and you will be well.' When I told him that I had nothing to take the water in, he brought a small jug out of his cell, repeating as he gave it to me his former words, and he said them over again on my return with the water from the well.

"On my arrival at the hospice, I at once carried out exactly all Father Seraphim's instructions without the least fear of using water in a case of dropsy. And by the prayers of His Saint the Lord God worked a miracle on me a sinner. To the surprise of everyone, especially of those who had forbidden me to pour water over my body saying that the dropsy did not like it, I rose on the next day quite cured, and I had so changed for the better that those who had seen me on the previous night did not recognize me in the morning. All the water which had been under the skin and which had made me look unnaturally fat, had run out, the swollen appearance had disappeared, and the yellow colour of my body gave place to a natural complex-

---

[94] Russian: Polumantia.

Amazing Wonderworker

ion. My pain ceased completely. In a word, I seemed reborn.

"Just before setting out on my return journey Father Seraphim sent me and my two companions, with his blessing, a symbolical sign to each of us: to me a staff with a crook, to another a stick with four stems, and to the third a simple stick. We did not understand then the meaning of these symbols, but subsequent events showed us both their full significance and Father Seraphim's spiritual insight. I, unworthy as I am, entered a Convent and now carry the staff of an Abbess. My other companion embraced monasticism with her two sons and her daughter, and the third also entered a Monastery, but alone. And so everything was fulfilled according to the prediction of God's Elder."

Olympiada Lubkova wrote to Father Joasaph of how she was cured from cholera through the water from Seraphim's well.

"In August 1831 my Mother, Olga Petrovna Lubkova, went on a pilgrimage from Nizhny-Novgorod to Sarov with my eldest sister Mary. In the course of three days she was granted to see Father Seraphim several times and to talk to him. When she asked for his blessing for their return journey, Father Seraphim said good-bye to them, but a few minutes later he called them back, saying:

St. Seraphim of Sarov

"'Take this bottle of water with you. If anyone is taken ill, then give some of it. It is good for sick people.'

"They started back at once, arrived home safely and found everybody in good health. Before supper I felt a violent fit of dizziness and sickness, but hid it from my family, though I knew that such fits might be dangerous, because a violent epidemic of cholera was raging in Nizhny-Novgorod. After supper all soon went to bed, but my attacks of sickness became more and more violent, and I wanted to go into another room so as not to wake up my mother who was tired after her journey. But I had hardly left my bed, when the dizziness and sickness changed into unmistakable fits of cholera and I fell to the ground in utter exhaustion. All woke up and hurriedly put me to bed, and I remained unconscious until 7 o'clock in the morning. When the doctor came, he prescribed a medicine but ordered me to be bled first. His assistant was sent for, but in those difficult times he was always out visiting the sick. So for a time I remained without any kind of help. As for home remedies, they did not stop the fits of cholera in the least.

"Utterly exhausted by this prolonged and torturing nausea, I remembered the healing water which we had brought from Father Seraphim and spoke to my mother about it. She cried rapturously: 'Oh! I had forgotten it.' At once they gave me some of this water in a glass, I took about three swallows and suddenly, instead of the nausea, I felt a copious perspiration and an inclination to sleep. I was left alone.

Amazing Wonderworker

"While I was lying in a kind of pleasant exhaustion, in a state of semi-consciousness, for more than a hour, I suddenly felt as if something flashed past my eyes and a whisper reached my ears: 'Get up!' Opening my eyes I felt first of all an extraordinary freshness in all my body and a return of strength. Then I saw before me the glass of healing water; I at once took a few swallows, and got up well. Only the swelling which remained in the region of my heart testified to my recent illness.

"It is impossible to describe my mother's joy at what had happened. She wept for gratitude."

All Saints Who Shone Forth in the Russian Land
Commemorated by the Russian Orthodox Church on the Second
Sunday After Pentecost.

Chapter XVI

The Predictions of St. Seraphim

On many occasions and to many people St. Seraphim foretold the future which he foresaw with his spiritual sight. Nadezhda Feodorovna Ostrovsky relates:

"My brother, Lieutenant-Colonel V.F. Ostrovsky, often went to Nizhny-Novgorod on a visit to our aunt, Princess Gruzinsky, who had great faith in Father Seraphim. Once she sent him on some errand to the Sarov Monastery to the Elder. Father Seraphim received my brother very kindly and, in the midst of his instructions, suddenly said:

"'Ah, what a drunkard you will be, brother Vladimir!'

"These words made my brother exceedingly sad and unhappy. He had been endowed by God with many precious talents and always used them to the glory of God. He was deeply devoted to Father Seraphim, and to his subordinates he was a tender father. Therefore, he considered himself far from being a drunkard, which was incompatible with his calling and manner of life. The clairvoyant Elder, noticing his trouble, added:

"'But do not be troubled or sad. The Lord sometimes allows people who are devoted to Him to fall into such dreadful vices; and this is in order to prevent them from falling into a still greater sin--pride. Your temptation will pass by the mercy of God, and you

St. Seraphim of Sarov

will spend the remaining days of your life in humility. Only do not forget your sin.'

"This wonderful prediction of the man of God was actually fulfilled later on. As a consequence of various adverse circumstances my brother fell a prey to that unhappy passion--drunkenness; and to the general sorrow of his relations, he spent several years in this wretched condition. But at last owing to Father Seraphim's prayers and to his own simplicity of heart, the Lord had mercy on him. He not only abandoned his former vice, but also completely changed his manner of life and tried to live according to the commandments of the Gospel as a Christian should."

A.A.T. while still quite young (she was about twelve) once went to the Sarov Monastery with her mother in order to see Father Seraphim and get his blessing. This was in 1830. On her arrival at Sarov she heard from her nurse about some poor exhausted convict who was passing by the Monastery in heavy chains and looked very miserable. At the sight of this unfortunate man she was greatly touched by his condition, but did not give him any alms because she had no money with her at the time; then she found a silver coin of fifty kopeks and as she had nothing smaller, she decided to give it to the wretched man. When they came to Father Seraphim, the clairvoyant Elder who had never before seen them, called the girl, blessed her and said to her kindly: "It was good that you gave fifty kopeks to the beggar," and he quite unexpectedly addressed her as "your excellency." Her mother was surprised at this form of address and tried

The Predictions of St. Seraphim

to explain to the Elder that this title did not at all belong to them; but in talking to them the Saint continued to give the girl this title. And so they returned home without having learned the cause of this strange form of address from the Elder, and for a long time they wondered what it could mean. But afterwards it became clear, for when A.A.T. came of age, she married a general.

Two months before the appointment of Father Antony of Vysokogorsk as Superior of the Laura of St. Sergius, and while the former Superior Archimandrite Athanasius was still living and there was no talk of his being transferred, Father Seraphim foretold this appointment. This prediction was recorded by Father Antony himself.

In January 1831 Father Antony went to St. Seraphim in Sarov in order to ask his advice regarding his thoughts of death which had become almost an obsession and which greatly disturbed him. Having arrived in Sarov in the evening, he went straight to Father Seraphim's cell. But before reaching it, he met some brethren of the Sarov Monastery who told him that Father Seraphim had not yet returned to the Monastery from his hermitage. It was already about five o'clock and it was growing dark. The traveler stopped, and was wondering whether to go somewhere or wait for him there. Just at that moment the brethren who were standing with him saw the Elder coming in the distance and exclaimed: "Here comes Father Seraphim!" The Elder was walking in his ordinary garb with a sack on his back, leaning on an axe.

St. Seraphim of Sarov

Father Antony at once went up to him and bowed to him in the usual way.

"Well?" the Elder asked him.

"I have come to you, Father with a sorrowful soul," replied Father Antony.

"Let us go to my cell, my joy," said the Elder affably.

When they were alone in the cell, Father Antony asked St. Seraphim to tell him frankly whether his sorrowful thoughts would be realized. Was not his death actually at hand? "Whether I sit in my cell or walk in the Monastery," said Antony, "it seems to me that I see the Monastery for the last time. From this I conclude that I shall soon die, and that is why I have already arranged the place of my grave. I wish to know about my death solely so as to change my life, so that I may resign my post and consecrate my last days to quiet consideration. The news of my death will not frighten me," added Father Antony.

Father Seraphim listened without changing his position and holding Antony by the hand. When he had finished, the blessed Elder regarded him lovingly and said: "Your thoughts are not right, not right at all, my joy. The Providence of God is entrusting you with a large Laura."

Father Antony thought that St. Seraphim wanted to distract him from his sorrowful thoughts, and there-

The Predictions of St. Seraphim

fore he interrupted him saying: "Father, this will not quieten me, this will not set my thoughts at rest. I implore you, tell me frankly, are not my thoughts of death a sign from God that my end is near? And in that case I shall ask your prayers for my soul and will receive your word peacefully and thankfully. I want to meet the hour of my death with due preparation."

Father Seraphim replied with an angelic smile: "Your thoughts are wrong! I tell you, the Providence of God is entrusting you with a large Laura."

But the Superior of the Vysogorsk Monastery replied: "How can the Vysogorsk Monastery become a Laura? God grant that it may not become worse than it now is."

To Father Antony's still greater surprise, Father Seraphim without changing his mind, started asking him to receive kindly the brethren who would come to the Laura from Sarov, or anyone he might send. Remaining under the same impression, Antony continued: "Father! who will want to leave Sarov for the poor Vysogorsk Monastery? But if anyone wanted to or was sent by you, you know my constant readiness to do whatever you like. But it cannot really happen."

Father Seraphim said, as if following the same line of thought: "Do not leave my orphans, when the time comes."

Father Antony could no longer restrain himself, and under an impulse of unbounded love and veneration for the Elder, he rushed towards him, embraced him and wept copiously. Not understanding what he heard, he concentrated his attention on the word "orphans," and it seemed to him that the Elder was speaking of his speedy end. Blessed Seraphim went on: "Pray for the souls of my parents Isidore and Agathia." Then he advised him to submit himself in everything to the will of God, to be diligent in prayer, to carry out his duties strictly, to be charitable and indulgent with the brethren. "Be a mother, and not a father, to the brethren," he said and urged him to be kind to all in general and to be humble. "Humility and discretion," he said, "are the beauty of virtue." Then Father Seraphim repeatedly embraced him, blessed him with the cross which hung on his chest and said: "Now go in the name of the Lord. It is time for you to go; they are waiting for you."

On his way back Father Antony noticed that the Monk who was travelling with him was weeping. "Why do you weep?" asked Antony. The Monk replied that on his arrival in Sarov he had met Father Seraphim who was returning from the hermitage to his monastic cell, and who had said to him: "Well, you will soon have to part with your Superior."

Meanwhile time passed; January and February went by, and the Great Fast began. On the 2nd of March, Monday of the first week of Lent, the Superior took his turn at reading the Psalms (each Brother used to read for two hours, and this reading was continued day and night). Just then a letter was brought to him from the Metropolitan of Moscow. Father Antony

The Predictions of St. Seraphim

went to his cell. The letter which invited Antony to take the post of Superior of the Laura of St. Sergius, also enclosed an envelope addressed to His Eminence Athanasius, Bishop of Nizhny-Novgorod, concerning the speedy release of Father Antony from his post of Superior of the Vysogorsk Monastery and his transfer to Moscow. On March 4th he was released.

Saint Seraphim's prophecy about the death of Alexy Prokudin refers to the year 1832. Prokudin was a retired hussar and owned an estate in the Province of Nizhny-Novgorod. Being an extremely religious man, he regarded St. Seraphim's personality with profound reverence and lived according to his advice.

Being kind and sympathetic towards the sufferings of his neighbours, he carried his charity to such a degree that he gave away all he had to the poor.

In the summer of 1832 he was with St. Seraphim in the Sarov Monastery, accompanied by the Aksakovs.

When Prokudin went to say good-bye, St. Seraphim came out to him with a bunch of lighted wax candles in his hand and invited him into his cell. Having stuck four candles to the edges of his coffin which stood in the anteroom, St. Seraphim beckoned to Prokudin to come in and then looked intently and sadly into his eyes. He blessed the oaken coffin with a large Sign of the Cross and said in a hollow, but solemn voice: "On the Feast of the Protection."

St. Seraphim of Sarov

The holy Elder's words were interpreted both by Prokudin and the bystanders as a prophecy of his end.

St. Seraphim's prophecy came to pass that very year contrary to all expectations, as Prokudin felt quite strong on that day and cheerfully received the numerous guests who had come to congratulate him on his reception of the Holy Mysteries. Suddenly, at half past two, he whom rich and poor alike called the friend of the needy and destitute, sank down in his armchair, leant his head against its high back and died quietly and unobtrusively, as a baby falls asleep on its mother's lap.

Chapter XVII

Apparition of the Mother of God To St. Seraphim

One year and nine months before his departure from this world St. Seraphim was favoured by a wonderful visitation of the heavenly Queen. This was Our Lady's twelfth visit to him. It took place early in the morning, on the Feast of the Annunciation, 25th March 1831. It was a kind of premonition of his blessed end and of the incorruptible glory which awaited him. Mother Eupraxia, an elderly Nun of the Diveyev Convent who died on the 28th of March 1865, wrote of this wonderful event as follows:

"Father told me two days in advance to come to him on that day.

"When I came, Father announced: 'We shall have a vision of the Mother of God,' and making me bend to the ground, he covered me with his mantle[95] and read over me out of a book. Then, lifting me up, he said: 'Now hold on to me and don't be afraid of anything.'

"At that moment there was a noise like the noise of a forest in a strong gale. When it subsided, we heard singing which sounded like Church singing. Then the door of the cell opened of itself, it became light, brighter than day, and the cell was filled with a fragrance like that of rose-scented incense, only better.

"Father was kneeling with his hands raised to heaven. I was terrified. Father stood up and said:

---

[95] Russ. mantia.

St. Seraphim of Sarov

'Don't be afraid, child. It is not a misfortune, it is a mercy sent to us by God. Here is our most glorious, most pure Lady, the most holy Mother of God coming to us!'

"Two Angels were walking in front holding--one in his right hand and the other in his left--branches which were just bursting into blossom. Their hair looked like golden flax and lay on their shoulders. They stood in front. They were followed by St. John the Baptist and St. John the Divine. Their garments were white, shining with purity. After them came the Mother of God who was followed by twelve virgins.

"The Queen of Heaven was wearing a mantle[96] similar to the one painted on the Icon of Our Lady of Sorrows. It was glistening, though I cannot say what colour it was; it was of inexpressible beauty, fastened under her neck by a large round buckle or clasp studded with crosses variously adorned, but with what--I don't know. I only remember that it shone with an extraordinary brightness. Her dress which was covered by her mantle was green, girded high up by a belt. Over the mantle there was a kind of epitrachelion, and on her wrists were cuffs which, like the epitrachelion, were covered with crosses. She seemed taller than all the virgins. On her head was a high crown richly adorned with crosses; it was beautiful, wonderful, and shone with such light that my eyes could not look at it; nor could I look at the buckle or clasp, or at the face of the heavenly Queen herself. Her hair lay loose

---

[96] Russ. mantia.

Apparition of the Mother of God

on her shoulders and was longer and fairer[97] than that of the Angels.

"The virgins came after her in pairs. They wore crowns and garments of various colours. They were of different statures, and their faces were also different as well as their hair which lay on their shoulders. All were of great beauty, but some were more beautiful than others. They stood round us all. The Queen of Heaven was in the middle.

"The cell became spacious and its top was filled with flames which seemed like burning candles. It was lighter than at midday, but it was a special light unlike the light of day; it was brighter and whiter than sunlight.

"I was terrified and fell down. The Queen of Heaven came up to me and, touching me with her right hand, said: 'Stand up, girl, and don't be afraid of us. Just such maidens as you are, have come here with me.'

"I did not feel how I got up. The Queen of Heaven graciously repeated: 'Don't be afraid. We have come to visit you.'

"Father Seraphim was no longer on his knees, but was standing on his feet before the most holy Mother of God, and she was speaking to him as graciously as if he were one of her own family.

---

[97] Fairer, i.e. more beautiful (not lighter in colour).

St. Seraphim of Sarov

"Filled with great joy I asked Father Seraphim where we were. I thought I was no longer alive. Then, when I asked him: 'Who are these?' the most holy Mother of God told me to go up to the virgins and ask them myself.

"They were standing in order on both sides as they had come: first, the Great Martyrs Barbara and Katharine; second, the Protomartyr St. Thekla and the Great Martyr Marina; third, the Great Martyr and Queen St. Irene and Saint Eupraxia; fourth, the Great Martyrs Sts. Pelagia and Dorothea; fifth, Saint Macrina and the Martyr Justina; sixth, the Great Martyr St. Juliana and the Martyr Anicia.

"I went up to each of them, and each told me her name and the labours of her martyrdom and life for Christ's sake similarly to what is written of them in the *Lives of the Saints.* They all said: 'God did not grant us this glory for nothing, but for our suffering and revilement. You will suffer too.'

"Much of what the most holy Mother of God said to Father Seraphim the sharer of his vision could not hear, but this she heard: 'Do not leave my virgins' (the Diveyev Sisters).

"Father Seraphim replied: 'O Lady! I am gathering them, but I cannot manage them by myself.'

"To this the Queen of Heaven answered: 'I will help you, my beloved, in everything. Impose upon them obedience. If they do it, they will be with you

Apparition of the Mother of God

and near me; but if they lose their wisdom,[98] they will be deprived of the lot of these near virgins of mine. There will be no place or crown of this kind for them. Whoever offends them will be struck by me; whoever serves them for the Lord's sake will be remembered before God.'

"Then turning to me, she said: 'Look at these virgins of mine and at their crowns. Some of them left an earthly kingdom and riches, desiring the eternal and heavenly Kingdom. They loved voluntary poverty, they loved the Lord alone, and you see what glory and honour they have been granted. As it was before, so it is now. Only the former martyrs suffered openly, and the present ones do so secretly, through heartfelt sorrows, but their reward will be the same.'

"The vision ended with the most holy Mother of God saying to Father Seraphim: 'Soon, my beloved, you will be with us,' and she blessed him. All the Saints bid him farewell. St. John the Baptist and St. John the Divine blessed him, while the virgins and he kissed one another's hands.

"I was told: 'This vision was granted you by the prayers of Father Seraphim, Mark, Nazarius and Pachomius.' And then in an instant everything vanished. This vision lasted more than an hour.

"After that, Father turned to me and said: 'You see, Mother, what grace has been granted us sinners by the

---

[98] Cp. Mat.25:1-4.

St. Seraphim of Sarov

Lord. This is already the twelfth time that I have had such a vision from God. And now the Lord has granted it to you! We have had something which justifies our faith and hope in the Lord. Conquer the enemy--the devil--and be wise in all your dealings with him. The Lord will help you in everything. Call to your help the Lord and the Mother of God, and the Saints, and remember poor me. Remember and say in your prayer: 'O Lord, how am I to die? How shall I appear before the awful judgement, O Lord? What answer shall I give for my deeds, O Lord? Queen of Heaven, help me!'"

Chapter XVIII

The Last Year of St. Seraphim's Life, His Blessed End and Burial (1832-1833)

As the end of his life drew near, a year before his death, St. Seraphim began to feel an unusual exhaustion. Therefore he went less frequently to his near hermitage and did not always receive visitors in his cell in the Monastery. It made many sad, but the most fervent of his admirers, wishing to see him at all costs and get the benefit of his advice, would wait patiently for an opportunity and would stay for quite a long time in the Monastery.

At this time he was visited by a Diveyev Sister, Paraskeva Ivanovna. He was in the forest, in his near hermitage. After giving her his blessing St. Seraphim sat on a block of wood, and the Sister knelt near him. Father Seraphim started a spiritual talk and went into ecstasy. He stood up, raised his arms and turned his eyes towards heaven. The light of grace illumined his soul at the thought of the bliss of the future life. For the Elder had been talking about the eternal joy which awaits us in heaven in return for the brief sorrows of this temporal life. "What joy, what rapture floods the soul of a righteous man when, after its separation from the body, it is met by Angels who bring it before the face of God!" As he enlarged on this theme the Elder asked the Sister several times whether she understood him. But the Sister had been listening to everything without missing a word. She had understood the Elder's conversation, but she did not see that his talk implied his end. Then Father Seraphim began to repeat what he had already said:

St. Seraphim of Sarov

"My strength is giving out. Live alone now. I am going to leave you."

The Sister thought that he wanted to go into reclusion again, but Father Seraphim replied to her thought:

"I have been looking for a Mother (Superior) for you, but I could not find one. After me you will find no one to take my place. I leave you to the Lord and to His immaculate Mother."

The Sister still did not understand that the Elder was speaking of his death and thought that though Father Seraphim was entrusting them to the Lord and to the Mother of God, still the Convent could not remain without a spiritual director. But the Elder replied:

"You will not find a man, Mother, even though you search with a lantern by daylight.[99] I leave you to the Lord and to His immaculate Mother."

Then he spoke more plainly about his end. Thereupon the Sister fell down at his feet and sobbed so bitterly that she could neither speak herself nor hear what he said. Father Seraphim began to recite by heart the Gospel of St. Matthew, *Ye are the light of the world* (5:14) to verse 20, and when he had finished, he went on to the Gospel of St. John beginning

---

[99] This is an allusion to Diogenes who, when asked what he was doing with a lantern in the daytime, replied: "I am looking for a man." This anecdote was very popular in Russia.

The Last Year

with chapter 14:1: *Let not your heart be troubled.* He also read the 15th chapter and finished with verses 23-24 of the 16th chapter: *Amen, Amen, I say to you, whatsoever you shall ask the Father in My name, He will give it you. Hitherto you have asked for nothing in My name; ask, and you shall receive, that your joy may be full.* Here Father Seraphim stopped and said:

"Why are you still weeping, Mother? In time you will have a Saint for your mother."

When other Sisters of the Diveyev Convent visited Father Seraphim in his cell shortly before his death, he usually pointed to the Icon of Our Lady of Compunction[100] and often said to comfort them:

"I entrust you and leave you to the care of the Queen of Heaven."

Realizing that his end was near, St. Seraphim was preparing at this time for his departure. He went less frequently to his hermitage. He also received fewer visitors in his cell, in order to devote himself unhindered to the final preparation of himself for eternity. At this time he was frequently seen in his ante-room. He used to sit in his coffin immersed in meditation on the end of his life, the fate of man beyond the grave and his own too. These meditations were often accompanied by bitter weeping, and they began and ended with long prayers.

---

[100] Or, Tenderness, or Tender Emotion.

St. Seraphim of Sarov

Half a year before his death Father Seraphim said to many decisively when he took leave of them: "We shall see one another no more." Some asked his blessing to come in Lent for a retreat in Sarov, so as to see him once again. "Then my door will be shut," the Elder replied. "You will not see me."

It was becoming evident that the Saint's life was declining, though his spirit was as vigorous and alert as ever.

"My life is getting short," he said to some of the brethren. "In spirit I seem to have only just been born, but in body I am dead to everything."

Four months before his death, in August 1832, His Eminence Bishop Arsenius (Moskvin) of Tambov, on his first diocesan visitation, came also to the Sarov Monastery. St. Seraphim was in his hermitage at this time, yet he considered it his duty to go to the Monastery solely to meet his new archpastor together with the brethren. After the reception he went back to his hermitage. Bishop Arsenius inspected attentively and minutely all the Churches, the cells of the brethren, and the premises within the Monastery. Then he wished to see all the institutions and buildings which were outside the enclosure. Accompanied by the Sarov bursar, Hieromonk Isaiah, and a Priest of the Tambov Cathedral, Father Nikephor Teliatinsky, he visited the hermitages of Seraphim and Dorotheus. Father Seraphim was busy consolidating the bank of a small brook with stones. But as soon as he saw the

The Last Year

Bishop approaching, he left his work and, throwing himself at his feet, asked for and took his blessing.

"What are you doing here?" Bishop Arsenius asked him sympathetically.

"You see, holy Vladyka," replied the Saint, "I am reinforcing the bank with stones, so that the water may not wash away the bank and spoil it."

"It is a good work, old man of God," said the Bishop. "But now show me your little hermitage within your hermitage."

"All right, Father,"[101] he answered and led the Bishop genially into his cell.

According to the description of those who were present on this occasion, there was nothing special in his cell. It was an ordinary wooden cottage with a small ante-room. The furniture consisted of a simple unpainted table of lime-wood and two similar chairs. In a corner stood the holy Icons with a lamp burning in front of them. There were also two Service books. As they entered the cell Father Seraphim presented the Bishop with a prayer rope, a bundle of candles wrapped in homespun linen, a bottle of oil and some woolen stockings. The Bishop accepted the presents with paternal kindliness. Then he asked St. Seraphim:

---

[101] Russ. Batiushka.

St. Seraphim of Sarov

"But where in this hermitage have you the other hermitage, the other still more secluded place?"

But as he knew from hearsay where the place was, he did not wait for Father Seraphim's reply and made straight for the stove. Father Seraphim said naively in order to stop him: "Do not go there, Father, you will get dirty."

But the Bishop opened the door which screened the empty space between the wall of the cell and the stove, and there he saw a small space which was so narrow that a man could enter it and remain standing or kneeling only with difficulty, but to sit down or make yourself comfortable was quite impossible. Here too, as in the first cell, a small Icon with a burning lamp stood in the corner between the wall and the door-post. Evidently the Saint sometimes retired there for vigils and prayer.

Thence the Bishop went to the hermitage of Dorotheus, intending to visit Father Seraphim again on his way back. Father Nikephor remained with the Saint, spending the time in conversation.

When the Bishop returned, Father Seraphim took him by the hand and reverently asked him:

"You see, Father, the pilgrims come to me, poor Seraphim, and ask me to give them something as a blessing, and I give them dried bread, black or white, and a spoonful of red Church wine. May I do that?"

The Last Year

To this the Bishop replied: "You may, you may, but only separately, so that if you give dry bread to someone, do not give him any red wine. Otherwise the simple people, as I have heard, in their simplicity think and tell others that you give them Holy Communion. It would be still better," added the Bishop, "to give no wine at all, but only the dry bread."

"All right, Father," the Elder replied. "That is what I shall do."

And it was afterwards noticed that St. Seraphim actually did do that to the end of his life.

Soon after this conversation the Bishop bid farewell to Father Seraphim. The Saint took leave of him in rather an unusual way. Having taken the Bishop's blessing for the last time, he bowed down at his feet, and though the Bishop tried to lift him up and asked him to stand, St. Seraphim remained on his knees and continued bowing to him until the Bishop was quite out of sight.

On the following night St. Seraphim, as though to prove his obedience, brought a small vessel of Church wine to the cell where Bishop Arsenius was staying, and gave it to his cell-attendant, saying:

"Give it to Father from sinful Seraphim."

It subsequently became clear that all these presents were connected with the Saint's approaching end, and

St. Seraphim of Sarov

referred to his request to be remembered in prayer after his death, which he had also expressed verbally to his Bishop.

Bishop Arsenius on his part conscientiously carried out Father Seraphim's wish. The candles, oil and wine were used when the Bishop celebrated a Requiem Liturgy for the eternal repose of the blessed Elder Seraphim, while the prayer rope, the stockings and the homespun linen he kept himself.

A few months before his end St. Seraphim had letters sent to certain people inviting them to see him in the Monastery. As to those of his friends who could not come to him, he instructed people to tell them after his death what was needful and profitable for their souls, adding in explanation: "They will not see me themselves."

Not long before his end a Brother who came to him in the evening noticed that it was dark in his cell. But hardly had the Elder said that the lamp should be lighted--and crossed himself three times with the invocation: "My Lady, Mother of God!"--than the lamp was lit of itself. That same Brother came on another occasion at 7 p.m. according to an appointment the Elder had made with him, and saw him in his anteroom in front of his coffin. The Brother wanted to take a light from the cell which the Elder used to give him for a blessing. The Brother opened the door, and St. Seraphim said: "Oh! my lamp has gone out, but it ought to burn!" And he began to pray before the Icon of the Mother of God.

The Last Year

At that moment there appeared before the Icon a bluish light which stretched itself out like a ribbon and began to spin round the wick of a large wax candle, which it lit. The Elder took a small candle and, lighting it from the big one, handed it to the Brother and began talking to him. He then mentioned among other things that there would shortly be a guest from Voronezh, told the Brother his name and what he was to tell him, and then added: "Do not bring him to me. He will not see me!" During this conversation the Elder's face shone with light. At last he said: "Blow out the candle." The Brother blew, and extinguished the candle.

"There, that is how my life will go out," said the Elder, "and I shall be seen no more."

A certain Brother, seeing his ascetic life, asked him for his own edification: "Why don't we, Father, lead as strict a life as the ancient ascetics did?"

"Because," replied the Saint, "we have no determination to do so. If we had the determination, we should live as those Fathers did who, in olden times, shone with labours and piety; because God gives His grace and help to the faithful and to those who seek the Lord with all their heart now just as He did before. For according to the word of God, *Jesus Christ is the same yesterday, and today, and for ever* (Heb. 13:8).

This profound and holy truth which St. Seraphim had learned from actual experience in his own life

St. Seraphim of Sarov

was, so to say, his final message and the seal of his labours.

A week before his end, on Christmas 1832, St. Seraphim unexpectedly came to the Liturgy which was celebrated by Abbot Niphont. He had Holy Communion and after Liturgy talked to the Abbot. Among other things he interceded with the Abbot for many, especially for the younger brethren. He did not forget to mention for the last time that, when he died, he should be put into his coffin. Having said good-bye to the Abbot and the brethren, the Saint returned to his cell and gave one of the Monks, Jacob, who was afterward a Hieromonk in the Tolshevsky Monastery, an enamelled Icon representing the visit of the Mother of God to St. Sergius, saying: "Put this Icon on me when I die and put me into the grave with it. This Icon," he continued, "has been sent to me by the venerable Father Archimandrite Antony, Superior of the holy Laura, from the relics of St. Sergius."

On New Year's eve (1833) St. Seraphim measured his grave himself by the side of the sanctuary of the Cathedral of the Dormition, on the very spot he had marked with a stone on leaving reclusion.

On the 1st January, 1833, a Sunday, St. Seraphim came for the last time to the Hospital Church of the Wonderworkers of Solovtsy. He came to the early Liturgy, put candles before all the Icons and kissed them. Having received Holy Communion at the ordinary time, after the Liturgy, he said good-bye to all the brethren, blessed and kissed them all and com-

The Last Year

forted them with the words: "Save your souls, do not despond, be watchful. Crowns are being prepared for us today."

Then he kissed the Crucifix and the Icon of the Mother of God and, having made the usual acts of adoration in the sanctuary[102], he went round the altar and out through the north door, as if to indicate that man comes into the world by one door and goes out by another.

After the Liturgy Father Seraphim was visited by Hieromonk Theoktist of the Vysogorsky Monastery of Arzamas. Father Seraphim said to him at the end of the talk: "You had better serve here." But Theoktist was in a hurry to get home and he refused to serve in Sarov. Then Father Seraphim said to him: "Well, then you will serve in Diveyev." Of course, Father Theoktist did not understand the meaning of these words and, having taken the Elder's blessing, he left Sarov the same day.

Near St. Seraphim's cell was the cell of a Monk called Paul who, being his neighbour, performed the duties of his cell attendant. When he went from the Monastery to his near hermitage, St. Seraphim used to leave candles burning in his cell which he had lit from the morning before the Icons. Father Paul had often

---

[102] On entering and leaving the sanctuary, it is customary to make two bows (making the sign of the cross each time) and then to kiss the altar, after which a third bow is made.

St. Seraphim of Sarov

told him that the burning candles might cause a fire. To this St:Seraphim always replied:

"While I am alive, there will be no fire; but when I die, my death will be revealed by a fire."

His prediction was justified.

On the 1st January 1833, Father Paul noticed that St. Seraphim went out of his cell three times in the course of the day to the spot which he had assigned as the place of his burial. In the evening he heard Father Seraphim singing in his cell the holy songs of the Easter Canon: "Having beheld the Resurrection of Christ," "Shine, shine, New Jerusalem," "O great and holiest Passover, Christ."

About 6 in the morning on the 2nd January 1833, Father Paul, on leaving his cell to attend the early Liturgy, noticed in the ante-room near Father Seraphim's cell the smell of smoke. Having said the customary prayer he knocked at the door, but there was no answer. Then he went outside and told some of the brethren who were passing by. One of them, the Novice Anikita, rushed to St. Seraphim's cell and tore the door from its hinges. Entering the cell, Paul and Anikita saw that various presents made of coarse linen which had been given to the Saint by zealous pilgrims and which were lying in great disorder on a bench together with some books, had begun to smoulder. They had probably been kindled by a fallen candle whose candle-stick was standing nearby.

The Last Year

It was dark outside; there was no fire in the cell, and the Elder himself was neither to be seen nor heard. Meanwhile the early Liturgy in the Hospital Church was going on. They were already singing "It is truly meet," when the young Novice ran into the Church and informed the brethren of what had happened. The Monks hastened to St. Seraphim's cell. Father Paul and the Novice John, wanting to know whether the Elder was resting, began to grope in the dark in his cell, and found the Elder himself. They brought a lighted candle and saw that St. Seraphim was kneeling before the Icon of Our Lady of Compunction: He was in his usual white smock, bare-headed, with a brass crucifix hanging from his neck and with his arms crossed on his chest.

At first they thought that the blessed Elder had fallen asleep and began to try to wake him up, but there was no response. The great ascetic had already finished his earthly pilgrimage and was resting for ever in God. His eyes were closed. His face was animated by his last prayer.

With the blessing of the Superior the Monks lifted the Saint's body and, having dressed him according to monastic regulations in a mantle in the adjoining cell of Hieromonk Eustace, they put him into the oaken coffin which he had made with his own hands and carried him into the Cathedral.

Hieromonk Theoktist who had been at the Monastery and had left the day before, had passed the night in the village of Vertyanovo and had continued

St. Seraphim of Sarov

his journey on the following day. On the way, without any apparent reason, his sledge was slightly damaged, the horse got unharnessed and he was obliged to put up at the Diveyev Convent. There he found all the Sisters in deep grief and in tears. They were weeping over Father Seraphim's death. The Priest of Diveyev was absent on a tour of inspection. The Sisters begged Father Theoktist to serve a Pannikhida[103] for the repose of the soul of Father Seraphim. Their desire was fulfilled and the Elder's words came true: "Well, then you will serve in Diveyev."

The news of the blessed Elder's death quickly spread, and all who had known Father Seraphim during his lifetime flocked from all parts of the country to the Sarov Monastery to pray for the blessed Elder and to kiss his hand for the last time.

His body remained in the Cathedral of the Dormition for eight days and nights until all had had time to bid him farewell. During the Burial Service the Cathedral was so crowded that the candles standing near the coffin melted and went out owing to the insufferable heat. The Burial Service was performed by Abbot Niphont with the Hieromonks of the Monastery.

At that time there was a Novice in Sarov who later became an Archimandrite (Metrophan) and occupied the post of sacristan in the Laura of St. Alexander

---

[103] i.e. to conduct a short requiem service (lasting 15-20 minutes).

The Last Year

Nevsky. He reported the following miracle. When the confessor wanted to put the prayer of absolution into Father Seraphim's hand, the fingers loosened of themselves. The Abbot, the treasurer and other Monks who saw this were struck with amazement.

No sermons were preached over his grave. But the memory of his extraordinary life and the melodies of the Church hymns he so loved were more eloquent than any sermon.

The body of St. Seraphim was buried on the south side of the sanctuary of the Cathedral, beside the grave of the recluse Mark who died fifteen years before him. Later a funerary monument of cast iron was erected on the grave of St. Seraphim at the expense of a merchant of Nizhny-Novgorod called Stephen Yassyrev. The following inscription was engraved on the monument: "Under this monument is buried the body of the deceased servant of God, Hieromonk Seraphim, who passed away on the 2nd January 1833. A merchant of Kursk, he entered the Sarov Monastery at the age of seventeen and died at the age of seventy-three. All the days of his life were consecrated by him to the glory of the Lord God and to the spiritual edification of Orthodox Christians in whose hearts Seraphim even now lives."

Two remarkable circumstances accompanied St. Seraphim's departure from the world. On the actual day of the Saint's death Abbot Philaret of the Glinsky Monastery of the Mother of God (Province of Kursk) went out of the Church after Matins and, glancing up

St. Seraphim of Sarov

at the sky, he was astonished to see an extraordinary light. Then the Abbot saw in spirit that it was the soul of St. Seraphim ascending to the heavenly mansions, and he said to the brethren who were with him: "That is how the souls of the righteous depart. Father Seraphim has just passed away in Sarov."

Archbishop Antony of Voronezh who was renowned for his piety was also informed in an extraordinary manner of Father Seraphim's end. At that time Nikolas Alexandrovitch Motovilov, a landowner who had been previously healed through Father Seraphim, was in Voronezh. This is what Motovilov writes in his memoirs for the 2nd January 1833: "On the 2nd January in the evening I heard from Archbishop Antony that Father Seraphim had passed away on the previous night at 2 a.m. and that apparently he (St. Seraphim) had himself appeared to him and informed him of it. On the very same day Archbishop Antony served a Pannikhida for the Elder with all the Cathedral clergy."

As the distance between Sarov and Voronezh is about 500 kilometers, there could be no question of getting news in the evening by natural means in Voronezh of what had happened in the morning in Sarov on the same day.

Soon after St. Seraphim's death, I. J. Karatayev who was on his way to join his regiment in Kursk, passed through Sarov in order to take St. Seraphim's blessing as he always did. It was a great grief to find that the blessed Elder was no longer on earth.

The Last Year

"The news of his death," he said, "deranged my whole soul. I took it as a punishment for my sins. But after I had had a Pannikhida at his grave, I suddenly felt such peace of soul that it seemed as if I had received the forgiveness of my sins from the Elder himself and heard his promise to pray for me at the throne of God.[104]

Abbot Niphont asked him to see Father Seraphim's relations in Kursk, to convey to them some holy bread and his blessing and to tell them of the end of their blessed relative.

On his arrival in Kursk, Karatayev went at once to see Father Seraphim's relations, but he found Alexis, his brother, already dead. He had just passed away. A few days previously he had been perfectly well, only he had felt great sorrow though he had known nothing about the death of his brother and had been unable to account for his sadness. The afflicted state of his soul had constrained him to seek comfort in prayer. He had gone every day to Church; at last he had prepared for Holy Communion, and had made his confession and received the Holy Mysteries. Just at that time they received a letter from Sarov about Father Seraphim's death with a portrait of him. Then his brother began to prepare finally for his death. He received the Sacrament of Holy Unction, and shortly after this last anointing he died.

---

[104] Cp. Hebrews 4:16; 10:19; I Tim.3:13; Ephes.3:12.

St. Seraphim of Sarov

We have included this incident in St. Seraphim's biography because it was said that when he came to Kursk in 1775, he foretold his brother's end to him in the following words: "Know that when I die, your death will also follow soon after."

The Russian Orthodox people who venerated Father Seraphim during his life, continued to honour him even after his passing from this world of shadows. They came in crowds to his grave animated by a vivid faith in the power of his prayers. They came to the grave which enshrined his holy relics as they had come to him when he was still alive, in order to pour out their sorrows, confess their sins and tell him of their diseases; and according to their faith they received spiritual comfort, supernatural direction and even miraculous healing of their bodily ailments.

And why should they not come to the grave of the wonderful ascetic who had once told them prophetic words about his boldness[105] before God and his readiness to help all who would invoke him in their troubles.

"When I am no more," said the love-filled Father Seraphim to his reverent admirers, "come to my grave! Come whenever you have time, the oftener the better. All that weighs on your soul, whatever happens to you, whatever sorrow you have, come to me and bring all your troubles to my grave. Fall down on the earth and tell me everything as if I were alive. And I

---

[105] Cp. Hebrews 4:16; 10:19; I Tim.3:13; Ephes.3:12.

will hear you; all your sorrow will fly away and pass. Just as you always talked to me when I was alive, so here too! For you I am alive and will live for ever!"

The Blessed Repose of St. Seraphim of Sarov
The Saint was discovered, still in a kneeling position before the Icon of the Mother of God "Compunction".

Pilgrims at Sarov Monastery

Above: Pilgrims on the way to the holy places of Sarov at the time of the Canonization of St. Seraphim in 1903. *Below:* Pilgrims before the Shrine housing St. Seraphim's Spring, where they will bathe in the miraculous waters.

Chapter XIX

Supernatural Help and Miraculous Healings Obtained Through St. Seraphim's Intercession After His Death

The blessed Elder closed his eyes in prayer, but after his departure from this corrupt world into the Kingdom of eternal light and glory, he did not rest from his labours. Healings of the sick, comfort for the afflicted, advice to the erring flowed in a constant stream. Here in chronological order are a few instances of St. Seraphim's miraculous intervention after his death.

I

Captain African Vasilievitch Toplov wrote to Hieromonk Joasaph about the miraculous healing of his children.

"In 1834, already after Father Seraphim's death, I went to the Sarov Monastery with my family as was our custom. One of my children, my three-year-old daughter, had at that time diseased legs and could hardly stand. Therefore, after having attended a Pannikhida at Father Seraphim's grave, we all went to his hermitage and his spring, carrying the child in our arms and firmly believing that the Lord would have mercy on the suffering child through the prayers of the Elder.

"There we drank from the well, washed, and bathed the legs of the child. Then we took some of the water and went to the Monastery intending to have the

St. Seraphim of Sarov

Service of the blessing of water for her. But even before the Service we saw God's mercy to us. When we were entering the Monastery by the back gate, the little girl suddenly asked to get down from her nurse's arms with the evident intention of walking herself. The nurse opposed her for some time, but at last she decided to put her down, and began to lead her by the hand. Then the little girl pulled out her hand and to everyone's astonishment ran ahead by herself. Overjoyed at her miraculous healing we all hurried to St. Seraphim's grave and with tears thanked him for his gracious intercession for us sinners.

"In 1848 our second son twisted his leg and suffered from it for two years. Meanwhile the time had come to send the child to school. As I firmly trusted in the intercession and help of Father Seraphim who had already shown so many benefits to my family, I went with them to the Sarov Monastery. There we attended a Pannikhida at the grave of the Saint and I drove the children to the well in spite of the bitter cold and the deep snow (it was the 21st December 1848).

"On our arrival there we first prayed before the Icons at the spring that God would send down His blessing on us through the prayers of Father Seraphim. Then we drank some of the water and washed with it. My second son also washed himself and his bad leg. At last we returned to the hotel.

"A few hours later my children asked me for permission to go again to the well. My youngest son took a bottle with him, and on the way he outran his older

Miracles

brother in spite of the pain in his leg and the narrow way. Having reached the well before him, he dipped up some water from the well, undressed and poured it over himself. Then he dressed and knelt before the Icons at the well, asking God to have mercy on him through the prayers of Father Seraphim. His older brother followed his example and both prayed for some time in this posture according to their faith. Not only did they not feel the cold at all, but they even felt a slight perspiration. And so the Lord God accepted their fervour and had mercy on them for their childish zeal. On their return to the hotel my younger son declared rapturously that he no longer felt any pain in his leg whatever. In fact, through the intercession of St. Seraphim his leg has been quite well ever since, and he joined one of the cavalry regiments."

II

In 1858 Evdokia Otchkina from Penza was in the Diveyev Convent with her daughter Maria. This is what she related: "In 1843 I was walking in the garden with my three-year-old daughter Elizabeth. Somehow a thistle stuck to the fringe of my dress. As I removed it, probably a tiny bit flew off and settled in the child's eye. My Elizabeth suddenly screamed, shut both her eyes and began to weep copiously. All our efforts to help her were of no avail and she lost her eyesight completely. A year passed. A doctor came from Petersburg to Penza. I took my blind daughter to him, but he could not even examine her eye. It was impossible to open her eyelids, which were compressed as if they had grown together. The doctor

441

St. Seraphim of Sarov

was unable to help. A year later my blind daughter was sitting by me on the floor. I had just put some toys in her lap and she was handling them gropingly. As I looked at her, I wept and said mentally: "Father Seraphim! Pray to the Lord that the eyes of my blind daughter may be opened. I shall go to you on foot to Sarov." At that very minute the child jumped to her feet and started running around the room. From that time she began to see as before, but she died about two years later. As for me, sinner that I am, I completely forgot my promise of a journey to Sarov, and so I was punished a second time. My other daughter, Mary, also got a serious eye disease when she was three. No medicine could help her. Then I remembered that I had promised to go to Sarov. I set out on that very day, and as soon as we had had a Pannikhida for Father Seraphim, my baby was healed. Only on one eye a mark remained, not a cataract, but a tiny spot which does not effect her sight, as though in remembrance of the fact that her mother, through her forgetfulness, offended a man of God."

III

"In 1848," writes an Eletz merchant, Alexey Michailovitch Lavrov, "I was on business not far from the Sarov Monastery, in the Voznesensky factory belonging to Mr. Batashev.

"There I saw almost every day a portrait of an Elder of Sarov, Father Seraphim, whom I had long known from hearsay and whom I respected, though I had not known him personally. I wanted to have a portrait like that too, and so I told my clerk to find a good painter to make me a true and artistic replica.

"Two days later I went away and when I came back, on the 1st of November, my clerk handed me a portrait of Father Seraphim. But it was so badly done that I was angry and began to scold my clerk, and I said to him among other things that the place for that portrait was the wardrobe, because it was too disgraceful to put in a room.

"All that day I was angry with my clerk and as a punishment for my rude words I felt in the evening of the same day such a terrible tooth-ache that I could hardly bear it.

"That same night I called for the medical practitioner of the factory and implored him to help me. I told him moreover about my rudeness with regard to Father Seraphim's portrait in order to quieten my conscience by this avowal. The medical practitioner put some drops on my teeth and the pain apparently stopped, but it came on again, and from that time it tortured me daily, with rare moments of respite, for nearly three years, until the 4th August 1851, in spite of all the drugs and home remedies I tried.

"How many sleepless and agonizing nights I spent! How often I ran about my room half crazy and shouting with pain! How often I resolved to remove the diseased teeth! But as soon as a diseased tooth had been taken out, the one next to it began to ache. At last all my friends and relatives began advising me to

St. Seraphim of Sarov

walk to Sarov and ask Father Seraphim's forgiveness. At first I could not prevail upon myself to do so, but in the end, seeing the futility of every kind of treatment, I decided to apply to the portrait of Father Seraphim which had caused so much displeasure. I took it in my hands and began to ask God and the humble Elder with bitter tears for the forgiveness of my sins and for my healing. That was on the 20th of June 1851 in the town of Kassimov.

"On the following day my pain subsided a little. Then my wife urged me to go to St. Seraphim and to have a Pannikhida served at his grave. On the 30th of July I went with Father Nikolas Gratsianov and a colleague of mine, Leonty Perryzhoggin. We walked for forty versts, but I could walk no further and was obliged to ride. Twenty-five versts from Sarov my teeth began to ache again.

"We arrived in Sarov on the 3rd August and went to the late Liturgy. My teeth were so painful and I could not even stand on my feet. After the Pannikhida I made the acquaintance of an elderly colonel to whom I told my story and who advised me to bathe in St. Seraphim's spring and ask for a cure. I gladly agreed to this, but I could not walk, so my friends drove me in a cart.

"On our arrival Father Nikolas at once took some water in his mouth to see whether I could bathe in the spring or not. And he found the water so cold that his teeth began to ache, so that he did not advise me to bathe. But I had already decided to have recourse to

Miracles

Father Seraphim's help and did not want to listen to anyone's advice.

"When he saw that I was undressing, he said to me: 'What are you going to do?' I replied imperturbably: 'I am going to bathe.' 'But you will never come out again!' he rejoined. 'One cannot hold the water in one's mouth and you want to get in there with your aching teeth.' But I said to him resolutely: 'It won't be worse than what I feel now,' and making the Sign of the Cross, I hurled myself into the spring head first, saying: 'Lord Jesus Christ, by the prayers of St. Seraphim cure my unbearable toothache.' When I came out, I no longer felt any pain whatever, and I said from the fullness of my heart: "Glory to Thee, O Lord, and to thee, Father Seraphim!'

"Ever since then my teeth have been perfectly well. And I am not afraid to go out without goloshes in autumn and spring, which I never dared to do before for fear of the cold."

IV

Colonel V.A.P., a landowner of the district of Shatsk, providence of Tambov, suffered from continual headaches. In 1857 he came to Sarov on August 15th, the Feast of the Dormition of the most holy Mother of God. He attended the early Liturgy in the hospital Church and wanted to go to St. Seraphim's spring before the late Liturgy. But the thought that his wife was waiting for him at the hotel to have tea troubled him, and he was already making his way towards the hotel when, all at once, and without knowing how, he found himself on his way to the spring. On coming there, he hesitated for some time to pour water on his head which was buzzing and aching badly, especially as the morning was cold and damp and there was a drizzling rain. But the invisible hand of God miraculously effected his cure. Unexpectedly his feet slipped on the wet clay and he fell by the spring with his head under the spout. He was drenched against his will with the healing water. No longer afraid to catch cold, the patient rose to his feet and poured the water on his head several times without feeling the slightest pain.

On his way back to the Monastery, Colonel V.A.P. met a peasant who, in his turn, told him of his cure. "Father Seraphim has healed me today!" he said. "My arm was very painful. It was swollen, had become hard and I could not lift it. And so I came to Sarov with this disease. Today I bathed it twice with water from the spring, and now my arm is perfectly well again." On reaching the hotel, the colonel told everyone about these two cures.

V

Father Gabriel Galitsky wrote to the Abbess of the Diveyev Convent, Mother Maria, as follows: "In August 1861, I fell ill with typhoid fever as a result of catching a cold and still more on account of my grave sins. I was treated in the town of Orlov (province of Viatka), but the medicines brought me no relief, as I vomited everything I took. Besides that, I could not

Miracles

sleep, so that I despaired of my life. One night I said farewell to my wife because I felt the approach of death. But my wife said to me: 'If you do not hope to live any longer, you should at least die as a Christian.' I had no inclination to cleanse my conscience by repentance and to have Holy Communion, as I was in anguish and despondency. I told my wife this, but she implored me with tears to send for a Priest, though it was already midnight. I told my wife to give me some book, in the hope that the reading would drive away my dejection, and she gave me a book, *The Life of Hieromonk Seraphim, Hermit of Sarov*. Having read this book, I resolved at once to repent of my sins, and there and then sent for the Priest who came immediately and gave me the Sacrament. In about four days after Holy Communion I went for treatment to Viatka, where I arrived in the evening. It was at the beginning of September. In the morning of the next day, at 7 o'clock, an old woman came to my lodgings and offered to sell me a portrait of Father Seraphim of Sarov. I took two portraits from her and she said on leaving me: 'Batiushka, when the time comes, do not forget Agathia.' Regarding these two incidents as signs from God, I turned in prayer to St. Seraphim and promised to go to the Sarov Monastery and have a Pannikhida sung at the grave of Father Seraphim. From that time I began to feel better, so that the doctor even allowed me to go to the Monastery and to the town, and I began to regret my promise. And probably as a result of that regret my illness took such a bad turn that the doctors whom I invited refused to treat me, and the last of them said to me: 'I shall visit you,

St. Seraphim of Sarov

but I cannot promise to heal you. Look for a spiritual healer.' Then I again made the firm promise to go to the Sarov Monastery. And by the prayers of Father Seraphim I was completely cured of my illness. During my stay in the Sarov Monastery I bought *The Life of Elder Seraphim* (ed. 1863) and from it I learned that the first Abbess of the Diveyev Convent was Agathia. Then I remembered the words of the old woman from whom I had bought the portraits of Father Seraphim: 'When the time comes, remember Agathia,' and thought that I must pray also for this Saint, that she also was close to the Lord."

VI

A fourteen-year-old boy, Dmitry Sabanyeyev, fell ill in St. Petersburg, in 1864. His mother was very sad both at her son's illness and because he had to pass an examination just at that time in order to enter the institute of higher studies. His illness threatened to prevent his entering the institute.

Mrs. Sabanyeyeva who was fervently devoted to Father Serephim, had recourse to him in her prayer for help. On the very next night she saw the Elder in a dream, and he said to her: "Your son will get well and he will pass his examination." Waking with a feeling of joy, she went at once to the infirmary of the naval school where she expected to find her son still sick. But they told her that he was already well and had gone to sit for the examination. When they saw one another, they met with tears. The mother's joy changed into amazement when she heard that her son,

448

Miracles

who like her had a deep veneration for Father Seraphim, had also seen the Elder in a dream and had heard from him the same words: "You will get well and you will pass your examination."

VII

Alexandra Vinogradova, the wife of a Priest, reported the following about the cure of her son from stammering. "In 1865, as a punishment for my sins, my three-year-old boy who spoke quite fluently, suddenly began to stammer. This stammering became worse and worse, and it grew so bad at the beginning of 1866, that he could not say a single word at once, but for about five minutes would repeat: 'a...a...a...' growing quite red; then he would seize his jaws with his hands and run away in tears. He would hide and cry because he could not say what he wanted. For us, his parents, it was great sorrow to see this. We thought anxiously of the future, when the poor boy would have to answer his lessons in school. Often we used to say to him, 'Sashenka[106], think first, and then speak,' imagining that he had got into the habit of stammering so terribly through speaking too fast. Sometimes we would say to him: 'Better be quiet. It is very disagreeable to hear your stammering.' All this made the boy, who was clever beyond his age, very sad.

"In the Great Fast of 1866 some friends lent me *The Life of the Ascetic of Sarov, Father Seraphim.* I

---

[106] Diminuitive of Sasha.

read it aloud to my son. He listened to my reading with amazing attention and understanding, and from that time he began to have faith in the holiness of Father Seraphim and to cherish love for him. He expressed it by kissing with reverence pictures representing Father Seraphim. Easter passed. On Tuesday, Father sent Sasha from the front half of our house to a back room to tell me something. He opened the door, tried to speak, but couldn't, grew red, pressed his jaws (because from stammering a pain had developed in his jaws) ran out of the room and started to cry. Seeing him in this state both I and his nurse began to cry too. I comforted my poor boy and advised him to pray or even only to cross himself at the ringing of the bells before 'It is meet,'[107] wherever he might be, and to pray to Father Seraphim to heal him through his prayers. The boy accepted my advice with joy and promised to carry it out, which he did. At the same time I made a vow to have a Pannikhida served for the repose of the soul of Father Seraphim. I went to my husband and told him everything, but my husband who at that time had not yet read the life of St. Seraphim, listened indifferently to my vow and promised me to have a Pannikhida served some time. It is remarkable that from the very day we made the vow to have recourse to Father Seraphim and to pray

---

[107] In the Russian Orthodox Church there is a tradition of ringing the bells in particular ways to designate certain moments in the Liturgy so that those who were unable to attend may participate in spirit. "It is meet" is the hymn to the Mother of God that culminates the Anaphora (consecration of the Gifts) during Divine Liturgy. It is also the time when special commemorations are made for the living and the dead.--ed.

Miracles

for the repose of his blessed soul, our son suddenly stopped stammering and began to speak well and distinctly. We, sinners, thought in our folly: 'It was true after all what people said about his disease disappearing in time. Now it has, and we have not had the Pannikhida.' Still I thought in my heart that some time, should an opportunity occur, I would fulfill my vow. And so three weeks passed. And then the Lord deigned to enlighten us, careless people, and to show us that our son had not recovered by himself, but through the prayers of Father Seraphim. Our son began to stammer again as before, and again he could not say a single word at once. Then I, a sinner, understood the cause of all this and told my husband what I thought. Then he wanted to read the biography of Father Seraphim, and as he read it, he felt reverence towards the Saint and soon expressed the wish to serve the promised Pannikhida, which he did. Straight after the Pannikhida our child completely recovered. And not only that, but in the same year, being only four and a half, he insistently asked to be taught how to read."

VIII

Anna Simeonovna Rubtsova wrote to the Abbot of the Sarov Monastery as follows: "Wonderful is God in His Saints, the God of Israel, and even to me, a wretched, unworthy sinner, He has shown His mercy through His great Saint, the Sarov solitary, Hieromonk Seraphim. May his glory spread from end to end of the land of Russia! Here, on the frontier be-

St. Seraphim of Sarov

tween Russia and Poland, I sing Pannikhidas to him[108] with heartfelt tears of gratitude, and I ask you, Your Reverence, to convey my most respectful request to one of the Hieromonks to serve a Pannikhida at his grave and a Moleben of thanksgiving to Our Lady of All in Sorrow. And now do me the kindness to listen to how I learnt, while living several thousand versts away, that your holy Monastery possesses such a treasure.

"When I was still a child I often stayed in a Convent with my aunt. There I saw a wonderful oil-painting, 'The End of Hieromonk Seraphim.' My aunt used to tell me much of his sublime life and his incredible labours. Many years passed. My husband was appointed vice-governor of Kovno on the north-west frontier (of Poland). There, I do not know why, this picture often haunted my memory, though I had never thought of it before. A year later my husband was transferred to Vilno. On my arrival in Vilno, I became seriously ill and for almost four years I suffered from various maladies. At last I had a disease of the nose. A big tumour developed in my left nostril which became red outside. For eight months, I was treated by several doctors, but nothing helped me. Some said it was a polyp; others said it was a more serious disease. Finally they decided to operate on me in the spring if the tumour did not yield to treatment; but an operation would have been dangerous on account of my anemia. Once, after having wept my fill, I went to bed. Then I

---

[108] She was not strictly correct. Pannikhidas are sung *to* God *for* the departed.

Miracles

saw in a dream the picture which has remained so vividly in my memory that even now I could draw that fragile old man with white hair and waxen complexion, kneeling with his arms folded on his chest. He was in a white smock, holding a prayer rope. His eyes were cast down as if in contemplation, and he did not look like a dead man in the least. This picture so gripped my soul that for a long time I did not want to get up. I kept my eyes shut so as to enjoy it, and felt heartily sorry that now it was impossible to get it, for I did not know who had received it after my aunt's death. On the same day I asked Abbess Flaviana for some books, and you can imagine my surprise and joy when she sent me a life of Hieromonk Seraphim with six pictures, among which there was one with his hermitage and the spring.

"After reading about all the cures wrought by him during his lifetime and after his death, I applied that picture to my face and wept, saying: 'Those happy people! They saw you, Saint of God, and through your prayers and your blessing they received healing from this spring. But I can never do that, living so far away from that holy place.' I pressed my diseased nostril just under the representation of the spout, and to my amazement some blood came out of the nostril, after which it was a tiny bit easier to breathe. Next day I repeated the same thing, and again blood came out. And every time I did it, my nose began to bleed. The tumour and the swellings gradually disappeared, and my nose returned to normal."

IX

St. Seraphim of Sarov

Ivan Latkin, a merchant of Krasnoyarsk, wrote to Abbess Maria of Diveyev: "In 1860 I was ill for about two months in Krasnoyarsk. I could not even walk. But the master, in whose service I was, sent for me and took me with him to Tomsk. The medical practitioner who was treating me at the time told me that unless I changed the bandages on my wounded leg four times a day, I must die. In spite of this, though against my will, I had to go with my master. We sat side by side in a cart and on account of the bad roads, it took us more than three days to reach Tomsk. I dared not speak of my illness to my master and did not dress my wounds on the way. At Tomsk we went to some lodgings where, in the evening some time later, I lay down on a sofa and fell asleep. And I saw in a dream an old man, in a white smock reaching to a little above his knees and with a belt, who entered my room. Coming near me, he struck my leg with the palm of his hand and said: 'Well, you have stopped the treatment and you have recovered!' I woke up at once, struck a light and looked at my wounds which I had not dressed throughout the journey. To my amazement there were even no signs of the disease. I felt so overjoyed that I ran irresponsibly several times to the chapel of Our Lady of Iberia and back again with the intention of buying a book of the Lives of the Saints, but everyone was asleep because it was past midnight. When it began to get light I ran there again and to my delight saw a Monk sweeping away the snow near the chapel. I asked him whether there were any books of the lives of the holy Fathers, and he replied that there were. The Monk opened the chapel and handed me a book. Remembering the face of the old man whom I had seen in my dream, I took the book, opened it and saw unexpectedly that same old man. It was Father Seraphim, a Hieromonk of the Sarov Monastery, whom I had previously neither seen nor known."

X

Mrs. A., who was pregnant, felt extremely afraid at the approach of delivery, because child-birth had always been particularly difficult and dangerous for her. Just at that time a pilgrim came to their house and he had with him a biography of Father Seraphim. Mrs. A. read the book. Then she prayed to God and asked St. Seraphim for his help. After that she felt much better. All her fears passed and her soul was filled with joy. The time of delivery came. Without any human aid, invoking only the help of the Mother of God and St. Seraphim, without any of her previous sufferings Mrs. A. gave birth to a son whom she called Seraphim.

XI

"I suffered for a long time from an inflammation of the right side," wrote Mother Athanasia, a Nun of the Ponetayev Convent, "and though I used medicines, they helped me very little. Therefore I tried above all to have recourse to the help of Father Seraphim, asking him with sincere faith to raise me from my bed of sickness. And truly, the Saint of God appeared to me in a light sleep in his usual white smock and his kamilavka. He sat down by my bed and said to me with fatherly compassion: "Why do you weep all the time?' I put my head on his lap and said to him weeping: 'Father, I think that I shall not be saved, because I lead a slack life.' But he replied to me by way of comfort: 'Do not think that, my joy. All who call on my name will be saved.'

After these words of the wonderful Elder, I woke up at once and felt in my heart an unutterable joy and in my cell I smelt a fragrance.

From that time I gradually began to recover, and now I am perfectly well by the grace of the Lord and His Saint, the unforgettable Elder Seraphim. This happened at the end of 1882."

XII

Maria Michailovna Blinova, the widow of a merchant from Kotelnitch (province of Viatka), wrote on the 27th February 1903, that in July 1890 there had been in that town several fatal cases of cholera. Her servant was also among the dead. A little later she herself showed symptoms of the same disease. Her husband had gone on business to the fair of Nizhni-Novgorod. The illness reached a dangerous stage-- vomiting and convulsions. When all human means had been exhausted and had proved of no avail, Blinova was confessed and communicated by her parish Priest. Her strength had ebbed so low that she could not even raise herself on her bed, and the unbearable abdominal pain as well as the convulsions gave her no rest.

On the night after she had received Holy Communion she dozed off for a moment and suddenly saw a stooping old man in a Monk's habit with a cross on his chest who seemed to come up to her. The old man blessed her, kissed her on the head and said: "Live a little longer." Maria Michailovna asked with joy: "Who are you, Father?" "Seraphim of Sarov," he replied. When the sick woman woke up, she felt great relief. The pain in her abdomen had gone and the convulsions had subsided. Then her strength began to return and in a few days she had completely recovered. The following year Maria Michailovna went with her husband to Sarov, to venerate St. Seraphim at his grave and to thank him in prayer for the miraculous healing which had been granted her.

XIII

Doctor S. Apraxin recorded the following cure of the daughter of an inhabitant of Nizhni-Novgorod:

"On March 8, 1903, I was invited to Andrew Vasilievitch Vinokurov's house. After a talk about his own illness, I was asked by the parents to see their daughter, a thirteen-year-old-girl. They told me that just before Christmas, Mania who was a pupil in a college, became ill with acute arthritis. This illness was soon complicated by chorea in its worse stage, so that the patient could neither sit on account of the constant twitching of all her muscles nor speak on account of a motor trouble of the tongue. She could only lie down while her body kept tossing from one side to the other on her bed. After some time this serious illness was aggravated by a still graver one--namely, endocarditis. Besides the twitching of the limbs caused by chorea, the girl began to have fits of convulsions at night. The neuropathologists who treated her pronounced her case very serious and warned the parents to be ready for anything. After five weeks of unsuccessful treatment the parents of the girl, on the advice of a relative, had recourse to God's help through His Saint, Seraphim of Sarov. Abandoning all medical treatment, they hung in front of the bed of the sick girl a picture of Father Seraphim praying before the Icon of Our Lady of Compunction. And the sick girl's mother said to her: "Mania, pray to Father Seraphim. He will heal you. If you cannot speak, at least with your heart ask him to help you.' From that night the nightly convulsions stopped. In a few days the girl who had been unable to speak at all, began to say: 'He appeared...he appeared...' But she could not yet relate in detail what had happened. Meanwhile a distinct turn for the better took place, and in a few days the girl could already relate how one night Father Seraphim had appeared to her, blessed her, and said: 'Don't be afraid, you will be well.' And then he added: 'You are not the first I have healed. Your Anyuta[109] in Arzamas was also ill. I have healed her too.' The parents who were greatly struck by this, gave thanks to God and made a vow to go to Sarov as soon as their Mania got well. Then they anointed the body of the

---

[109] One of the diminutives for Anna (pro. Anewta).

Miracles

patient with oil from a lamp burning before the Icons, after which she gradually recovered. On the same day they went to Anyuta's mother of whose illness their daughter had told them, in order to learn whether Anyuta had really been ill at Arzamas. Anyuta's mother whom I personally saw at the time and to whom I talked, was very surprised and said that she had not had any letters from her daughter for a long time and had not heard of her illness. On the same day a letter was sent to Anyuta in Arzamas. Anyuta wrote in reply that she really had been ill with a severe attack of mumps, after which the school doctor had forbidden her to go to school for a week. The sick Mania recovered soon after this, so that she was able to go to Sarov with her parents in the third week of Lent in fulfillment of their vow. At the medical test no traces of chorea were visible. There was only a modification in the valves of the heart as a result of the endocarditis. The grateful parents had a large Icon of Father Seraphim painted in the Diveyev Convent, and this Icon was to be placed, after Saint Seraphim's Canonization in St. Elias' Church in Nizhni-Novgorod because the miraculous cure had taken place in that parish.

St. Seraphim of Sarov

XIV

Daria Feodorovna Tewtcheva[110], lady-in-waiting to the Empress Alexandra Feodorovna, and daughter of the famous poet, related the healing of the Grand-Duchess Maria Alexandrovna as follows: "My sister Anna Feodorovna was in charge of the education of the Grand-Duchess Maria Alexandrovna. In early October 1860 the five-year-old Grand-Duchess became ill with an inflammation of the throat and this illness soon became dangerous. My sister was very anxious. Moreover, the Empress, her mother, had not yet recovered after the birth of the Grand-Duke Paul Alexandrovitch. Towards evening the Grand-Duchess grew worse. She groaned continually and complained of an unbearable pain in her throat. The doctor looked very worried, and my sister was in despair. Our sister Yekaterina Feodorovna was her guest at the time. At 9 o'clock she came to the apartment of the Grand-Duchess and told Anna that a Nun, Sister Glykeria, had come from St. Petersburg and had brought with her a short cloak which had belonged to Father Seraphim. Anna gave orders that this cloak was to be brought and the patient covered with it. The Grand-Duchess immediately fell asleep and whenever she woke up during the night, she would grope with her hands for it and say: 'Give me that black thing.' And she pulled it over herself. In the morning Doctor Hartman ċame and was amazed to find her on the way to recovery. The illness was transformed into a bad cold in the head which passed in two days, so that the

---

[110] Tew pronounced like dew.

Miracles

Grand-Duchess left her bed and had completely recovered. The joy of the Emperor and the Empress knew no bounds.

The Empress Alexandra Feodorovna believed in the prayers of Father Seraphim. She used to say: 'Je sais que ce petit vieux m'aidera à bien mourir.' (I know that that little old man will help me to die well). The Emperor allowed St. Seraphim's cloak to be put on the bed of his dying mother. Her Majesty at once felt relief and afterwards wished to bid farewell to her court. At 8 o'clock in the morning the Empress died. I was on duty that day. I went to my room for a minute, and on the way I looked in at the little Grand-Duke's. There I found the Priest who had been sent for to serve a Pannikhida for Father Seraphim. The Pannikhida had not yet finished when I told the people there of the Empress' death. At the Pannikhida the Priest mentioned her name with that of the holy Elder so that the Empress' soul was borne to heaven on the wings of prayer offered for Father Seraphim."

XV

St. Seraphim also often helped people who were in danger or in difficult circumstances.

A merchant of the province of Kostrosa who afterwards visited the Diveyev Convent every year, related the following about his first visit there. Returning home from Sarov he stopped with his clerk at Diveyev. After Vespers, he wanted to continue his journey. The Sister who attended to the travelers in

St. Seraphim of Sarov

the hostel urged them to stay the night so as to see next morning the things which had belonged to Father Seraphim and were kept in the Convent; but they went. About one verst from Diveyev a black cloud overtook them and such a snowstorm arose that, though they were following the high road, they lost sight of the track completely. The postilion began to freeze.

The prayers they addressed to many Saints did not help them. All at once the merchant exclaimed: "Ah, brothers, how foolish we are! We have just been on a pilgrimage to Father Seraphim, and we do not ask for his help. Let us ask him to help us!" They had not yet finished their prayer when suddenly they heard someone shuffling in the snow nearby, and a voice said: "Hey, you! Why are you sitting there? Come on, follow us. We will show you the way!" Then they saw an old man and an old woman pass them by pulling a sledge which left a wide tack. The sledge moved on quickly and they drove behind it. When they reached the village, the old couple suddenly vanished. Undoubtedly they were Father Seraphim and Mother Agathia Simeonovna.

XVI

A pilgrim was going through the Mouromsky Forest. In a deserted place she heard terrible shrieks and groans. She had with her a picture of Father Seraphim. She took it out and crossed herself with it as well as the place from which the shouts came. All became quiet. She went further. On the road stood a

Miracles

cart and close by it lay two mutilated men. They said that robbers had wanted to kill them, but that all at once they had run away. After some time a police officer passed by, took all three of them, and suspected the woman of being a party to the robbery.

After this the robbers remained for a long time at liberty and were caught for another misdemeanor. They repented and also confessed the robbery they had committed in the Mouromsky Forest. They had just been going to deal the last blow to their victims when they had seen a stooping white-haired Monk in a crumpled kamilavka and in a white smock running at them from the forest. He shook his finger at them and shouted: "Just you wait!" Behind him ran a crowd of people with sticks.

The robbers were shown the picture of Father Seraphim which had been taken from the pilgrim and they at once recognized him as the old Monk who had scared them away and prevented them from murdering the two men in the forest.

XVII

In 1865, in Mrs. B's house the customary distribution of Christmas presents to the needy took place before the feast.

A stooping white-haired old man came separately from the rest and having prayed, said: "Peace and blessing be upon this house!"

St. Seraphim of Sarov

The servant who distributed the gifts asked him: "Have you come for alms?"

"No, not for that."

"Anyway, take it if you want it."

"No, I do not want anything. I only want to see your mistress and to say a few words to her."

"The mistress is not at home. If you have something to say, tell us."

"No, I must do it myself."

One of the servants said softly to another: "What does he want? Let him go. Perhaps he is a tramp."

The old man said: "When your mistress is at home, I shall come. I shall come soon." And he went out.

The distributor saw the old man's bad shoes. She felt remorse and a certain uneasiness. She ran out of the house, but there was no one near it. He had disappeared. The servants did not tell their mistress. But the maid heard someone telling her in her sleep: "You talked inconsiderately. He who came to your house was not a tramp but a great Saint of God."

On the following morning a parcel came by post to Mrs. B. It contained a picture of Father Seraphim (who was greatly venerated by the family) feeding a bear.

Miracles

Great was the general surprise when those who had talked to the old beggar recognized him in the picture of St. Seraphim.

Early Icon of St. Seraphim
Based on a portrait by Serebryakov painted five years before the Saint's death. The artist himself became a Monk at Sarov.

The Canonization of St. Seraphim, 1903
Above: The Imperial Family of Tzar-Martyr Nicholas II at Sarov
Monastery for the Canonization of St. Seraphim.
Below: Clergy and dignitaries leaving the Church of St. John the
Baptist at the time of the Canonization of St. Seraphim.

Chapter XX

The Canonization

The festival of the solemn glorification of the holy relics of St. Seraphim of Sarov, which took place on the 19th July 1903, necessitated a whole series of preparations on the part of Bishop Innocent, the local diocesan. These preparations were undertaken with a view to giving full religious satisfaction to all the pilgrims who, as it afterwards proved, gathered from the remotest confines of the Russian Empire in numbers exceeding 200,000.

Sarov Monastery is situated in a dense forest. The nearest village is 6 versts away. Round the Churches of the Monastery, there are only the buildings where the brethren live and a few hostels (four in number) outside the Monastery enclosure. Obviously the crowds of pilgrims who were expected for the festival could not possibly be accommodated in the Monastery buildings. Therefore rows of huts were erected by the civil authorities in different directions, near the roads leading to the Monastery and in open spaces free from overgrowth. The diocesan authorities considered it necessary to erect a chapel near each group of huts and to provide it with everything necessary for the serving of Pannikhidas and Molebens. If the group was a large one, two or three chapels were erected. Each chapel was beautifully adorned with Icons, the principal Icon being that of St. Seraphim. In these chapels there was always a Priest on duty and singers for the performance of Services. There, during the festivities, Icons of St. Seraphim, pamphlets, "Trinity Leaflets", lives of the Saint and pieces of dry

St. Seraphim of Sarov

bread blessed in his memory, were distributed to the people. Bishop Innocent summoned for this purpose 30 Hieromonks from 3 dioceses, and as many Priests from the province of Tambov which lay nearest to Sarov Monastery, and up to 150 Novices and sacristans, for the performance of Pannikhidas and Molebens as well as for other needs. These measures proved to be fully justified, as it was naturally quite impossible for each and every one of the pilgrims to attend the Services in the Monastery itself.

Metropolitan Antony of St. Petersburg gave orders that some of the clergy of the capital, his own choir and other Church attendants should be sent to Sarov in order to take part in the Services and processions during the festivities of the exposition of the holy relics of St. Seraphim. He also dispatched two of the secular clergy of the capital---Archpriest Philosoph Ornatsky and Father Alexander Rozhdestvensky--both of whom acted as public preachers during the Sarov festival.

On the 3rd July 1903 Metropolitan Antony of St. Petersburg arrived in Sarov Monastery. Assisted by Bishop Nazarius of Nizhny-Novgorod and Bishop Innocent of Tambov, he transferred the relics of St. Seraphim from their original burial place to the Church of Saints Zossimus and Sabbatius, and placed them in a new cypress coffin which had been made by the zeal and devotion of their Imperial Majesties. On the morning of the same day, the Lord Metropolitan celebrated in the Cathedral of the Dormition of the Sarov Monastery a Requiem Liturgy in memory of

The Canonization

the blessed Elder, Hieromonk Seraphim, in the presence of a large concourse of pilgrims. At the same time, with the blessing of Metropolitan Antony and under the supervision of Bishops Nazarius of Nizhny-Novgorod and Innocent of Tambov, some preparatory work was done in the chapel enclosing the tomb of St. Seraphim in order to lift the Saint's coffin from the grave. To this end, the grave-stone with its covering of glazed white brocade was removed, the marble slabs which covered the grave were taken out, and the oaken coffin with the remains of the Saint was raised to the surface of the earth.

After the Liturgy, the Lord Metropolitan went in procession from the Cathedral of the Dormition to St. Seraphim's resting-place, and there he celebrated a Pannikhida for the repose of the soul of the holy Elder before his grave, assisted by Bishops Nazarius and Innocent. Then the Priests lifted the coffin with the relics of the Saint on to their shoulders and carried it in procession to the Church of Saints Zossimus and Sabbatius (which was within the Monastery walls) to the accompaniment of the impressive singing of "Holy God, Holy Mighty, Holy Immortal" by the brethren of the Monastery. This procession made a deep impression on the pilgrims who by this time had gathered in large numbers in the Monastery. The coffin was brought into the Church and put in the middle, on the tombstone which had formerly covered the Saint's grave. At the insistent request of the fervent pilgrims who wanted to see and at least touch St. Seraphim's coffin, Metropolitan Antony gave his

blessing to allow the people free access to it for some
time. For the space of an hour a continual stream of
people poured into the Church to see the precious and
sacred relics and venerate them. After the people had
left the Church the coffin with the holy relics was carried by Hieromonks into the sanctuary (by way of the
north doors), and there the relics were transferred to
the new cypress coffin by Metropolitan Antony, assisted by Bishops Nazarius and Innocent and other
persons. What was specially remarkable was that all
who were present in the sanctuary smelt a distinct fragrance coming from the holy relics which bore no re-
semblance to ordinary perfumes. The cypress coffin
with the holy relics was inserted into a specially prepared oaken coffin which was then placed in the middle of the Church where it was to remain till the
solemn opening of the holy relics on the day of the
Saint's Canonization.

At a distance of two versts from the Monastery, a
small "town" comprising more than a hundred huge
huts had been built for the reception of the pilgrims. A
whole row of shops for the sale of food products was
also built. In spite of the fact that there still remained
more than a week before the festivities were sched-
uled to begin, life in the "town" was already in full
swing. Crowds of pilgrims settled in the huts, men in
one block and women in another. These simple people
who had come to enjoy the spiritual festival presented
an extremely picturesque and motley spectacle. Here
had gathered representatives of almost all the various
peoples of the Russian Empire. The majority of pil-

The Canonization

grims, of course, were from Great and Little Russia, but among them there were also many White Russians, Morduates, Korelians, Zyrians and various other nationalities. All these people who at home lived in ways differing widely from one another, here seemed to be one family. One thought animated them- -to venerate the holy relics of St. Seraphim and to find life, strength and consolation in fervent prayer to him. And what enormous crowds had gathered here in the hope of receiving spiritual help and the healing of various diseases through St. Seraphim's intercession. At almost every step one could meet the lame, the blind, the paralyzed, and all kinds of other sufferers. And many were, in fact, healed according to their faith.

At St. Seraphim's spring manifestations of God's mercy occurred continually. On one day more than ten cures of lame people were registered. In order to bear testimony to God's mercy which had been so miraculously manifested in them, these people collected their crutches and burnt them on the banks of the River Sarovka in the presence of crowds of people.

Out of the many cases of healing which took place at this time, we shall select five for brief mention.

1) A peasant boy, Basil Yovlev, 12 years old, who came to Sarov with his grandmother from the village of Ilisskoyé in Eniséisk Province, had been dumb from birth and had a certificate to this effect from his

St. Seraphim of Sarov

parish Priest. He bathed in St. Seraphim's spring and began to speak.

2) A peasant girl, Agripinna Elizarovna Tabayeva, 18 years old, from the village of Taznéevo in Simbirsk Province, had been blind from birth. She bathed three times in St. Seraphim's spring. After the second bathing, she began to see the light of the sun, trees and other objects. After the third bathing, her sight became normal.

3) A peasant called Michael Tifkin from the village of Nikolskoyé in Viàtsk Province, to use his own words, "had not been able to move (his) neck for 23 years, on both sides of which were swellings, and (his) head hung on it as on a string (lit. bast)." After bathing in St. Seraphim's spring, the swellings went down, the neck became normal and the head straight.

4) A man of the lower middle classes called Basil Nikolaevitch Bogomolov, 50 years old, from the town of Spassk, Ryazàn Province, had lain for 7 years in a state of paralysis, without the use of his legs; his tongue and hearing were also paralyzed. He was brought to St. Seraphim's spring and bathed. After that, he began to hear, talk and walk. He threw away his crutches.

5) A widow called Anna Ivlev, 43 years old, who lived 40 versts from the town of Verny, had suffered from bad eyesight for 19 years. In spite of the fact that it was extremely difficult for her to leave her house as she had four young orphans to take care of, she nev-

The Canonization

ertheless set out for Sarov and walked the 900 versts on foot. After bathing in St. Seraphim's spring, she completely recovered her sight.

Besides the spring which drew a constant stream of pilgrims, another place of attraction was the vast Monastery square with its Churches and the Monks' cells. Here the special attention of the pilgrims was attracted by the two-storied stone Church of Saints Zossimus and Sabbatius. In front of this Church could be continually seen kneeling pilgrims who well knew that here was hidden for a time a precious treasure-- the holy relics of Father Seraphim.

From July 10th the numerous hostels which had been built for well-to-do people began to fill.

Wednesday, July 16th, was the first day of the Sarov festivities. At noon the tolling of bells from the Monastery belfry summoned the people to a solemn Pannikhida in the Cathedral of the Dormition. The officiant was Metropolitan Antony, assisted by an Archbishop, two Bishops, eleven Archimandrites, and 19 members of the monastic and secular clergy. The Cathedral was packed with people. The wonderful singing of the Metropolitan's choir conducted by Mr. Ternov made a deep impression on everyone. The Archbishop of Tambov's singers formed the left choir. The names of the Emperors and Empresses beginning with the Empress Elizabeth and ending with Alexander III inclusive, then the names of the deceased Bishops of Tambov, the builders and Abbots of Sarov Monastery, the Saint's parents Isidore and

St. Seraphim of Sarov

Agathia, and "the ever-memorable Hieromonk Seraphim", were mentioned in the litanies. The Pannikhida lasted more than an hour and a half. Vast numbers of pilgrims could not get into the Cathedral, and remained outside. At the same time Pannikhidas were celebrated in the Church of the Life-Giving Font and in other Churches of the Monastery. The concourse of pilgrims increased from day to day.

At 6 p.m. on the same day in the Cathedral of the Dormition and in the Church of the Life-Giving Font, as well as in other Churches of the Monastery where confessions were not going on, all-night Vigils were celebrated with the great Pannikhida--Parastas.[111] The name of the ever-memorable Hieromonk Seraphim was mentioned in the litanies. The pilgrims who were in the Cathedral of the Dormition could enjoy the beautiful singing of the Metropolitan's choir "Bless the Lord, O my soul" (composed by Kastalsky), and "Blessed is the man" (Kiev melody) in the wonderful interpretation of the choir evoked a profound sense of awe and devotion and a realization of the marvellous beauty of the Orthodox Services.

On Thursday, July 17th, from early morning there was an unusual stir among the pilgrims. They were expecting the arrival of processions from Diveyev and Ponyetayev, St. Seraphim's two Convents. At exactly 7 a.m. a procession went out the gate of Sarov Monastery to meet those who were expected. It was a beautiful, clear and sunny day. The crosses, Icons and

---

[111] Requim all-night Vigils--ed.

The Canonization

banners were carried by representatives of guilds of bannerbearers who had come from various towns for the festivities. Bishop Innocent accompanied the procession with large numbers of monastic and secular clergy. After crossing the River Satis the procession stopped in a wooden chapel open on all sides which had been temporarily erected there, and waited for the expected processions.

About 8 a.m. the procession from the Diveyev and Ponyetayev Convents emerged from the famous Sarov forest. It brought to Sarov the Icon of Our Lady of Compunction before which St. Seraphim used to pray and which was kept in the Diveyev Convent. The processions merged into one and formed an imposing pageant. This giant column then moved towards the gates of the Monastery. Throughout its course innumerable crowds of pilgrims lined the roads.

At 9 a.m. the bells began to ring for the late Requiem Liturgy. There was a beautiful Service in the Cathedral of the Dormition which was celebrated by Metropolitan Antony and Bishop Nazarius. In the Church of the Life-Giving Font the Liturgy was celebrated by Archbishop Dimitry. The sermon was preached by Father P. Ornatsky. After the Liturgy, Pannikhidas were served in both Churches for the repose of the soul of Hieromonk Seraphim.

On the previous day, after the Liturgy the people had usually retired for some time to their huts and hostels. But this time they did not leave the court of the Monastery, for news had been received that His

St. Seraphim of Sarov

Majesty the Emperor accompanied by Their Majesties the Empresses and other persons of high rank were on their way to Sarov.

Thousands of pilgrims lined the road in dense walls. Beyond the gates of the Monastery, in front of the people, in orderly rows stood the Nuns of the Diveyev and Ponyetayev Convents. All eyes were turned towards the majestic Sarov forest whence the carriages with the august travellers would first appear.

About 4 p.m. the big bell of the Monastery belfry began to ring, announcing the speedy arrival of Their Imperial Majesties. At 5 o'clock all the bells of Sarov, which are renowned for their mellow tone, began to ring. At 5:30 the first carriage emerged from the forest, in which sat Their Imperial Majesties the Emperor Nikolas and the Empress Alexandra. The deafening cheers of a crowd of many thousands rent the air. The enthusiasm of the people was indescribable. In the next carriage was the Empress Maria Feodorovna. Then followed Their Imperial Highnesses the Grand Duke Sergius Alexandrovitch with his wife Elizabeth Feodorovna, the Grand Duchess Olga Alexandrovna with her husband His Highness Prince Peter Alexandrovitch of Oldenberg, the Grand Dukes Nikolas Nikolaevitch and Peter Nikolaevitch with his wife the Grand Duchess Militza Nikolaevna, and His Highness Prince George Maximilianovitch with his wife Her Highness Anastasia Nikolaevna, Duchess of Leuchtenberg. At the gates of the Monastery Their Imperial Majesties alighted from their carriages and were met by Metropolitan Antony with all the other

476

The Canonization

prelates and clergy who were taking part in the Sarov festivities.

From the Monastery gates Their Imperial Majesties and Highnesses walked through a pathway covered with red cloth, following the Lord Metropolitan and the other clergy to the Cathedral of the Dormition where a short Moleben was celebrated. From the Cathedral Their Majesties went to the Church of Saints Zossimus and Sabbatius where the coffin with the venerable remains of St. Seraphim stood. On entering the Church with the Lord Metropolitan and the other Bishops, Their Imperial Majesties venerated the holy relics of the Saint. Then Their Imperial Majesties went to the Abbot's house where rooms had been prepared on the upper floor for the Emperor and Empress, and on the ground floor for the Grand Duke Sergius Alexandrovitch and his wife the Grand Duchess Elizabeth Feodorovna. At the entrance to their rooms Their Majesties were met by the brethren who offered them bread and salt, according to Russian custom.

At 7 p.m. in all the Churches of the Monastery Requiem All-Night Vigils (Parastas) were celebrated by specially appointed Priests.

On Friday, July 18th, at 5 a.m. the bells began to ring for the early Liturgy, which was celebrated in all the Churches of the Monastery. Their Majesties the Emperor and the Empresses Alexandra Feodorovna and Maria Feodorovna attended the Liturgy in the Antony Chapel of the Cathedral of the Dormition and

St. Seraphim of Sarov

partook of the Holy Mysteries. They had made their confessions on the previous evening with Hieromonk Simeon. On that day the number of communicants was colossal.

At 8:30 a.m. the bells started to ring for the late Requiem Liturgy for the ever-memorable Hieromonk Seraphim. Specially appointed Priests celebrated the Liturgy in the Cathedral of the Dormition. After the Liturgy the bells were rung to invite the faithful to a Pannikhida in the Cathedral, to pray for the repose of the soul of Hieromonk Seraphim for the last time. Their Imperial Majesties and Highnesses attended the Pannikhida in the Cathedral. Just before the Pannikhida, Metropolitan Antony came out of the sanctuary on to the ambon and preached the following sermon:

"Wonderful is God in His Saints! To all of us who are here assembled in prayer the Lord has granted the great privilege (lit. mercy) of taking part in the splendid solemnity of the glorification of the ever-memorable ascetic Hieromonk Seraphim. Glory and thanks to the Lord Who is so good to us. Be glad and rejoice, holy Sarov Monastery, which is being glorified and has been glorified with the glory of your Saint!

"We are now about to offer our last prayer for him as a departed servant of God. Henceforward, and at all times, Orthodox Christians will turn to him in prayer as to a glorified Saint of God. And his venerable remains which for 70 years have rested in the bosom of the earth, have now been brought out to be put into

The Canonization

this shrine for the veneration of the faithful who in prayer have recourse to him for help, healing and consolation. Truly in this glorification an image of the Resurrection shines forth for us. The words of the Apostle insistently come to our mind: *It is sown in dishonour, it is raised in glory; it is sown in weakness, it is raised in power* (I Cor. 15:43).

"In the apparent deadness of the relics of Saints there is hidden by the grace of God the power of life. Through their instrumentality the Lord grants to people various cures from pain and sickness. The glory of the venerable Father Seraphim resides in just such miraculous cures. His boldness in prayer before God always attracted, even before, crowds of pilgrims to Sarov Monastery. And now the Lord has glorified him in the eyes of the whole Orthodox world, having gathered in this place hundreds of thousands from the remotest confines of Russia, and even from distant Siberia from West and East, North and South. And this great multitude of people is headed by the Orthodox Tsar himself, the pious Tzarinas and many members of the Imperial Family who are prayerfully taking part in the solemnity.

"In this vast but united gathering of pilgrims at the holy relics of the Saint is expressed the basic sense of life, as it has been understood by the Russian people from time immemorial. Russian people know their country and their history not so much from political or historical events as through their ascetics who stand for faith and truth, love and goodness. They know Kiev through Saints Antony and Theodosius of

St. Seraphim of Sarov

Petchersk, the Laura of the Holy Trinity and Moscow through St. Sergius and the Holy Metropolitans of Moscow, the North and Solovky through Saints Zossimus and Sabbatius, Siberia through Simeon of Verhotursk and St. Innocent of Irkutsk. From year to year, from age to age, the people visit the holy places which have been glorified by the ascetic labours of God's Saints, and learn from them the rules of life, and strengthen themselves in faith and truth, goodness and love. And now in the person of St. Seraphim the Lord has raised up a new light, a new teacher, a new spiritual stronghold for the Russian people. Glory be to our God Who is wonderful in His Saints.

"Through the prayers of the Saint numerous miracles are performed here every day. And if anyone were to ask us about them, we should answer such a questioner with reverent boldness, and in full conformity with the actual facts, in the words of the Saviour to John's disciples: *The blind receive their sight, the lame walk, the deaf hear, and the poor have the Gospel preached to them* (Luke 7:22).

"Let us then pray fervently, reverently and with heartfelt warmth for the last time for the repose of the soul of the servant of God, the ever-memorable Hieromonk Seraphim, and let us give the glory to God Who is wonderful in His Saints. Amen."

Then began the Pannikhida in which all the Archpastors who were present at the festival took part, with the wonderful singing of the Metropolitan's choir. The Pannikhida ended in a litia[112] at the tomb of St. Seraphim in front of his former coffin, whither all the clergy and singers went in procession from the Cathedral. After the Pannikhida Metropolitan Antony, on entering the Cathedral, stopped at the newly erected Shrine and read the prayer which is appointed to be said at the blessing of holy Icons, and sprinkled with holy water the Shrine and the holy Icons depicted on it.

At 6 p.m. the bells were rung for an all-night Vigil. This Vigil had a special significance. It was the first Church Service in which St. Seraphim began to be glorified by the Church in the choir of God's Saints, and in which his holy relics were exposed for public veneration. In view of the significance of this Service the people who had gathered for the festivities rushed to the Monastery in thousands. About one hundred thousand pilgrims arrived. As the actual enclosure of the Monastery cannot hold even one-third of that number, on the last days pilgrims were admitted inside the Monastery walls only with special tickets.

The Lord Metropolitan with all the clergy in procession entered the Cathedral of the Dormition. He was soon followed by Their Imperial Majesties and Their Highnesses who stood near the right choir. Until the litia, the Service followed the usual order; only in the stichera the name of St. Seraphim was already sung. But at the beginning of the litia all lit their candles. During the singing of the stichera a procession

---

[112] Litia - abbreviated memorial service.--ed.

issued from the western doors of the Cathedral of the Dormition and proceeded towards the Church of Saints Zossimus and Sabbatius. Their Majesties and Their Highnesses also took part in the procession. They were followed by Ministers of State and other persons of high rank. The doors of the Church flew open and the procession entered. At the sight of the relics which stood in the middle of the Church, all knelt. The Metropolitan censed the coffin all round, and then the coffin was carried out by His Imperial Majesty and Their Highnesses the Grand Dukes with the assistance of some specially appointed clergy.

After carrying it out of the Church, the coffin was put on a stretcher and raised high above the heads of the multitude. The moment of the appearance of the coffin with the holy relics outside the Church was profoundly moving. As it was carried to the Cathedral, peasant women strewed the way with homespun linen, towels and skeins of thread. On both sides of the way all kinds of sick people and cripples were lying.

At the western entrance of the Cathedral of the Dormition the first little litany was said. There were four more stations at other points as the procession made its way round the Cathedral, and each time there was a little litany. After the litia prayer had been read at the western entrance, the procession entered the Cathedral, and the coffin with the holy relics was placed in the middle of the Church on an elevated platform. The Service continued.

The Canonization

During the procession with the holy relics there were several cures. A peasant woman from the village of Promyslovky in the province of Astrakhan, called Vera Tchernysheva, 29 years old, who for 5 years had been crippled with paralysis and had contracted legs, got up and began to walk without help. Another peasant woman called Theodora Slezheva, 26 years old, was healed from attacks of epilepsy from which she had continually suffered.

Between the kathismas[113], Bishop Innocent preached the following sermon:

"*The Saints shall rejoice in glory* (Ps. 149:5). Before this coffin with the holy relics of a Saint, human thought is involuntarily drawn to the realm of faith. Only then do we see what different (and sometimes opposite) meanings things have in ordinary life and in the sphere of faith. In ordinary life a coffin is for us all a source of affliction and sorrow, a cause of lamentation and tears. At the sight of a coffin we involuntarily imagine the unhappiness involved, the sad separation, the bereavement. But in the sphere of Christian hope, a coffin is for a Christian a resting place until the general resurrection; and in the light of faith, it sometimes becomes by God's mercy a source of heavenly revelations, a testimony of God's power, a clear sign of heavenly reward for

---

[113] The Psalter is divided into 20 sections or kathismas, during the reading of which it is customary to sit. Each kathisma takes from 15 to 20 minutes.

St. Seraphim of Sarov

righteousness on earth, a cause of the most exalted Christian sentiments.

"The coffin which lies before us evokes in each believing soul just such a sense of spiritual joy, tears of compunction and reverence. As we stand round it, headed by our most pious Emperor and Empresses, we all know that it conceals the precious relics of a righteous man who was pleasing to the Lord, a man of prayer and asceticism, who was great in his simplicity, who was crowned with humility and meekness, and who was burning with Christ's love for every man.

"The persecuted and oppressed Church of the first three centuries knew her martyrs and confessors who suffered for the name of Christ. She buried their bodies with full honours, and carefully collected their bones. The calm and peaceful Church of our days knows her intercessors and ascetics; she also honours the graves of her righteous members and venerates their holy relics. When St. Polycarp, Bishop of Smyrna, suffered martyrdom and was torn to pieces by the wild beasts, the citizens of Smyrna sent to the other Churches an epistle in which they informed them that they had collected the bones of the martyr into a vessel and that they would keep and venerate these sacred remains as a most precious treasure. Following the example of that ancient Church of those early Christians, our Orthodox Church has extracted from the bosom of the earth the bones of her ascetic and man of prayer, St. Seraphim. Henceforward she will surround them with reverence,

The Canonization

psalmody and veneration, as a precious and sacred treasure.

"What message will the holy relics of God's Saint convey to the Christian world? Henceforth they will speak to the world of God's power which is wonderful in His Saints, of God's love for His righteous sons whose very bones He keeps (Ps. 33:20). Henceforth they will testify to God's glory which envelops God's Saints in the heavenly abodes. And even their holy relics on earth participate in this glory. They shed fragrance, and they give healing, comfort and spiritual help to all who have recourse to them. By means of this help the Saint's holy relics will clearly say to all that the abode of God's glory, the place of His omnipresence, is surrounded not only by a world of Angels, but also by God's Saints--that people would not get this unseen help if there were no prayerful intercession for it in heaven. The source of this supernatural help would be unknown if there did not exist an invisible though spiritually discernible prayer-connection between the Church on earth and the heavenly Church.

"But the significance of this holy coffin is revealed to us who are children of the Orthodox Church from yet another angle. In it we recognize the truth of our Holy Orthodox Faith. That Church does not err but stands firmly in the right way for whom the heavenly world of God's Saints is a constant guide, on which it moulds its dispositions, which inspires its prayer, and which is a source of spiritual consolation, help and protection. In these holy relics of a new intercessor

485

St. Seraphim of Sarov

for the Russian Church we feel the heartbeat of the life of our Church. For a Church which is constantly being adorned with new Saints of God is not dead or frozen or fossilized, but is alive and flourishing, and enjoys perennial youth. In this tomb is the source, the light and the joy of our faith. Our faith would be cold and dim if it did not receive the obvious encouragement that prayer and an ascetic life are always rewarded and glorified by the Lord. In these holy relics we see a new sign of the mercy and goodness of God to the Russian people and the Orthodox Church. It is as if the heavens were opened and a new intercessor and mediator for us sinners stood at the throne of God. And we see clearly the fruits of his prayer to the Lord: the blind see, the deaf hear, the dumb speak, the paralyzed rise.

"In a moment the lid of this salutary grave will be thrown open, and the holy relics will be exposed to our view. New streams of miracles will flow from them. And the image of St. Seraphim will rise even more distinctly before us, the image of him who is now wonderful among God's Saints, but who was meek, humble and poor in earthly life. And under the spell of his wonderful personality we shall sing to him with penitent joy which is a fruit of faith: We bless thee, holy Father Seraphim. Amen."

After the reading of another kathisma, at the singing of "Praise the name of the Lord", all the officiating clergy came out of the sanctuary into the middle of the Church. Metropolitan Antony opened the lid of the coffin. All knelt and the clergy sang the

The Canonization

magnification to the Saint: "We bless thee, holy Father Seraphim, and we honour thy holy memory, O director of Monks and converser with Angels." After the reading of the Gospel, the Lord Metropolitan and the other Prelates kissed the holy relics. Then Their Imperial Majesties and Their Highnesses kissed them, followed by the officiating clergy and all the pilgrims who were in the Cathedral.

After the all-night Vigil the Cathedral was left open throughout the night for the veneration of the relics of the Saint. All through the night the pilgrims passed before the coffin one by one, kissed the holy relics and were anointed with oil by the Priests on duty.

On the following day, July 19th, the late Liturgy in the Cathedral of the Dormition began at 8 a.m. It was celebrated by Metropolitan Antony together with the other Hierarchs, 12 Archimandrites, and 8 Protopresbyters and Priests. Their Imperial Majesties as well as Their Highnesses the Grand Dukes and Grand Duchesses were present. At the little entry with the Gospel, the following was sung: "O come let us worship and fall down before Christ. O Son of God, Who art wonderful in Thy Saints, save us who sing to Thee: Alleluia!" At the beginning of this singing, the Archimandrites lifted the cypress coffin with the holy relics which was standing in the middle of the Cathedral and together with the Hierarchs carried it round the altar, and then placed it in the Shrine prepared for it.

St. Seraphim of Sarov

Just at this time, the following case of healing took place. Among those who were praying in the Cathedral was a certain Mrs. Evodokia Maslennikov from Moscow with her 12-year-old daughter Katharine, who was suffering from catalepsy and who for two years had not spoken a word. Doctors had been unable to help her. As the coffin with the holy relics was carried past the sick girl, her mother touched the coffin with a handkerchief and wiped her daughter's face with it. To everyone's amazement Katharine there and then pronounced her mother's name and began to speak. The healed girl was afterwards given Holy Communion by the Lord Metropolitan.

At the end of the Liturgy, Archbishop Dimitry preached a sermon which ended with the following words: "By his prayerful intercession before God may he help us also to accomplish our earthly journey to heaven without stumbling or falling, in the love, joy and peace of our Lord and Saviour Jesus Christ."

After the Liturgy a Moleben was sung to St. Seraphim. When the troparion to Saint Seraphim was sung, the Archimandrites went up to the Shrine and took out of it the coffin with the holy relics. Then a procession took place from the Cathedral round the Churches of the Monastery. The coffin was carried by the Emperor and Their Imperial Highnesses, assisted by the Archimandrites. As on the eve, the crowds formed a living wall on either side of the way and were deeply moved. On all sides could be heard the weeping and sobbing of women. When the procession

The Canonization

returned to the Cathedral, a prayer to St. Seraphim was read by Metropolitan Antony while all knelt. The Moleben ended with the usual singing of "Many years!" Their Imperial Majesties and Highnesses kissed the holy relics and left the Cathedral.

On the following day, July 20th, the Emperor and Empress with the other members of the Imperial Family who had attended the Canonization visited Diveyev Convent on their way back from Sarov.

Long before July 20th the Convent had been preparing for the worthy reception of their most exalted and honoured guests. The whole way was adorned with greenery, flags and triumphal arches. The people (both the local inhabitants and those from distant lands) met the Imperial visitors in their best and most festive national costumes and gave them a joyous and enthusiastic welcome. Inside the Convent enclosure, the Imperial route was lined on both sides with Nuns with the children of their schools in front of them. At about 10 a.m. the Imperial carriages drew up at Diveyev amid deafening cheers and the ringing of the Cathedral bells. The exalted guests were met at the entrance to the Cathedral by Bishop Nazarius and a number of clergy, with the cross and holy water. His Lordship greeted the Emperor and Empress with an address of welcome. After the customary litany and "Many years", the Imperial Guests prayed before the Icon of Our Lady of Compunction (it was while praying before this Icon that St. Seraphim had breathed his last) and before a locally venerated Icon of the Saviour "Not-made-with-hands", and then

St. Seraphim of Sarov

kissed them. All the Imperial Pilgrims were then presented with Icons painted by the Sisters of the Convent: Icons of St. Seraphim, Our Lady of Compunction, Apparition of the Mother of God to St. Seraphim, etc. The Emperor and Empress then visited the north side-chapel in the Cathedral, designed to be consecrated in honour of St. Seraphim; they also inspected such of the paintings in the Cathedral as were of special merit (all the Icons and paintings were the work of the Diveyev Sisters themselves). From the Cathedral the exalted guests went to the apartments of the Superior of the Convent, the Abbess Maria, and attended the Liturgy in the house-chapel in the Abbess's apartments. Breakfast was served in the Abbess's house. After breakfast the Imperial guests looked over the Convent and its institutions. At about 2 o'clock the Emperor and Empress visited the Convent school with its orphanage for orphan-girls. From the school they went to the Church of the Transfiguration, in which they inspected the sanctuary and souvenirs of St. Seraphim's ascetic labours.

Thence the exalted guests went to the so-called Diveyev "hermitage"; that is the hut which St. Seraphim built himself for his "near hermitage" in Sarov, at the spring by the River Sarovka. The Imperial visitors prayed in St. Seraphim's cell or hut and inspected various souvenirs of his labours. After that, they visited the Icon-painting studio of the Convent. The Diveyev studio has several departments: Icon painting, photographic, lithographic, chromotypographic departments. All the Imperial

The Canonization

Family visited the studio. Bishop Nazarius met them there and introduced them to the work of the Sister-artists. The senior "painter", Mother Seraphima, as well as two other Nuns, Anastasia and Lydia, gave explanations. The Empress in the presence of the Emperor, was pleased to award Mother Seraphima with a gold cross, saying as she put it round her neck: "You work very well. We have been very pleased with all we have seen."

At 3:10 p.m. the Imperial visitors took their departure. Nuns, schoolchildren and people lined the route. Amid the ringing of the bells and deafening cheers, the exalted guests left the Monastery enclosure, signing themselves with the Sign of the Cross as they passed the Convent Churches. Immediately after the departure of the august guests, Bishop Nazarius served a Moleben in the Diveyev Cathedral, assisted by all the clergy, for their safe journey, ending with "Many years" to the Imperial Travellers.

The Sarov festivities ended with the consecration of two Churches in honour of St. Seraphim. The first Church in Russia to be dedicated to him was consecrated in Sarov over his monastic cell. The second Church was consecrated on July 22nd in Diveyev Convent.

Icon of the Mother of God, Our Lady of Compunction
The Icon depicts the Mother of God at the moment of the Annunciation. The lettering around her halo reads in Slavonic, "Rejoice, Unwedded Bride" and she is shown in humble submission to the will of God as she says, "Let it be done unto me according to Thy word." Saint Seraphim died praying before this Icon.

Chapter XXI

The Mingling of Heaven and Earth

"Seek first the Kingdom of God and His righteousness." In the Kingdom of God--the world of men, women and children as planned in the mind and intention of God--people will be so alive, so filled with the eternal life of heaven and the powers of the age to come, that the spirit of friendship, creative energy and joy will be such that it is difficult for us at present even to imagine it. Human life is bound to undergo a great change. There will, in fact, be 'a new heaven and a new earth.' At the very beginning of the Christian era, the holy Mother of Jesus saw clearly the vast change in the social order that her Divine Son's life and teaching is destined to bring about. She saw, as in a vision, how "the old things have passed away, all things have become new", and exultingly she sang her revolutionary and prophetic hymn:

"He has put down princes from their thrones
And has exalted the humble.
He has filled the hungry with good things
And the rich He has sent empty away."

This vision tends to become dim, and where there is no vision the people perish. In the life of St. Seraphim we realize that the glorious Queen of Heaven who spoke those remarkable words is still alive and active, close to us in that invisible world which interpenetrates this world, able and eager to help us to build that new order of love and justice which will fulfill her vision. Let us therefore close our brief study of the life of our Saint with the words of

493

St. Seraphim of Sarov

Archimandrite Evdokim (later Bishop of Volokolam), for they also have a definitely prophetic ring about them. In the concluding pages of his article, "At the Relics of Saint Seraphim of Sarov", he writes:

"The glorification (or Canonization) of St. Seraphim of Sarov is undoubtedly one of the greatest events of our times. Such days are of rare occurrence in the life of a nation. It was impossible to remain indifferent to July 19th (1903), whatever one's outlook on life may have been. That day, it seems to me, ought to be called a test-day for the Russian people, a day by which they examine themselves and their cherished beliefs, hopes and aspirations. And so, let us all stand mentally at the Saint's Shrine and examine ourselves and our life ideals.

"Casting a rapid glance over the Saint's life, one is involuntarily struck by the heights of its attainments. As one studies the life more closely, one begins to think that the holy Elder did not live in our days, but in the days of the great ascetics of antiquity--Antony, Pachomius, Makarius, Sabba, Hilarion, Euthymius and the rest--so closely was his life interwoven with the lives of the great ascetics. And actually it is difficult to point to anything in the life of St. Seraphim in which he suffers by comparison with the early ascetics. For he went through all the various forms of the old asceticism. He lived as a solitary, as a stylite, as a recluse, in silence, as a hermit, and as an Elder ministering to his neighbour by word and deed. The ancient ascetics earned their piece of bread with their own hands. And he procured his food with his own

494

The Mingling of Heaven and Earth

hands. The ancient ascetics had no spare clothing. Neither did he. The ancient ascetics had no possessions, so that they always left their huts unlocked. And he had nothing of his own and left his hut open for all. The ancient ascetics slept on the bare earth and ate little food. And he did not sleep on luxurious beds, and his food was poor and scanty. The ancient ascetics lived for years in the desert. And he lived for 55 whole years in his Monastery. The ancient ascetics worked miracles. And by his prayers many miracles are performed. They were great men of prayer. And so was he. In a word, if we compare the lives of the ancient ascetics with that of our Saint, we find a striking similarity everywhere and in everything. This similarity is so great that after a time you begin to wonder whether he is really ours and lived in our time.

"Undoubtedly the monastic life is difficult. The monastic craft constantly has to weather the most violent interior and exterior storms. Not all the wrestlers stand their ground in the fight. In many cases, page after page is gradually torn out of the book of life, from those most sacred writings by which they once promised to be guided throughout their whole life. The monastic vows begin to seem almost impracticable, and the lives of the ancient ascetics, whose feats illumined the whole world, are little understood and seem to be very remote and even impossible at the present day. Thus life is gradually knocking people off the old foundations and putting them on new ones

St. Seraphim of Sarov

which are sometimes entirely alien to the principles of ancient monasticism.

"Come and stand at the Shrine of the holy Elder, the Russian Monk. There you have the true monastic life which has blossomed so splendidly and wonderfully almost before our eyes in the forests of Sarov. The times of the ancient asceticism would seem to have returned to us. Only now we are not reading or hearing about them, but see them with our eyes and touch them with our hands. But do not lose courage, Monk! Go firmly straight ahead, sanctifying each step of your life with the teachings of the holy ascetics and Elders.

"And you, Russian people, come to the Shrine of the holy Elder. Grievous and difficult has been your lot. In spite of all your national misfortunes and failures, you have not lost your ardent faith in God's will on earth. You have kept the rules of the Church. You have loved above everything on earth to think of the Kingdom of God, and while enduring great hardships, you have not complained of your fate. You have firmly believed that God's righteousness and justice can be everywhere on earth. It can dwell in the hut of the poorest peasant. The Kingdom of God is not measured by palaces and wealth. But lately new self-appointed teachers have begun to worry you and to undermine your agelong beliefs and hopes. Some of the simple folk have already begun to waver. Others have gone further and have deliberately begun to shelve the ancient traditions. Many have abandoned the faith of

The Mingling of Heaven and Earth

their Fathers. Many are already finding various new faiths.

"Russian people, go to the Shrine of the holy Elder and learn that it was not for nothing that you kept your ancient faith. Therein is your strength and power, and not in vagaries and novelties. The holy Elder is your hero and your guide to eternity. He embodied and realized all your beliefs and all your dreams of salvation and happiness on earth. There you will see that the meaning and end of life is not in struggling for a piece of daily bread into which you are sometimes dragged by force and even by deception, but in God's righteousness and justice. You will see that God's righteousness found a congenial home in the forests of Sarov, in a breast covered with little better than rags, in a man who slept on stones and earth, and who for years lived only on vegetables. You will see that this justice, God's justice, and not any other kind of justice of merely animal interests and outward advantages and privileges, gathered round itself hundreds of thousands of people. Everything has now bowed before this justice: wealth, fame and wisdom. To the poor solitary of the Sarov forests all have come with the Tsar at their head: princes, courtiers, nobles, the rich, the learned, archpastors, pastors, Monks, Nuns, the poor, the wretched, old men, children, young men and girls, old women, fathers, mothers. Who gathered them there? They were gathered there by God's righteousness embodied in the life of the poor Elder of Sarov. How otherwise could such vast numbers of guests have been drawn to

St. Seraphim of Sarov

the holy Elder? The people of Russia went to Sarov to worship God's righteousness there, in order to confess and bear witness to their burning faith in divine justice. Keep that faith in God's righteousness on earth; guard your peace of soul. Do not yield to any temptations. Be firm and unbending. And teach it to your children. And it will be well with you. But if you forget your spiritual inheritance, you will perish with curses in a bloody struggle for existence.[114]

"And Russian educated society will not go away from this holy Shrine without edification. There is no need to speak of the progress that science has made in the various spheres of learning. That would be merely a dull repetition of old outworn platitudes. But is man happy with all this visible glitter[115] and the various blessings of culture and civilization? Not at all. How many complaints do we hear nowadays from all quarters against modern life! 'Educated society is going through a severe moral crisis,' says Ternavtsev. 'The need for something higher than one's own knowledge and attainments, for a more profound peace than one can obtain by one's own efforts, is burning the soul. All natural knowledge with its thousand-eyed science is proving to be inhuman and empty, for it is powerless to solve our torturing doubts as to the supreme meaning of existence or to answer the riddle of the universe. The socialistic schemes of

---

[114] This was prophetic, for it was written in 1903, years before the Red Revolution of 1918-1948. Unfortunately, for the most part such warnings fell on deaf ears.
[115] There is a proverb: "All is not gold that glitters."

Obedience to the
Holy Spirit!

1) Maintain silence

2) Enter into silent prayer as
often as possible

3) Pray the Jesus prayer when
unable to be in silent prayer

4) Seek the Lord with all your ?

5) Drop intellectual ministries
& seeking worldly interests

6) Know thyself - watch, confess sins
pray & praise & thanksgiving

7) humbly confess sins then turn
from them - renouncing them

8) hate sin, pray for sinners

9) ask Jesus continually for His grace
to overcome sin

10) Be obedient to these urgings
from the Holy Spirit.

11) Read from each gospel a day
1 proverb, 5 psalms